PEREGRINE BOOKS
Y 80
BERKELEY

BERKELEY

G. J. Warnock

PENGUIN BOOKS

Penguin Books Ltd, Harmondsworth, Middlesex, England
Penguin Books Inc., 7110 Ambassador Road, Baltimore, Maryland 21207, U.S.A.
Penguin Books Australia Ltd, Ringwood, Victoria, Australia

—

First published in Pelican Books 1953
Reissued in Peregrine Books 1969

—

—

Made and printed in Great Britain
by Hazell Watson & Viney Ltd,
Aylesbury, Bucks
Set in Georgian Linotype

CONTENTS

PREFACE TO
THE PEREGRINE EDITION

I т is just fifteen years since this book was first published; and
no doubt if I were writing it *de novo* today, it would come out
differently in many respects. However, to stitch new passages
into an old text, or to seek to amend its defects by sporadic
rewriting, is apt to be a confusing, unsatisfactory procedure;
and I have thought it best to reprint the original text without
alteration. But there are some important matters on which I
shall comment briefly in this preface, and, on several minor
matters, I have added notes at the end. I have also added a
short bibliography. Neither comments nor notes aspire to be
exhaustive; there would be a certain absurdity in treating a
fairly unambitious text of one's own with the full apparatus
of weighty philosophical scholarship, and I have not tried to
do so.

First, there is something to be said on the question of the
interpretation of Locke. Professor A. D. Woozley, in a review
in *Philosophy* in 1955, expressed the judgement that, while I
had written a respectable book about Berkeley, it was nevertheless a bad – though not the worst – book about Locke. A
point of some importance is involved here. I had taken the
view – which is, indeed, in a sense quite plainly correct – that
Berkeley arrived at some of his characteristic doctrines largely
as a result of critical reflection on the difficulties, and even
dangers, which he discerned in the doctrines of Locke's
Essay, published when Berkeley was a child and familiar to
him in his student days in Dublin. I had suggested that there
were indeed gross difficulties in Locke's position, and that
Berkeley's rejoinder gained a good deal of its plausibility from
its appearance (albeit deceptive) of being the only possible out-

come of his clearly effective critical argument. It is Woozley's contention that Berkeley, and I, and indeed most philosophers from that day to this, have seriously misunderstood Locke's position, have attributed to him absurd views which he did not really hold, and thus have used him, most unjustly and unhistorically, as a sort of whipping-boy for Berkeley's wit and critical invective.

The main points are these. Berkeley supposed that he found in Locke the doctrines: (1) that all meaningful words are a sort of proper names, and hence that there must be strange – according to Berkeley, logically impossible – items in our minds for them to be the proper names of; (2) that, since we are acquainted only with 'ideas' in our own minds, the 'external' objects which Locke took to be their causes must – though, according to Berkeley, Locke quite failed to see this – be perfectly unknown to us, and their very existence a quite gratuitous and useless supposition; and (3) that, while there must be such a thing as *substance*, it is something wholly unknown to us, and indeed is in principle not even describable. However, in his Introduction to his valuable new abridgement of the text of Locke's *Essay* (Fontana Library, 1964), Professor Woozley argues that Locke did not hold, either explicitly or implicitly, any of these views; that accordingly Berkeley was tilting at a straw-man of his own invention; and that commentators who imply, as I did, that what Berkeley saw in Locke was really there, are giving Berkeley much more credit, and Locke much less, than each deserves, and incidentally are perpetuating a tidy but highly inaccurate picture of the history of philosophy.

The historical question cannot be settled here – if, indeed, it could conclusively be settled at all. Locke's text is very long, and not very perspicuous or careful or precise, and there are many points at which one might be tempted to conclude that he held more than one view, or no definite view at all, or at least that no definite view could be identified with anything like certainty as his. I believe, however, that there is at least more room for argument as to what Locke's views really were than, when I wrote this book, I allowed for, and that on this point at least I was probably too much disposed to take Berkeley's word for it; and accordingly, while I have not amended my text, I would ask readers to bear in mind, particularly in reading chapters 4 and 5, that what are there presented as 'Locke's views' had better be understood as 'what Berkeley *took* to be Locke's views', and that there is at least to be reckoned with the allegation that Berkeley, and most others, have not understood Locke correctly.

Second, about my own interpretation and criticisms of Berkeley. A minor point is that I was, I think, inclined to over-stress his role as a defender of 'common sense'. It is true that he was fond of claiming this reassuring role for himself; and I wished to bring out with emphasis both that this was so, and that the claim was not so absurd as all that, for the reason that it is so easy, and has been so common, to see Berkeley as *merely* a fantastic metaphysical speculator. But perhaps I went too far. One might get the impression from my book, I think, that Berkeley's queer ontological doctrines were a perfectly understandable, perhaps almost inadvertent, by-product of what was essentially a sober critical exercise in philosophical analysis. But Berkeley, if one may put it so, was crazier than that. In a sense he really did like to think, and not merely to speak, 'with the vulgar'; he was also seriously concerned to defend religious orthodoxy; but besides that he had, in no way at all by inadvertence, his own personal, extraordinary vision of the true nature of reality. In my book I do not deny this, but I mention it, I think, too seldom and too apologetically.

This raises, in fact, the next point that I should like to discuss. If I understand my own book correctly (it may well be that I do not), I had the idea that Berkeley was offering (a) a set of ontological, or 'metaphysical', doctrines, and (b) a certain programme of conceptual analysis – specifically, an analysis of propositions about the material world; that (a) and (b) could and should be considered separately; and that, while the proposed analysis could be usefully examined and appraised, it was not clear that argument about the metaphysical doctrines would be profitable or even, perhaps, possible at all. This seems to be the conclusion I reach at the end of chapter 6. However, I seem to have been in some confusion about this, for I find that I say, in chapter 13, that the ontological propositions 'alleged to support his analysis were in fact disguised assertions of that analysis itself' – which seems to conflict with the earlier supposition that there were here two distinguishable issues, detachable from one another.

These are matters on which I am still very far from clear; but I am inclined now to think that I probably was mistaken in suggesting that Berkeley's 'metaphysical' doctrines could be detached from his conceptual claims – and also, perhaps, in implying that I myself could make analytical points here without 'ontological commitments'. J. W. Yolton (in *Philosophical Quarterly*, 1961) has argued that my rejection of Berkeley's analysis presupposes a 'realist' view of the material world, an ontology which unfairly prejudges what I represent as non-committally conceptual questions; and a similar point was made, in more knock-about terms, in Ernest Gellner's *Words and Things* (1959). Conversely, it was claimed by J. L. Austin in *Sense and Sensibilia* (1962) that a modern, professedly non-ontological version of a (somewhat Berkeleian) phenomenalism 'really rests squarely on the old Berkeleian, Kantian ontology of the "sensible manifold" ' – a remark which might well suggest that Berkeley's own analyses were not really detachable from his metaphysics. It may be, then, that Berkeley's 'version of the world', if one may so call it, should be represented, not as an ontology conjoined with and detachable from a programme of analysis, but as a single 'version' having, according as it is 'read', *both* ontological *and* conceptual implications. This seems to be more or less what I say at the very end of my book, though not in its earlier stages; but to say only this, of course, is not to say anything very clear or very helpful; and in any case, if I was going to say this about Berkeley, I should have considered the possibility that he would have been entitled to say the same thing about me.

A further point now arises. If, as has been urged, my contention that Berkeley's theory does not allow him to offer an acceptable analysis of ordinary propositions about the material world *presupposes* an ordinary 'realist' ontology which Berkeley also rejects, then what has been established? Nothing, surely, but that Berkeley's 'version' differs, both ontologically and conceptually, from mine, and from (perhaps) that of most other people as well. And to show that, of course, is not to show that Berkeley is wrong; it is only to place him in a numerical minority. There is something in this. In my book I do, in fact, rather cautiously claim only to show that Berkeley's 'version' *differs* – as he was apt to claim that it did not – from 'common sense'; but perhaps I do hint that, if so, then Berkeley was wrong; and if I do so hint, then doubtless more should have been done to show why Berkeley was wrong, and not merely an eccentric. I believe that this is true – that I should have been, so to speak, more metaphysically aggressive, and not have nervously shied away, as I sought to do, from full-scale engagement on the metaphysical front. For these matters are surely not, in fact, unamenable to argument. Berkeley was, of course, an extreme exponent of 'subjective idealism'; though he strenuously asserts that there is a common world, perceived and inhabited in common by many persons – though indeed he constantly derides the very idea of any sceptical doubt on such topics – yet, according to him, what any 'spirit' actually encounters in his experience is absolutely private to him, is 'in his own mind'. And it could be argued, I think, on lines first sketched by Kant and recently filled in by many others, that this picture is not merely eccentric, but strictly incoherent. The world could not be a class of absolutely private worlds, even with a God thrown in to guarantee their cohesion; if Berkeley wishes to say about the world what he does not question the possibility of saying, then he must be wrong about 'what there is'; there could not be *only* 'spirits' and their private data. I cannot, of course, argue this large matter here; but I mention it as something which I should have argued in my book, instead of leaving, as perhaps I timorously did, a certain impression that Berkeley's 'version', though indeed unusual, was a perfectly conceivable and possible one. Of course, I still do not wish to deny that his reaching the view he did was perfectly understandable, even though that view may not really be understandable in itself; it is still true that to his classic (if disputable) interpretation of Locke, he set out the classic and, dialectically, wholly natural rejoinder.

Next, about my particular way of formulating Berkeley's views. It seemed to me, naturally enough, that a major obstacle in the way of judging the merits of his case – an obstacle, probably, to him as well as to us – was the extreme unclarity of his ubiquitous term *idea*, with the resultant constant uncertainty as to what exactly he was asserting in sentences, of which there are so many, in which that term occurs. Accordingly many pages of my book are devoted to an attempt to get this clear; I was trying to define the term *idea*, as philosophers used to say, 'in use', by devising a form of words in which the term itself did not occur but which, as a whole, would mean the same as what Berkeley meant, and which at the same time would be reasonably clear in its sense and implications. I hope that this was worth doing, and that the results may still be worth reading; but it must be admitted that this enterprise has attracted, one way and another, a good deal of criticism. The complaint I anticipated was that my procedure was unhistorical – that, in translating Berkeley out of his own language, I was distorting his opinions. Was he really asserting, as I make out that he was, that propositions about how things objectively are, are equivalent to indefinite arrays of propositions about how things subjectively seem? But what in fact has been chiefly objected to is not this translated version of Berkeley's meaning, but my further comments on that version, even assuming it to be a fair one. My case for denying the equivalence alleged in this version of Berkeley has been declared by Jonathan Bennett to be insufficient (*Kant's*

Analytic, 1966, pp. 194–6). My suggestion that 'seems' stands
to 'is' much as evidence stands to a verdict has been subtly
criticized by W. F. R. Hardie (*Philosophical Quarterly*, 1955).
And any assimilation of saying how things are to giving a
verdict has been strongly deprecated by J. L. Austin *(Sense
and Sensibilia*, pp. 140–41) as playing straight into the hands
of scepticism. Austin in fact, if I understand him rightly, was
inclined to deplore this whole section of my argument as over-
indulgent to doctrines of the Berkeleian variety; to represent
them as falling, so to speak, at the last fence is perhaps to
insinuate, quite falsely in his view, that all goes quite smoothly
up to that point. 'The right policy is to go back to a much
earlier stage, and to dismantle the whole doctrine before it
gets off the ground' (op. cit., p. 142). I hope that the reader will
not conclude straight off that those central chapters are a pure
waste of time, but I must, I think, call his attention to such
criticisms as these. They are not, of course, the only criticisms
that have been made.

Berkeley almost invariably followed the practice of number-
ing his paragraphs, so that in references to his texts it is not
necessary to mention the pages on which quoted passages occur
in the various editions. I have given almost all references in
the form of a capital letter, or letters, followed by a number –
the letters indicating the work, and the number being that assigned by Berkeley to the paragraph, from which quotation is
made. I refer to the *Principles of Human Knowledge* by the
letter P; to the *Essay towards a New Theory of Vision* by E;
to *Siris* by S; to the Introduction to the *Principles*, the paragraphs of which are separately numbered, by I; and to the
Philosophical Commentaries by P.C. The latter work, which
consists of two note-books kept by Berkeley for his private use
in early youth, was first published by A. C. Fraser and called
by him *The Commonplace Book*. I have adopted the title more
recently proposed by Professor A. A. Luce, which though not
ideally appropriate seems less wide of the mark than Fraser's.
The paragraphs of the *Three Dialogues* were not numbered

by Berkeley; but as each dialogue is fairly short, I have taken it to be sufficient simply to indicate from which of them my few quotations are taken.

An excellent, exhaustive, and authoritative biography of Berkeley, by Professor Luce, is published (1949) by Nelson, uniformly with their recent complete edition of his works (nine volumes, 1948–57).

1968

1

INTRODUCTION

THAT philosophers are often misunderstood is a well-established though regrettable fact, in many cases not hard to explain. They often seem to assert, or to deny, what they do not really intend to assert or deny, and thus appear to be allies, or even leaders, of schools of thought which they would not in fact approve. Sometimes they themselves do not notice the natural outcome of their own arguments; and it is of course a familiar fact that later generations, or writers with quite other interests, are apt to seek comfort in isolating and misapplying fragments of ancient and respected philosophical doctrine. Berkeley has had his fair share in all of this; he has been constantly praised or blamed, condemned or supported, for the wrong reasons. But his case is more than usually curious and interesting. For, from the first moment of publication, he was taken to be propounding opinions the very reverse of those that he wished to convey; and his most convinced opponents were exactly those people from whom he might have expected, and at first did expect, unhesitating support. He soon came to see that this was so, and did his best to clear up the tangled issues. But in spite of his efforts, those that he thought should agree with him persisted in believing that he was so obviously wrong as scarcely to deserve their serious attention.

'Mem: to be eternally banishing Metaphisics etc. and recalling Men to Common Sense' (P.C. 751). This early note gives vigorous expression to his predominant aim. He and his contemporaries were the immediate heirs to the remarkable achievements of the seventeenth century. In 1700 Isaac Newton was nearly sixty. Galileo, Harvey, and Boyle were not long dead. In philosophy Hobbes, Descartes, and Spinoza had breathed new life into argument and speculation; and Locke, Leibnitz, and Malebranche were still alive. Nevertheless, in spite of all this activity and achievement, it seemed to Berkeley that men's minds had become clogged and burdened with new and old errors; that, in every inquiry and all branches of science, progress was obstructed by a mass of mistakes and complications. Accordingly he set before himself as his primary concern the task of simplification, of clearing the air.

For this work he was indeed admirably equipped. He was the most acute of critics, a writer of perfect grace and lucidity, and by temperament an enemy to all dullness, pedantry, and needless sophistication. He was, at least in his youth, deeply convinced that most branches of learning were in reality far simpler than their professors made them appear, and that the appearance of difficulty was due, if not to deliberate obscurantism, mainly to confusion of mind and to muddled exposition. The philosophers of the Scholastic tradition were, he thought, most seriously to blame for stirring up the 'learned dust', but the mathematicians seemed to him hardly less culpable. Newton alone he regarded with wary respect, and for Locke he felt admiration mingled with pity. 'Wonderful in Locke', he wrote, 'that he could when advanced in years see at all thro a mist that had been so long a-gathering and was consequently thick. This more to be admired than that he didn't see farther' (P.C. 567). (Locke was, in fact, less than sixty years old when his most important work was published; but Berkeley, when he wrote this note, was not much more than twenty.) However, in spite of this certainly sincere tribute, it is Locke who is most openly and frequently attacked in Berkeley's writings; for by his very success he had given new currency to some of the doctrines which Berkeley proposed to annihilate. Lesser antagonists are for the most part ignored or refuted anonymously.

Nor did it seem to Berkeley that his task of clarification was an affair of merely academic importance. For the whole of learning, including mathematics, he took to be of value only so far as it was of use, so that blunders in theory were also practical misfortunes. Atheism and vice, moreover, he thought could flourish only if supported by intellectual mistakes. And so, if once the encumbrance of metaphysics could be thrown off, the sciences could be expected to bring innumerable bene-fits to a universally devout and virtuous public. In the pursuit of this goal Berkeley emphatically claims the alliance of Common Sense; he is on the side of 'the vulgar' against the professors. The opinions, or rather the unformulated assump-tions, of plain men are to be vindicated in his philosophy, and defended against the confusing attacks and questionings of open or covert scepticism.

The response of the public was, however, unsympathetic. On the publication in 1710 of his most important book, the *Principles of Human Knowledge*, a doctor diagnosed insanity in the author; a bishop deplored his vain passion for novelty; some said his fantastic paradoxes were at any rate amusing, and were inclined to excuse him on the ground that he was an Irishman. Even his friends, though respectful of his talents, were quite unconvinced. Dean Swift is reported (perhaps apocryphally) to have left him standing on the door-step when he came to call, saying that if his philosophical views were correct he should be able to come in through a closed door as easily as through an open one. This tale is indeed typical of the common view of Berkeley's doctrines; it was said that he represented the whole of our experience as a dream, and the material world as a collection of 'ideas' in the mind, depen-dent for its very existence on being observed. After all, he explicitly denied the existence of Matter; he asserted that we perceive only 'our own ideas'; and what is this but to say that we are all in a dream? Why open the door if there is really no solid, impenetrable door to be opened? So far from being acclaimed as the rescuer and defender of Common Sense, Berkeley was charged with an absurd and almost frivolous in-difference to the plain and fundamental convictions of all sensible men.

So extreme a divergence as this between Berkeley and his readers cannot wholly be explained away. Certainly he was, as he has often been since, misunderstood; but more is involved than mere misunderstanding. The fact is that Berkeley was himself, in his own way, a metaphysician. He employed without question the same technical vocabulary as that used by his predecessors; whatever his loyalty to Common Sense, he had no great respect for common language. He even had, as they had, a general answer to the most typical of all metaphysical questions – the question what there really *is*. Locke had listed the contents of the Universe as being minds, or 'immaterial substances'; 'ideas'; and material substances, 'external bodies'. Berkeley does not question the value or propriety of such a queer and general catalogue, but boldly offers a rival list of his own. There are, he says, *only* 'spirits' and their 'ideas'. This persistent tendency to oppose strange metaphysical claims with a no less metaphysical counter-assertion naturally puts some strain on his fidelity to Common Sense. He claims, indeed, only to formulate clearly opinions already latent in the untutored mind; and there is no doubt that, in protesting that his views are not so strange as they may seem, he was sincere and to a great extent justified. He did not intend to subvert the accepted opinions of unphilosophical men, and he really believed that he had not done so. But his purpose of vindicating Common Sense was in fact only half fulfilled. Plain men might follow with respect and agreement the work of criticism, of demolition; but the reconstruction would leave them justly uneasy.

*

Berkeley was born in Ireland, in the neighbourhood of Kilkenny, in 1685. His grandfather was English, but both he and Berkeley's father had lived in Ireland. Berkeley himself was brought up and educated there, never visiting England till 1713; and he seems always to have been regarded, and to have regarded himself, as an Irishman. His family was comfortably off, and his education was well provided for. At Kilkenny College, a school with many distinguished names on its roll, he was shortly preceded by Swift and was contemporary with Congreve; and in 1700, at the early age of fifteen, he was sent to Trinity College, Dublin. He would probably have fared worse at that time in England. Many years of war and disturbance in Ireland had only recently ended with the battle of the Boyne and the surrender of Limerick, but Trinity College was full of life. He studied Latin and Greek, French and Hebrew; he was by no means ignorant of mathematics and the works of Newton; and Locke's *Essay concerning Human Understanding*, published ten years before, was already established as a work of great importance. There were societies for discussion among students which Berkeley joined, and the Provost himself was modernist enough to encourage the study of Locke.

He took the degree of B.A. in 1704, and being already marked out for academic distinction, he decided to stay on in the college as a graduate in the hope that a fellowship might before long fall vacant. The opportunity came in 1706; he was admitted as a fellow on June 9th in the following year, and shortly afterwards ordained as the statutes required. It is clear that in these three years of waiting he was far from idle, but it is impossible to say how far he had travelled towards his later opinions. Of three short works which can with plausibility be assigned to this period, all are more or less directly concerned with mathematics; and he evidently gave much attention to this subject, even though he deeply disapproved of most of its exponents, was at times inclined to question its value, and himself held very extraordinary views particularly about geometry. But in 1707 he began to fill a note-book with reflections on a wide field of philosophical topics, and it is from internal evidence clear enough that he was not approaching these problems for the first time. There are two of these note-books, with nearly nine hundred entries – a rare, unusually detailed specimen of the informal comments and remarks of a great philosopher, intended for his own use and not for publication. One or two of the more elaborate entries are evidently designed for incorporation in a book, but they are for the most part brief and colloquial, often dogmatic, and some are almost rude. 'I'll not admire the mathematicians,' he writes, 'I see no wit in any of them but Newton'; and elsewhere he finds even 'Newton in sad plight'. The words 'absurd', 'ridiculous', and 'impossible' occur many times; iconoclasm and defiance are on every page.

It would, of course, be a mistake to look in these *Philosophical Commentaries* (as the notes have recently been called) for any connected, coherent argument.[1] The note-books were filled in a little over a year, but Berkeley at the time was not much more than twenty years old and his opinions were not yet firmly settled. Some of the entries clearly conflict with others; they are not set down in any order of logical sequence; and most of them are of interest mainly as the seeds from which his later publications developed, and so do not need or deserve separate consideration. He has already framed what he calls 'ye immaterial hypothesis', the view that 'matter does not exist'; and he already believes and repeatedly affirms that this is in no way in conflict with common sense. But at first he seems to have embraced an 'ontology' even more strange than anything he advocated later: 'Nothing properly but persons i.e. conscious things do exist, all other things are not so much existences as manners of ye existence of persons' (P.C. 24). This would indeed have scandalized his readers; however, he soon reminds himself (P.C. 79) not to 'fall in with Sceptics', but 'to make bodies exist certainly, which they doubt of.' But perhaps the most interesting feature of the *Commentaries* is that they seem to contain sketches and notes for the treatment of a much wider range of problems than those actually dealt with in Berkeley's published works. The bulk of his published writing is concerned with the nature of perception, though he also deals at some length with problems about mathematics and the natural sciences. Among his notes, however, are numerous remarks about ethics, and many more about Volition, Desire, the Will, Understanding, and the Mind. It is as if he had intended, after discussing our knowledge of the material world, to discuss also our knowledge of our own and other people's minds and characters, and of the moral rules that should govern human conduct. The *Principles* was in fact published as 'Part I'; and he said, many years later, that he had by about

1715 made considerable progress with the later parts, but had lost the manuscript while travelling in Italy. And, he then said, 'I never had the leisure since to do so disagreeable a thing as writing twice on the same subject.' His original plan seems to have been to cover, probably in several volumes, the entire field of philosophical, scientific, and mathematical inquiry. This project appears, no doubt, rather grandiose; but Berkeley believed that he had found a key. He had, he thought, hit upon a single and simple truth in the light of which the whole field of human inquiry could be easily surveyed, simplified, and set in order. It seemed to him, too, that this momentous truth must be, if freely considered, accepted by everyone. 'I wonder not', he wrote (P.C. 279), 'at my sagacity in discovering the obvious tho' amazing truth, I rather wonder at my stupid inadvertency in not finding it out before.'

Many philosophers before, and also long after, Berkeley's day thought of their task as that of rendering clear and intelligible the complex phenomena of ordinary experience by 'analysing' them into their simplest elements, and showing how from these simple elements the complex facts could be reconstructed. Berkeley accepted this aim. But he believed that his predecessors, notably Locke, had fallen into most serious errors: they had in fact presented a supposedly clear, 'analytic' view of the world, which however made it appear that we were necessarily quite ignorant of that world's true nature, and which played into the hands of irreligion and vice. And he thought he knew how this had come about. Most theorists, he suggested, who had put forward absurd or unintelligible doctrines had done so 'through not knowing what existence was'. In making up their picture of the world they had asserted the existence of various entities which they *could* not have taken to exist, if they had grasped the meaning of that word. ' 'Tis on the Discovering of the nature and meaning and import of Existence that I chiefly insist' (P.C. 491). In the light of this discovery, so Berkeley thought, we could at last see the correct and only possible way in which, from its simple elements ('ideas'), the 'mighty frame of the world' must be constructed;

and we could see also that this construction *cannot* raise the baffling problems on which Locke and others (he believed) had come to grief. The true picture of the world is luminously clear; atheism vanishes before it as self-contradictory; and Common Sense (so he repeatedly affirms) 'receives no manner of disturbance'.

His great 'discovery' is this – that existence is '*percipi* or *percipere*'; to exist is either to be perceived or to perceive. He claims that the word is in fact 'vulgarly restrained' to this sense; philosophers, however, have introduced the notion that existence and perception can be distinguished, and hence have flowed all their confusions and difficulties. If once this distinction is disallowed, we shall find 'a vast view of things soluble hereby'; and at first (P.C. 604) Berkeley was sanguine enough to say that 'I am persuaded would Men but examine what they mean by the word Existence they would agree with me.'

Most of the difficulty of all Berkeley's doctrines is contained in embryo in such remarks as these, and a proper examination of them must be left to subsequent chapters. It can however be seen at once that (with one conspicuous exception) he is putting forward an extreme, dogmatic, and very simplified version of empiricism. No assertion of existence is to be accepted unless what we assert to exist not only could be, but actually *is*, perceived; or unless it is itself a perceiving 'spirit'. He is, as he himself says, asserting 'the evidence of sense as high as you please', indeed rejecting any other kind of evidence. He does not, he insists, wish to deny any statement for which there is actual evidence, but only to unmask the confusions of theorists by clarifying the meanings of words: if this is done we shall see what assertions *can* be significantly made; what does, and what could not conceivably, *exist*. The exception to his empirical principles is that, in his view, every part of the universe is necessarily and always 'in the mind of God'; God is an omnipresent, infinite spirit whose power is seen in every event, and whose purposes direct the course of everything in nature. The things that we ourselves perceive are 'in the mind of God';

his mind and his will uphold, and alone uphold, 'the whole choir of heaven and furniture of the earth.' Berkeley thinks he can show that this is demonstrably true.

When he was writing his major works Berkeley was very young and conscious of his youth, but already widely read and thoroughly confident, prepared to take issue with his predecessors however eminent. On the 'meaning of existence' he was utterly convinced; his principle that '*esse* is *percipi* or *percipere*' appeared to him almost as a revelation. He was not a 'piecemeal' philosopher, dealing with limited problems one at a time; he was not merely the critic of other men's errors, nor a cool practitioner of 'philosophical analysis'. He believed that he, and he alone, had noticed a vital and neglected truth, in the light of which whole departments of supposed learning, whole batches of problems, could simply be swept away. He could state, with lucid finality, what there really *is*. In this he diverges from the philosophical tradition in which he is often regarded as a transitional figure. In point of time, indeed, he stands between his predecessors Descartes and Locke, and his successors Hume and Kant; and certainly Locke's influence upon him, as his upon Hume, was very great.[2] But in many ways their problems were not his. He did not, or did not merely, ask what can be known with certainty and how it can be known; he was wholly uninterested in 'philosophic doubt', and never thought of questioning that on most points men (unless they are also philosophers) know well enough what they ordinarily think that they know. For questions such as these would have seemed to him relatively trifling. His task was rather to assert the fundamental, illuminating truth that to exist is either to perceive or be perceived : that there is God, there are 'spirits' and 'ideas', and nothing else whatever.

*

While Berkeley was filling his note-books in 1707, already planning his vast and comprehensive survey, he turned aside for a time to examine some particular problems in visual perception. The results of this inquiry were published in 1709 as

An Essay towards a New Theory of Vision. In this work his most novel contentions are kept out of sight; but it is both an admirable piece of argument, and a useful stage on the way to his developed doctrines. It is important to bear in mind that the views here stated are not Berkeley's final views, and are open to objections which his other writings evade. With this reservation, however, we may accept the chronological starting-point as also the first step in our exposition.

2

THE *ESSAY*: (1) THE PROPER
OBJECTS OF VISION

IN writing his *Essay* Berkeley was influenced by several considerations. There was at the time a general demand for books on Optics, stimulated by the recent work of Newton and by the rapidly increasing availability of optical instruments; as a result of which, partly, the *Essay* was at first the most successful of his publications. A second edition was issued within a few months of the first, and the book attracted attention on the Continent as well as in Ireland and England. Its doctrines, too, were not so strange and unfamiliar as those that earned a cold reception for the *Principles*; on the contrary, more than a hundred and fifty years later a philosopher could refer to what he called 'the received (or Berkeleian) theory of vision'. But Berkeley had also an axe of his own to grind; he wished to prepare the way for his projected major work. In that work he was to maintain that what is seen is, strictly speaking, 'in the mind': and he realized that to some readers it would appear that this is simply and obviously untrue. Do we not 'in truth see external space and bodies actually existing in it, some nearer, others farther off'; and does this not 'carry with it some opposition to what has been said of their existing nowhere without the mind'? Berkeley plans to remove in advance this likely and natural objection to his main case. 'The consideration of this difficulty it was that gave birth to my *Essay towards a New Theory of Vision*, which was published not long since' (P. 43). For our purposes the *Essay* merits close attention, for in it Berkeley explains at length certain strange statements which are later taken almost for granted, and as a result seem needlessly cryptic and puzzling.

*

He begins with a statement of his precise, limited intentions. 'My design is to show the manner wherein we perceive by sight the distance, magnitude, and situation of objects. Also to consider the difference there is betwixt the ideas of sight and touch, and whether there be any idea common to both senses.' In following out the second part of this design Berkeley winds his way into some awkward problems; but at first all goes well.

Berkeley saw clearly, as too many writers on the 'theory of vision' did not, that questions of several different kinds can be asked about seeing, and that serious mistakes will be made unless each kind is properly distinguished from the others. There is, to begin with, the geometry of optics. Questions about refraction, reflection, magnification, or the curvature and focal length of lenses, can be asked and answered in purely geometrical terms; and the eye for this purpose can properly be regarded simply as an adjustable lens. On the other hand, investigation of what Berkeley calls 'the mechanism of the eye' is a different matter and, as he says, 'appertaineth to anatomy and experiments'. Here we have to deal with the muscles of the eye, its anatomical structure, the physiology of the retina and the optic nerve. Berkeley's own inquiry is different from both of these. When he asks about 'the manner wherein we perceive by sight the distance, magnitude, and situation of objects', he does not want a geometrical account of the properties of such a lens as the eye nor does he wish to know how light stimulates the retina, the optic nerve, and the brain. He wishes to know what it is that enables us to estimate by eye the distance from us, the size, and the position of the various objects that we see; and what leads us to make the particular estimates that we do.

One puzzling expression crops up at the outset. It is, Berkeley says, 'agreed by all that distance, of itself and immediately, cannot be seen'. What are we to make of this? Someone might say 'There's a gap between those two trees', and I might properly say 'Yes, so I see.' But if he had said 'The distance be tween those two trees is exactly 54 feet 3 inches', my remark would not have been in place. I might claim to have guessed, or judged, that the distance between them was something of that order; but I could not claim to *see* that it was exactly that. Does Berkeley, then, intend to call our attention to the fact that we do not speak of 'seeing' distance? If so, he is on firm ground.

One might, however, feel inclined to object to what he says on the ground that, though certainly we do not speak of 'seeing' distance, yet simply to say 'Distance cannot be seen' is to suggest that, when we see things, they do not *look distant*. But in some sense at least they certainly do. We often say 'It looks a very long way off', 'I saw him in the distance', and so on; we claim to see things that are at all sorts of distances from us, and which look as if they are; and does not saying 'Distance cannot be seen' suggest, at any rate, that this is not so?

But the point which, in this rather odd way, Berkeley is seeking to make is a different one. Consider again the two trees. There is, we said, a gap between them; I see that there is a gap, and there is a familiar device for measuring such visible gaps by the breadth of one's fingers held out at arm's length. But I cannot in the same way 'see the gap' between either of the two trees and myself. If I hold up a finger it will probably obstruct my view of the trees altogether. The gap between myself and any object at which I look is a gap which, we might say, I can only look at from one end; and of course from the end it does not *look* like a gap – not like the gap that I can see between the two trees. It is this that Berkeley wishes to point out. 'For distance being a line directed endwise to the eye, it projects only one point in the fund of the eye, which point remains invariably the same, whether the distance be longer or shorter.' I invariably remain at one end of the gap between myself and the objects at which I look: I cannot move to one side and so see the gap between myself and them.

Now in view of the agreed fact that the 'point in the fund of the eye ... remains invariably the same', however near or far the objects may be, many writers on optics had found it hard to explain how we ever contrive at all to estimate the distance of objects from us. However, in the current orthodoxy, at least part of the difficulty was supposed to have been met by appeal to the fact that most people have two eyes. If both eyes are directed upon an object, the two straight lines from the eyes to the object (the 'optic axes') will converge; and if the object is very close to the eyes, the angle of intersection of the optic axes will be fairly large. It was then supposed that, at least in the case of an object very close to our eyes, we are able to calculate its distance from us from the angle at which the optic axes converge on it – the larger this angle, the closer the object must be. The same theorists had also made some provision for those who have, or for any reason wish to use, only one eye. Their argument here was that the rays of light emitted or reflected from an object very close to us must converge quite sharply upon the eye; and that this angle of convergence decreases as the object is moved further away. In this way the distance of the object could be worked out from the angle at which the rays converge on the eye. It was admitted in this case, and in the former too, that unless an object is very close to us we cannot work out its distance in the way described; for as it recedes, the angles of convergence soon become so extremely small that we could not reasonably be supposed to detect any further variations in them. But, with this restriction, the problem was widely held to have been solved.

Berkeley rejects the whole of this account, and for the right reasons. He points out, in effect, that what leads me to form a particular judgement on any occasion must be something of which on that occasion I am *aware*, even if I do not go through any deliberate reasoning process or consciously make any inferences. Suppose, for example, that on meeting an acquaintance I formed the opinion, or got the impression, that he was angry. What gave me this impression? He looked pale, perhaps; he frowned; he was drumming with his fingers on the table. That is why I thought he was angry. Now his looking pale and frowning could not have been what gave me the idea that he was angry, if in fact I could not see his face. His drumming fingers could not have given me the clue, if I could neither see nor hear what his fingers were doing. Also, the

possible fact that his heart was pounding could not have contributed to my impression, if either I did not know that this
was the case, or did not know that a pounding heart had any
connexion with being angry. However difficult it may be to
say just what made me think that he was angry, it must be
wrong to mention circumstances of which I was totally unaware or totally ignorant. These could not have influenced my
judgement in any way.

But the orthodox writers on optics had, as Berkeley saw,
committed exactly this sort of mistake. Their statements about
variations in the angle of intersection of the optic axes or in
the angle of convergence of light rays might be perfectly correct, and even of great theoretical value. But it is obvious that
we do not in fact make use of these doctrines in estimating the
distance from us of objects, or in explaining why we have
made a particular estimate. A man who has never heard or
thought of the geometry of optics may judge distances as well
as, or better than, an expert in the subject. But worse than
that, we could not, even if we tried, make use of geometry in
judging distances – though we might, of course, in the process
of *measuring* them. For we do not actually see lines from our
eyes converging upon an object, or lines from the object converging upon each eye: and so we see no angles of intersection or convergence. These lines and angles are to be found
only in the theorists' diagrams; and the diagrams are not pic-
tures of visible rods, nor of anything else that we actually see.
(Similarly, though contour lines are a useful device in map-
making, it would be absurd to say that they help us to *judge*
the height of hills.) Thus, the orthodox explanation of our
judgements of distance by eye mentions circumstances of
which, in judging, we cannot possibly be aware and about
which many competent judges are wholly uninformed. What
is said may be true enough, but it cannot be the right answer
to the problem proposed.

Having thus got the orthodox theory out of the way, Berkeley turns to his own account of the matter. He considers the
sort of case with which the official theory was supposed to deal

satisfactorily, namely the case of an object that we judge to be very close to us. He finds here three features. First, we sometimes (not perhaps often) actually feel the muscular strain required to turn both eyes inwards upon an object; second, the object is often, as we say, 'out of focus' – 'the nearer it is brought the more confused appearance it makes'; and third, if we try to keep our eyes focused upon it, we usually feel the increasing muscular effort required to do so. In other cases quite different factors are important. If an object looks 'faint', or if we 'perceive a great number of intermediate objects, such as houses, fields, rivers, and the like', we tend to judge that the object is a long way off. (Conversely, in a very clear atmosphere, or on a relatively featureless surface such as the sea, our estimates of distance tend to be much too small.) Further, judgements of distance and size are interdependent. If I see a car coming down a long, straight road, and the car is much smaller than I ordinarily expect cars to be, I will be apt to think that it is further away than it actually is; I will tend, as it were, to compensate for its sub-normal size by exaggerating its distance.

Berkeley does not pursue these inquiries in much detail: they are of course matters of very great detail indeed, but this is not his primary concern. He wishes mainly to set the whole question on the right lines, and in this broad aim he is entirely successful. He sees that there is an essential distinction to be drawn between estimating or judging, and measuring or calculating, distance and size; and he sees that what leads us to make our particular estimates must be something to do with how things look, combined with our normal beliefs and assumptions about them and (in a few cases) actual feelings in the eyes. In particular he is eager to insist that there is a purely contingent connexion between the clues that we use in judging, and the actual states of affairs about which we make judgements. If the base of a triangle is kept constant and the angle at the apex diminished it is obviously necessary that the height of the triangle should increase; this can be geometrically demonstrated. The orthodox theory, which Berkeley has rejected, contended that in judging, for example, that an object is receding from us we use as the basis for our judgement the decrease in the angle of intersection of the optic axes – an alleged clue which is necessarily, demonstrably, connected with increasing distance. But the clues that we actually do use have no such necessary connexion with our conclusions. It *happens* to be the case that we have difficulty in focusing our eyes on objects very close to us; it *happens*, owing to the nature of the atmosphere, that remote objects tend to look 'faint'. The connexion between the clues and the conclusion is 'habitual or customary', not necessary and demonstrable; it has to be learned and tested by experience; peculiarities and variations in the looks of things are no further bases for estimates of distances 'than as by experience they have been found to be connected with them.'

With Berkeley's discussion of what he calls 'situation' we find ourselves in deeper waters. He considers under this heading only one problem, and that a problem newly raised by the scientists 'of the last age'. It had been noticed that, if light is passed through a lens resembling the eye and projected on a screen behind it, the resulting pattern on the screen is upside down. If, that is, the source of light has the shape of a pyramid standing on its base, the shape projected on the screen is that of a pyramid standing on its apex. Thus, if we take the figure of a man as the source from which light is reflected into the eye, the pattern on the retina will have the same shape, but will be exactly inverted. How then, it was asked, does it come about that the man is seen as the right way up, and not standing on his head?

Berkeley's treatment of what he appositely calls this 'knot' is surprisingly complicated. He is here, as in the former cases, concerned to reject the orthodox solution of the difficulty, 'allowed by all men as satisfactory'; but his own account is extremely difficult to follow. It certainly contains many hints at a proper solution, but much of it is highly idiosyncratic and puzzling.

The official solution was as follows. We know, it was argued, that the rays of light emitted or reflected from objects cross each other in the eye; and so, 'perceiving an impulse of a ray of light on the upper part of the eye', we regard this ray as emanating in a straight line from the lower part of the object; conversely with the impulses that we perceive on the lower part of the eye. It is, it was said, as if we felt at an object with a pair of crossed sticks; in this case we would realize that the stick held in the upper hand touched the lower part of the object, and the stick in the lower hand touched the upper part of it.

'But', Berkeley observes, 'this account to me does not seem in any degree true.' It would imply, for one thing, that no one could escape from the difficulty unless he were familiar with the theory of optics, and were constantly correcting his impressions by reference to it – constantly reminding himself on theoretical grounds that the things he sees are not *really* upside down. But this is quite untrue. People who have never heard of or thought about the theory of optics feel no difficulty. They do not constantly make foolish mistakes because the world seems to them to be upside down and they do not know how this impression ought to be corrected. But the account works no better for those who do know about optics. For it is in any case not true to say that we *perceive* rays of light impinging on the retina, in the way in which we might perceive a stick that we held in our hand. When I look at a tree it is the tree that I see; it is not the rays of light reflected from the tree, nor is it the pattern produced by them on my retina. The fact is that it is really nonsensical to suggest that the whole world, including the observer's own body, *could* look to anyone to be upside down. A man might indeed stand on his head; but then he would be perfectly aware that his head was nearer to the ground than his feet, whereas the people he saw had their feet firmly planted on the earth – which is, of course, to say that they were the right way up. Whatever may occur to our retinas (and we hardly ever stop to consider what does occur), we do in fact see people's feet, the bases of trees, and so on, closest to the ground, and people's heads and the tops of trees farthest from it; we know that our own feet and heads are similarly placed; and this is exactly to be, and to see other things as being, the right way up. 'The head is painted farthest from, and the feet nearest to, the visible earth; and so they appear to be. What is there strange or unaccountable in this?'

The official theorists had, as Berkeley intermittently seems to appreciate, made a fundamental but oddly tempting mistake. From speaking of the inverted 'image' on the retina – they sometimes called it a 'picture' – and from pointing out that such an image is always present when anything is seen, they had slipped into thinking that it is this inverted image or picture that we really see. They had the idea of a man living, as it were, behind his own retina, upright inside his own head, peering at the retina as if at a screen on which everything appears upside down. And it seemed then that this man must either work out, in terms of optical theory, how the 'external world' comes to project on the screen an inverted image; or else he would mistakenly take for granted that the world beyond the screen is itself the wrong way up. But such a picture as this is wholly inappropriate. The retina is not a screen at which we peer; so far from seeing nothing but images on our own retinas, we actually never see such things at all. We do not lurk behind our eyes and between our ears, seeing and hearing only what goes on in our own heads. If we resist the influence of this queer but curiously seductive notion and 'confine our thoughts to the proper objects of sight, the whole is plain and easy.'

But Berkeley believes that there is much more to be said. He suggests that there is another, quite different absurdity in the statement of the problem. He argues that the correct application of such expressions as 'erect' and 'inverted' is really to be determined by the sense of *touch*; that sight has nothing to do with the matter at all; so that the expression 'It *looks* upside down' is strictly illegitimate, as would be, for example, the expression 'It *sounds* pink.' We are apt, he says, to suppose that we can 'judge of the situation of visible ob-

jects with reference to their distance from the tangible earth' –
we think, for instance, that we can properly say that the visible
top of something is close to the ground, and so that the thing
looks to be the wrong way up. But this is a mistake, in Berkeley's opinion. For he says that the 'tangible earth', by reference to which positions are really determined, 'is not perceived
by sight'; and we cannot, therefore, speak of the position rela-
tive to it of any object that *is* perceived by sight. 'The two distinct provinces of sight and touch should be considered apart,
and as if their objects had no intercourse, no manner of relation one to another, in point of distance or position.' Thus, the
supposed problem of the inverted retinal image cannot arise.
We cannot say that things *look* to be situated otherwise than
as they really are; for there is in fact no relation at all, either
right or wrong, either usual or unexpected, between what we
see and things, 'tangible' things, as they really are.

These puzzling contentions are offered as part of the solution of the puzzle about the retinal image, but they raise the
whole topic of the second part of the *Essay* – namely, 'the difference there is betwixt the ideas of sight and touch, and
whether there be any idea common to both senses.' So we will
go on to consider this topic in general, without special reference to that particular problem.

*

In Sec. 41 Berkeley argues that, since judging distances and
sizes by eye is a skill or knack that is acquired by experience
and practice, a man born blind and suddenly enabled to see
would at first be quite at a loss. In fact, having acquired his
notions of size and distance solely by experience of movement
and touching, he would not at first see how such expressions
as 'broad' and 'narrow', 'near' and 'far', could have any application in the quite new field of experience suddenly opened
to him. He would not consider that any such expressions could
be applied to objects merely by looking; he would rely as before on his old techniques of feeling and moving about. Berkeley is inclined to suggest that a man in this (seemingly)

unfortunate position is in many ways nearer to the truth of things than normal people.

Let us, he says, 'carefully observe what is meant in common discourse, when one says that which he sees is at a distance from him.' Suppose I look at the moon, and say that it is 240,000 miles away. I cannot, Berkeley thinks, mean to say this of the 'visible moon', the moon that I see. for that is only a quite small, flat, illuminated disc; and if I moved in its direction for 240,000 miles, I should no longer see anything of the kind. What I saw at first, and what I said was 240,000 miles away, is simply not to be found if I were to make the journey; I must have been wrong, then, in saying that *it* was 240,000 miles away. So that Berkeley now goes further than he did at first, and says that 'I neither see distance itself, nor anything that I take to be at a distance.'

We must be careful at this point. Berkeley is not, presumably, denying that we take ourselves to see things at a distance; for this we certainly do. Rather he is suggesting that what we actually *do* see is not at a distance, and is not even what we take to be at a distance. I may take myself to be seeing the moon at a distance of 240,000 miles; and the moon really *is* at that distance away; but then it is not, strictly speaking, the moon that I see. What I actually see is 'a small, round, luminous flat'; and this neither is, nor is considered to be, at the distance and of the size of the moon itself.

To illustrate and support this unusual doctrine Berkeley compares the case of hearing. Just as I might say that I *see* a coach half a mile away, I might also say that I *hear* a coach half a mile away. Berkeley admits that we commonly speak in this way, but he believes that such ways of speaking are loose and misleading. In the case of hearing this is, he thinks, plainly so. For when I say that I hear a coach half a mile away, I hear, *strictly speaking*, only a certain sound. This sound 'suggests' to me that there is a coach in the distance; but the 'proper object' of hearing, the sound that I actually hear, is not itself at any distance at all. And the case of seeing, he contends, is exactly analogous. I might loosely say that I saw the coach in the distance; but here too the 'proper object' of sight is not at a distance, but serves merely to suggest to my mind that there actually is a coach at a distance from me.

At this point a question naturally arises. If (strictly speaking) what I hear and what I see is not at a distance, what *is* at a distance? This is for Berkeley a decidedly awkward question, but let us for the moment merely record his answer to it – 'tangible objects', he says, are really at a distance, 'in circumambient space'. Most tangible things, my ash-tray for example, are thought to be visible too; but to this Berkeley has his answer ready. 'The objects of sight and touch are two distinct things' – what I touch when I pick up the ash-tray is not the same as what I see when I look at it.

His contention, then, is this. In ordinary speech we often say that we see, hear, and touch the very same thing. Berkeley often writes as if he regarded this as false; he certainly regards it as dangerously inaccurate, concealing the nature of the case and suggesting wrong views of it. For in his view each sense has its 'proper objects', and if we spoke correctly we would always assign to each sense only the objects proper to it. If we speak otherwise we do so at our peril.

He admits that 'it may perhaps require some thought rightly to conceive this distinction.' And it is in fact curiously difficult to work out – much more so than he seems to have realized. Clearly, it must be asked what *are* the proper objects of the various senses. What is it that, if we speak really *strictly*, we shall say that we see and hear, touch, taste, and smell?

Let us begin with hearing. In this case the answer seems obvious enough – we hear sounds. And sounds are 'proper' to the sense of hearing in the way that Berkeley requires. Sounds, that is to say, can only be heard – it would be nonsense to speak of seeing or touching, tasting or smelling, a sound; and furthermore, if anything at all is heard, what is heard is necessarily a sound. Perhaps we might say that the word 'sound' is the 'tautologous accusative' of the verb 'to hear'; it is logically necessary that, if I hear at all, I hear a sound, and it would be obviously incorrect to use 'sound' as object to any of the verbs 'see', 'touch', 'taste', or 'smell'. So far, then, so good.

And now what about seeing? What here is the 'proper object' or tautologous accusative? No word springs to mind so readily as did 'sounds'. Indeed, as Berkeley says, 'the difficulty seems not a little increased, because the combination of visible ideas hath constantly the same name as the combination of tangible ideas wherewith it is connected.' It seems that most possible objects of the verb 'to see' could also be objects of, at least, the verb 'to touch' – for we ordinarily say that we see and touch the same things. But in the end Berkeley hits upon a curious answer – we see 'light and colours'. For presumably, whenever we see at all, we can be said to see light and colours – even if the colour be black or the light very faint; and light and colours can only be seen, not heard or touched, tasted or smelled. Leaving aside for the moment the sense of touch, we may complete the list with the senses of taste and smell, whose 'proper objects' are obviously tastes and smells.

This list has at least one important peculiarity which Berkeley does not bring out. It is not, so to speak, a homogeneous list; the supposed 'proper object' of sight is oddly unlike those of hearing, taste, and smell. We can speak of the sound *of* a car, the taste *of* an orange, the smell *of* a geranium. But in the case of sight there is nothing analogous to this. We do, no doubt, see light and colours, although we would not ordinarily *say* that this is what we see; but we cannot speak of 'the light and colours *of*' anything. I heard the sound of a car; I smelled the smell of the geraniums : I saw the . . . of a tree. There is no expression that fills the gap in the last of these sentences, in the way in which 'sound' and 'smell' find an ordinary, natural place in the others. Certainly 'light and colours' would be completely out of place in this context.

There is, as one would naturally expect, an explanation of this asymmetry. We do in fact locate and recognize the objects in our environment mainly by the senses of sight and touch, predominantly by the sense of sight. It is, indeed, obvious that we could hardly do otherwise. Many things are

tasteless, or for a variety of familiar reasons cannot in practice
be tasted. Inanimate objects often do not make any noises, and
even animate objects emit detectable sounds only intermittently. Comparatively few things have characteristic, easily
detectable and distinguishable smells. In addition, the range
of these senses is very limited, and it is often extremely difficult to tell where a smell or a sound is coming from; they are
often, so to speak, pervasive, and give us few clues to the
direction and position of their sources. Thus, we do and we
must normally establish the presence and existence of objects
without reference to how (if at all) they taste and smell, or
what noises (if any) they make from time to time. We may
add these tests, of course, for special purposes; we might decide whether what is in the decanter is whisky by taking a
sniff, or whether a coin is genuine by ringing it on the counter.
But even in these cases, we would ordinarily bring our noses
and ears into play only when we had already established, by
other means, that there was a decanter with something in it on
the table, or a metal object of some sort in our hands. In this
primary task our hands and our eyes play the principal role.

All this being so, we can *distinguish* the object whose presence and existence we have thus established, from the smell of
it and its taste, and the noises it makes. I can speak of the
sound of a car, because I already know, or could have known,
of the presence of a car, independently of hearing anything. I
can speak of the *taste of* an orange, because the question
whether there is an orange to hand can be settled without my
tasting anything. We cannot, however, distinguish in a similar
way between the object, and what we see and touch; for what
we see and touch is, precisely, the object – it is *essentially* by
the use of these senses that the existence of common objects is
established. If an object makes no sound and has no taste and
no smell, we are not in the least put out; there are doubtless a
great many objects of which this is true. But if there is nothing
to be seen or felt, there is no object there (though there may
seem to be so).

Thus, Berkeley's claim that we see (strictly speaking) 'light

and colours' is by no means, as he implies, exactly analogous
with the statement that we hear sounds. It shares, however,
with this latter statement the character of being oddly un-
informative. But this, after all, is inevitable. If there is anything which, whenever I hear at all, I can be said to hear; and
which I could not without absurdity be said to see or touch,
taste or smell; then to *say* that I hear this cannot be to say
more than simply that I hear. (To know that people hear
sounds, it is only necessary to know what hearing *is*.) Similarly, if light and colours are indeed, in Berkeley's sense,
'proper objects' of sight, then to say that this is what we see is
to say no more than barely that we see. Hence, to say that
(strictly speaking) the objects of sight and of hearing are not
the same, would be to say no more than that seeing is not
hearing.

We can now understand why Berkeley is certain that there
is 'no idea common to both sight and touch.'[3] The notion that
there are such common ideas had been put forward by Locke.
Locke's use of the word 'idea' is hopelessly vague, but what he
seems to have meant in the present case is this. There are at
least two obvious ways of deciding (roughly) what shape an
object is – we can look at it, or we can feel it. We can say 'It
feels round' as well as 'It looks round.' Thus, Locke would say
that the word 'shape', and words for shapes, denote ideas common to two senses, the senses of touch and sight. But Berkeley
is not willing to say this. He might allow that we do speak as in
the examples cited, but he would think it improper to do so;
for in his own terminology, as we have seen, to say that the
ideas, 'proper objects', of sight are not the same as the ideas of
touch amounts to saying that seeing is not touching; and this
is certainly true. Locke, of course, had not intended to say
that seeing is the same as touching; so that, when Berkeley
says that there are no ideas common to both sight and touch,
he is not denying what Locke had intended to assert. But however this may be, in his own terms Berkeley's contention is
certainly, even necessarily, correct.

He next seeks to re-inforce his point, however, by considerations which are mistaken. Although he would, it seems, be on strong ground if he insisted merely that an *idea* (in his usage) cannot be the 'proper object' of more than one sense – for him this would be true by definition – the fact remains that there are some *words*, such as 'round', which we use in saying both how things look and how they feel. We suppose, in fact, that a round shape can be recognized both by looking and by feeling. (This is the point Locke had in mind.) But if this is so, there remains a strong temptation to think that at any rate some things, shape for example, can be seen as well as felt; and hence that 'the two distinct provinces of sight and touch' cannot really be so distinct as Berkeley makes out.

Now Berkeley might, I suppose, have suggested that the word 'round' is simply a loose and misleading word, which would not be used at all in a 'strict' language, a language in which we associate with each verb of perception those words, and only those, that are 'proper' to it – colours to 'see', odours to 'smell', and so on. Instead, he chooses to say that such words as 'round' are *ambiguous*. There is, he says, tangible shape and, an entirely different thing, visible shape. We may use the word 'round' to refer to a visible or to a tangible shape, but we are not referring to the same thing in each case. Consider a man who has been blind from birth. Clearly he could have learned to use the word 'round'; he could learn that objects which affect his sense of touch in a certain way are ordinarily said to be round. Now suppose that a tennis-ball is set before him and that he is suddenly made to see. Would he forthwith, without touching the ball, correctly apply the word 'round' to that object which he now, for the first time, sees with his eyes? Berkeley answers that he would not; and no doubt he is right. And he infers that the word 'round' and other words for shapes, when they are applied to things that we touch, do not *mean the same* as when applied to things that we see; for if they did, he argues, the suddenly healed blind man would at once ascribe the correct shape to any object he saw. If the word 'round' is unambiguous, and he understands it, surely he would be able to say immediately that the tennis-ball is round. 'If the same angle or square which is the object of touch be also the object of vision, what should hinder the blind man at first sight from knowing it?'

But the answer to this question is very simple. What 'hinders the blind man at first sight' is exactly the fact that he has hitherto been blind. He has learned to apply the word 'round' not, as normal people do, by looking at objects as well as touching them, but only by touching them; even if he never applies it incorrectly, he has still not learned to use it in the ordinary way. Part of its ordinary use is inaccessible to him, because he lacks the use of his eyes. Of course he does not know how a round object looks; he has never seen such a thing: he has never seen anything, and has no notion how words refer to what is seen. Berkeley's example thus begs the whole question. In seeking to show that the word 'round' does not describe a shape that things look as well as a shape that things feel, he cites the case of a man who does not and could not use the word 'round' as it is normally used. But this is not the way to show what it really means. It is not at all the case that 'round' is commonly used with *two meanings*, or in two senses, of which a blind man could learn one but not the other. It is rather that there are two conjoined criteria for its use – how things look and how they feel. If an object felt round but looked square, or felt square and looked round, we would never say that it was round 'in one sense', but not in another; we would not know what to say about its shape at all. The normal conditions in which we use the word 'round' would simply have broken down; and the plain fact that in this case we would be utterly baffled, and would not at once speak of its being round 'in one sense of the term', shows that there is no *ambiguity* about it. There are *two ways* of telling what shape an object is; but this does not mean, as Berkeley suggests, that there are *two shapes*, one visible and the other tangible.

However, his use of this example does help us to see more clearly what his view is. He argues that the word 'round' is ambiguous, that visible shape is not the same as tangible shape, because he does not wish to drop the word entirely and yet will not admit that, in the *strict* use of language, a word might characterize univocally both what we see and what we touch. And this brings into prominence his notion of what a strict language would be. It would be a language in which to each verb of perception would be appropriated its own list of grammatical objects and adjectives; if any words appeared on more than one list they would be ambiguous words, with as many different senses as there are different lists on which they appear. The point of having such a language is, in Berkeley's opinion, this: it would enable us, in reporting what we perceive, always to distinguish accurately between what is actually present to our senses and what, as a result of our experience, is merely suggested to us. The statement 'I hear a car' he regards as 'loose', in the sense that I could only make this statement if I had *learned* to associate the sound that I hear with cars. I am, he thinks, *immediately* aware of the sound, but of the car only by 'suggestion' – by a learned, customary association of sounds of that sort with the things called cars. Similarly, if I say that I see a round tennis-ball, this is not a report of what I actually *see*; what I actually see is a round, white area of colour. The statement 'I see a round tennis-ball' is one that I would not and could not make, unless I had learned to associate areas of colour shaped in this way with the presence of tennis-balls. But in every case we ought, in speaking *strictly*, to distinguish what we actually see, hear, and so on, from what is merely suggested to us by experience of customary associations.

Curiously, Berkeley does not seem to think of this 'strict' way of speaking as requiring an alteration or reform of language as it is. He thinks rather that his ideal language is what our existing language would be, if we used it really properly. For practical purposes he regards a certain laxity as tolerable, even advantageous; but in reality, he maintains, we are breaking the rules when we speak as we ordinarily do. The advantage in doing this, he thinks, is mainly that of brevity. It would take much longer to say that I hear a certain sound (hard to describe) which suggests to me that I will in time see a train, than it takes to say that I can hear the train in the cutting. And the price paid for this advantage is not too high, since in practice it leads to no undesirable consequences. When I hear that characteristic sound, there nearly always is in the neighbourhood the object that I have learned to associate with it; so that when I say, loosely, that I hear the train, neither I nor my audience are disastrously misled.

But this, Berkeley insists, might not have been so. Just as there is a merely customary connexion between visible faintness and great distance, so there is a merely contingent, customary connexion between the deliverances of the various senses. It is clear enough that what looks and feels like a rose might have had a smell quite other than it actually has, or might have had no smell at all; but equally, if less easily, it is conceivable that what looks like a rose might not have felt like a rose. The look of an object might conceivably not have been any sort of guide to how it would feel, taste, or smell. If so, we could not of course have used a language which relies on there being such regular connexions as this. I could not say 'I hear the train in the cutting', if there was no reason at all for associating the noise that I hear with the presence of a train; I could not say 'I saw a cat in the garden' if what I saw was in no way connected with what I might have felt or smelt on closer inspection. If in so wild and chaotic a world as this there could be any language and any speakers at all, they would be obliged to satisfy Berkeley's standards of strictness. They would have to speak only of the 'proper objects' of sight and the other senses, for what they saw would be no indication of what might be heard or felt; what they heard would not suggest to them what might be seen. It would be as if they were subject to what we should now call (though they would not) a perpetual hallucination – apparently an elephant, but nothing like it to be heard or felt; a sound like a rocket but no such thing to be seen; a blow on the head struck soundlessly by no visible instrument. Useless to ask (as *we* should) what was really there, or what actually happened; it could only be said that a certain sound was heard, a pattern of colours was seen, and a shock was felt.

Berkeley was immensely impressed by the fact that this sort of continuous nightmare, which might after all have constituted human experience, in fact does not. He seems to assume, however, that we ought *strictly* to be linguistically prepared for it – though we ordinarily say that we see and touch the same things, we ought *not* to say this, in view of the possibility that the customary correlation of sight and touch might conceivably break down. He need not, of course, have said that we do *not* see and touch the same things, for as things are it is entirely proper and correct to say that we do; he should rather have argued that the *possibility* of saying this, of there being a language in which it is the proper thing to say, depends on certain actual correlations which, conceivably, might not have obtained. If I look out of the window and say 'It looks cold outside', this is not an *improper* thing to say. It is certainly true that the decisive test for cold is feeling, not seeing; but there is in fact a well-established connexion between cold weather, and a certain look that things and people have in cold weather. Hence I can properly say 'It looks very cold': or similarly, 'It looks heavy', or 'It sounds hollow'. It would be absurd to say 'It feels pink' or 'It sounds vermilion' – not, however, because the adjectives 'pink' and 'vermilion' are linguistically improper as associates for 'It feels ...' and 'It sounds ...', but because there is simply no reliable correlation between how things feel or sound and what colour they are. Thus, the fact that many of the things we commonly say *could not be said* if the facts were other than they are, does not establish that it is *not correct* to speak in that way; if the correlations on which we rely so heavily are indeed reliable, then it can be and is quite proper to speak as we do.

Strangely enough, Berkeley was more than usually confident that the correlations on which we rely are and always will be reliable, so long at least as we are reasonably careful in studying the ordinary course of events. For he regards these reliable correlations as being attributable to the benevolence of God towards us. It is, he says, by God's ordinance that what looks like a rose also (in most cases) smells and feels like a rose; that when I see what looks to me like a chair I am usually safe if I proceed to sit down on it. 'The proper objects of vision constitute a universal language of the Author of nature.' By presenting us with certain patterns of colour God tells us what objects are about, and so instructs us 'how to regulate our actions in order to attain those things that are necessary to the preservation and well-being of our bodies.' But, he insists, the things we see are only *signs*. The connexion between a particular pattern of colour and the presence of a tiger is no closer than the connexion between a man's name and the man himself; nevertheless, on seeing just that pattern of colour I can conclude that evasive action is appropriate, just as I may do when I hear a visitor announced. There is in each case between the sign and the signified no more than 'an habitual connexion that experience has made us to observe between them'; but God maintains this connexion in practice, and so tells us what to expect and what to do.

*

This notion of a 'divine visual language' brings clearly into view one curious point that, so far, we have left in the background. Why does Berkeley say that it is a specifically *visual* language? Why does he regard the objects of sight as signs, but not, apparently, the objects of touch? Here is a distinction that must be further scrutinized. All through the *Essay* Berkeley takes for granted a sharp distinction between the sense of touch and the other senses. The real distance, size, and 'situation' of anything is determined solely, he says, by the sense of touch. Furthermore, the 'proper objects' of sight and hearing, taste and smell, are said to be 'not without the mind' – not (he here evidently means) actually at a distance from the observer. But what we touch, he asserts, really *is* at a distance; it really has quite definite size and shape; it is this that is really in 'circumambient space'. This, then, is why God's language is (predominantly) visual. What we see is a sign of what we could touch, that is to say, of what is really there; just as a man's name painted on a door indicates that the man himself is to be found behind it. As the man himself is not a sign, so also what we touch is not a sign. It is the real thing; and God's visual language merely serves to point it out to us.

3

THE *ESSAY*: (ii) THE PROPER
OBJECTS OF TOUCH

I t is possible that Berkeley never took quite seriously his assertions in the *Essay* about 'tangible objects'. In the *Principles*
(44) he claims that in making these assertions he was merely
falling in with what he knew to be a 'vulgar error'. He was
prepared to say that tangible objects are 'without the mind',
in physical space, not because he really supposed that this was
so, but because it was beside his purpose to argue the point 'in
a discourse concerning vision'. It may be, too, that he did not
wish to give offence by attacking too many 'vulgar errors'
simultaneously. However, there is perhaps some ground for
suspecting that, when Berkeley was actually writing the *Essay*,
he was not so sure that some parts of its doctrine were mistaken as he later claimed that he had been. In any case what
he then wrote is well worth considering, whether or not he
believed at the time that it was true.

*

It is, after all, natural enough to regard the sense of touch as
a special case. It is certainly different in important respects
from the other senses; and we are perhaps apt to think that
touching is peculiarly 'direct' and 'immediate'. When, later,
Berkeley contended that nothing that we perceive is 'without
the mind', Dr Johnson tried to show how absurd was this
doctrine, not by looking or listening or sniffing, but by kicking
a stone. And this seems natural. Doubts and questions are perhaps easily raised about what we see and hear, taste and smell;
but if I can actually land a kick on something then surely
something is really out there to be kicked. According to the
doctrine of the *Essay*, though not of the *Principles*, Dr John-

son's instinct was perfectly correct; what he kicked was indeed 'without the mind.'

A first point, though Berkeley does not make much use of this, is that there are fewer ways of going wrong about what we touch than there are about what we see. Our eyes may deceive us, and our eyes may be deceived. Mirrors, sleight of hand, queer conditions of light or atmosphere, mirages and visions, optical illusions, even ordinary perspective – in all sorts of cases, for various reasons and in various ways, we may be led into mistakes. It is much less easy, though not of course impossible, to play tricks on the sense of touch. After all we are always very close to what we touch, and we are not dependent upon a variable intervening 'medium'.

But the peculiar character of touching can best be brought out by asking about it what would seem to be the natural question for Berkeley to ask – what is its 'proper object'? What sort of thing is it that, *strictly speaking*, we touch?

We naturally begin by saying that we touch *things* – physical objects like tables, pens, and doors. Since Berkeley has argued that with none of the other senses do we actually, strictly speaking, perceive physical objects, one might expect that he would not be satisfied with the answer that it is physical objects we touch. However, in the *Essay*, he accepts this answer.

It is in fact easy to see that no other answer could be maintained. Suppose, for instance, that one offered as an 'alternative' the suggestion that we touch surfaces. It is clear that this is not really an alternative at all; for surfaces are precisely the surfaces of *things* – of the wall, of the desk, of the painting, and so on. It could not be said that I might touch a surface and yet there be no physical thing whose surface it was: for if there is no physical thing there is in fact no surface, though perhaps there may seem to be one. (Surfaces do not have even that degree of independent existence which we might, with caution, be prepared to allow to sounds and smells.) Nor is it, of course, at all to the point to suggest that we touch only *parts* of things, or of the surfaces of things; for it is exactly when I touch some part, or some part of the surface, of (say) my desk, that I can properly be said to be touching the desk itself. Touching part of the desk is no more an *alternative* to touching the desk than falling into some part of the sea would be an alternative to falling into the sea; it is the same state of affairs eccentrically described. And to support this point, so to speak, from the other flank, it should be noticed that where we would *not* use the expression 'physical object' we also would not speak of touching. We might see 'diversity of light and colours' in, for example, the sky or the flames of a fire; but the sky and the flames, though we see them, would not ordinarily be called 'physical *objects*'. And just for this reason we do not say that flames or the sky can be touched. I may put my hand in the fire or fly in an aeroplane, but in doing so I would not be described as *touching* the sky or the flames.

It is easy, too, to see why touching has this (at first sight) peculiar status. We have already rejected as pointless the suggestion that, when I say I am touching my desk, I am strictly speaking touching only part of it. An equally trivial but not unilluminating suggestion would be this – that (strictly speaking) *I* do not touch my desk – my fingers, say, touch it. This is trivial, certainly, since it is precisely when my fingers touch the desk, or part of the desk, that I myself may properly be said to be touching the desk. But it is worth observing that to say 'My fingers touch the desk' is neither so trivial nor so peculiar as it would be to say 'My eyes see the desk.' There are at least two important differences. First, I might have touched the desk with any part of my body, whereas I could not see it except with my eyes – so that to say 'My fingers touch the desk', though not incompatible with, tells us rather more than, saying simply that I touch the desk : it adds a detail, that I touch the desk with my fingers, and not with my elbows or my feet or anything else. But second, and this is more illuminating, the verb 'touch' does not, as the verb 'see' normally does, demand a personal (or at least an animate) subject. Not only can I say quite ordinarily that my fingers touch the desk : I can also say that the desk touches the wall, or I could move the desk so that it touched the piano. People see things; but things touch each other. If there were no life anywhere there would be no seeing; but there would still be plenty of touching. For this there do not need to be any senses.

A person who is deaf cannot hear. A person who is blind cannot see. But there neither is nor well could be such a thing as a person who could not *touch* anything. For he would only be in this latter predicament if he were floating in mid-air, and paralysed so that he could not touch his own body. He would have to be incapable of all physical contacts; and this brings out the fact that to touch something just *is* to be in physical contact with it.[4] I am in physical contact with my desk; and the desk is in physical contact with the wall and the floor.

We may, then, re-write the question 'What is it that we touch?' in the form, 'What is it with which we can be in physical contact?' And now it is obvious that the answer can only be 'physical objects'; or, to speak plainly, things. It *must* be impossible to find any different answer.

Why then, if touching does not entail the presence of senses, do we speak of the 'sense of touch'? The answer is, I suppose, sufficiently obvious. When (say) my fingers are in contact with my desk, I normally have some feeling in my fingers. It is by such feelings that I know when I am touching something – though of course we often touch things without knowing or noticing. But the occurrence of ordinary 'sensations of touch' is neither necessary nor sufficient for the occurrence of touching. It is not necessary, since we frequently touch objects without feeling (or noticing, or knowing) that we do so; and it is not sufficient, since sometimes it feels as if we were touching something when in fact we are not. When one puts down a heavy suit-case, it often feels at first as if one had still got hold of it. Furthermore, as has been already pointed out, inanimate objects, though not sensitive, may properly be said to touch each other.

One who, as we say, has lost all 'sense of touch' is not unable to touch anything, as one who has lost the sense of sight is unable to see; it is rather that, when he touches anything, he feels nothing.

*

In view of all this, one might feel inclined to say that Berkeley's plan has at least in some degree broken down. He has, in the belief that thereby he was rectifying the looseness of our ordinary ways of speaking, set out to discover 'proper objects' for each of the senses, or (to put the same point in another way) tautologous accusatives for each verb of perception. But has he not failed in this case, with the verb 'to touch'? What he allows us to say that we hear and see we could *only* be said to hear and see; sounds can only be heard, light and colours can only be seen. But if he allows me to say, as certainly he must, that I touch my desk and my pen, can I not say also that I see my desk and my pen? If this be so, then the sense of touch is recalcitrant to Berkeley's treatment; it cannot be assigned a 'proper object' at all, since its only possible objects are not proper to it.

There is, however, a possible answer to this which at first sight seems to be effective. Berkeley could argue that, in the last paragraph, we have slipped back into that loose way of speaking which he is exhorting us to correct, and would not have supposed that we had found an objection to his case unless we had erred in this way. We suggested that physical things are not 'proper' to the sense of touch, since they can also be said to be seen; but Berkeley, of course, would not admit this. It is not, he claims, correct to say that we see desks and tables; we actually see only light and colours, which serve to suggest the presence of those things. The things themselves can be touched, and can *only* be touched; they cannot, in propriety of language, be said to be seen or smelled, tasted or heard.

But there is something strange about this reply. Touching remains in some way a peculiar case. It would be at once admitted by everyone that sounds can only be heard, smells can only be smelled; no one ever speaks of hearing colours or seeing tastes. In order to show that, in Berkeley's sense, sounds (etc.) are proper to hearing (etc.), it was quite sufficient to appeal to everyone's acquaintance with ordinary English. But in the case of touching this is not so. In order to maintain that physical objects can only be touched, an appeal must be made, not to ordinary English, but to Berkeley's own supposedly 'stricter' way of speaking. It is only Berkeley who assures us that it is wrong to speak of seeing and tasting an orange; we normally speak in exactly that way. Here, then, we have the curious position that part of his doctrine can only be supported by appeal to other features of that same doctrine; he is no longer able to rely on our ordinary acquaintance with the English language.

But, quite apart from this rather disturbing point, Berkeley's position is both more peculiar and less reasonable than it appears, or than he himself seems to realize. The 'tangible object' is not the source of comfort it may seem to be. When I say that I see and hear the train in the distance, Berkeley says that, strictly speaking, neither what I see nor what I hear is at any distance from me; colours and sounds do not have positions in physical space, they are 'not without the mind', not 'external' to the percipient. What then, one asks, is really in the distance? If the answer is 'Nothing', then surely we are all of us under a most remarkable and persistent misapprehension. Surely it would be too fantastic to say that *nothing* is really ten miles, or half a mile, or ten yards away from the place where I now am. Berkeley, it seems, can avoid this fantastic conclusion. For he is prepared to say that 'tangible objects' really are in 'circumambient space'. When I say that I see the train in the distance, the train really is in the distance; my mistake, or my inaccuracy, consists only in saying that I see it. If I had said that I see such a pattern of colour as suggests to me that there is a train in the distance, all would have been well. I should then have been interpreting what I saw as a sign of the presence and approach of a tangible object; and since God speaks to us in this language of signs, I can safely rely on this interpretation.

But a moment's reflection shows that this is still a very extraordinary doctrine. For if what is really in space, really 'external', is a tangible object and is, as Berkeley insists, not visible nor audible, then it can actually possess only those properties that we can ascribe to objects by touching them. It cannot be said that the train that is in the distance is red or green or of any other colour, if the train itself is not a visible thing. It could be said that the presence and approach of this train are signified by colours predominantly red or green, but not that it *is* red or green. The train itself might be, for instance, hard and heavy, hot in some places, angular in parts, smooth and flat in others; for we could tell by touching it that it had these properties. But our eyes and ears, noses and palates, would not, it seems, enable us to assign any properties to it; they enable us only to perceive the signs of its presence and its doings. But to those who wish, as surely as we do all wish, to maintain that there are about us physical objects at various distances from ourselves and each other, it is not consoling to reply that this is in fact so – but that these objects are invisible and inaudible, tasteless and odourless, actually possessing only those properties that can be detected by the sense of touch. It is not, we might say, *this* sort of object that we mean when we say that the train is now half a mile away. And how curious too, in other ways, is the manner of speech that Berkeley recommends. Suppose that one morning I go out to the hen-house, and find a gap in the wire, a couple of dead birds, one missing, and feathers everywhere. 'Ah,' I might say, 'there are signs that a fox has got in during the night.' For the next few nights, accordingly, I sit up keeping a watch. At last I see (as we should ordinarily say) a fox stealthily approaching the wire, creeping through and setting to work among the hens. Now, according to Berkeley, even when I am watching these proceedings with my own eyes from a few yards away, I should still say 'There are signs that a fox has got in.' I could, he suggests, properly say 'Here *is* the fox' only if I performed the risky and improbable feat of actually taking hold of it; short of that, however good the light and my view of the affair, I can only claim to have found some signs of a fox. But how strange it would be, and how undesirable too, to obliterate in this way the distinction between finding feathers and dead birds, and actually watching the fox's depredations.

But it is not only that this way of speaking is strange and surprising, nor yet that it would be most inconvenient in practice. (Berkeley would admit both these points with equanimity.) It is also that to accord, in this curious way, a special and pre-eminent status to the sense of touch is not a *reasonable* thing to do. Berkeley's own words help us to see that this is so. At one point he observes that the 'ideas of sight' (God's visual signs) indicate to us 'what tangible ideas are by the wonted ordinary course of Nature like to follow.' Now this is all very well. But by the 'tangible ideas' which are 'like to follow' he clearly means the sensations of touch that we may expect to have; and these 'ideas' or sensations are no more actually at a distance, no more 'without the mind', than are the 'ideas' of sight, the light and colours. 'The object which exists without the mind, and is at a distance' obviously cannot be an *idea* of touch; that idea is the sensation I may expect to have, if I traverse the distance towards that object. I may say that, if I move three yards to my left (and bump into a wall), I shall have certain sensations of touch, be 'affected with' certain ideas: I cannot say that these sensations or ideas actually *are* three yards away on my left. This I could only say of the wall itself, which is a tangible object but not a 'tangible idea'. Thus, in Berkeley's view, I look at the wall, and conclude from the 'ideas of sight' that I then have that I *could* (in certain circumstances) have certain 'ideas of touch'; and having these ideas of touch is to count as actually touching the wall. But if to have these ideas of touch is to count as *touching* the wall, why should not having the ideas of sight be counted as *seeing* the wall? In each case, it appears, I have certain ideas – ideas of sight, ideas of touch; but in one case I am allowed to say, not only that I have these ideas, but that I am touching a wall, while in the other case I am allowed to say only that I have certain ideas. But why should there be this distinction? Why should I regard the ideas of touch that I have as conclusive grounds for saying 'Here is a wall', while I am to regard the ideas of sight as entitling me to say only 'There are signs of a wall?' It is clear that sensations of touch, 'tangible ideas', are treated by Berkeley in a way quite different from that in which he treats all other ideas; and yet there appears to be no ground for making this distinction.

The plain fact is that, in the *Essay*, Berkeley has only gone part of the way, and has reached a position in which he cannot be allowed to halt. He must either be much less, or much more, radical and unorthodox. If he persists in saying that there are, variously located in space, physical objects that we do or could touch, he cannot reasonably maintain that we do not see or hear, taste or smell, any of these objects. For the reasons that we could find for concluding, on the basis of 'ideas of touch', that we are actually touching physical things, are no better than the reasons that could be offered for saying, on the basis of 'ideas of sight', that we *see* physical things, and sometimes hear, taste, and smell them as well. Apart from the *oddity* of maintaining that all the senses except that of touch reveal to us only signs of the presence of objects, there is no *reason* for maintaining this. If we are allowed to go beyond our ideas of touch, to conclude that we are touching some thing and to say what it is, we cannot reasonably be forbidden to go similarly beyond the ideas of the other senses. Nor need Berkeley have been unduly reluctant to admit this point; for much that he says remains unaffected by it. His remarks on our estimates by eye of distance and size remain substantially correct and (in their day) novel, and at least part of his solution of the puzzle about the inverted retinal image stands undamaged. Also, he could still have argued quite correctly that there happens to be (and conceivably might not have been) a regular correlation between the way things look and the way they feel, between the sounds we hear and the things we see, between the smell in the kitchen and the cheese in the larder. It is true that we have to learn by experience to correlate and interpret correctly the data of our various senses, and that this is not wholly unlike learning a language; and it is true that, if there were no such correlations to be discovered and learned, we could not have used a 'physical object' language at all. But the fact that there happens to be a regular correlation between the way things look and the way things feel should have been cited as explaining how we *can* say that we see and touch the same thing, instead of being brought as a reason for denying that we do.

But Berkeley might, on the other hand, have chosen an even more radical course. He might have continued with his attempt to devise a 'strict' use of language; he might have carried on with his search for 'proper objects'. But if so, he would have had to abandon the verb 'touch' entirely; it can have no place in such an enterprise as this. It is true that touching can, apparently, be assigned as its 'proper objects' physical things; but it is precisely this peculiarity which makes it incompatible with the more radical verson of Berkeley's doctrine. For it means that the verb 'touch' can only have a place in a language which permits us to speak of physical things; and if we are to have such a language at all, there is no possible case for refusing to allow that physical things can be seen, heard, tasted, and smelled. If Berkeley's 'strict' way of speaking is to be consistently worked out, our perceptual experience will have to be described in terms of 'diversity of light and colours', sounds, tastes, smells, and feelings – what we would ordinarily call 'sensations of touch', but which would have to be characterized merely as a certain sort of sensations. (Berkeley does, in speaking of 'tangible ideas', occasionally flirt with this more radical programme, but he does not stick to it; he soon reverts to speaking of tangible *objects*.) In such a strange but consistent terminology as this, it could not be said that anything at all, strictly speaking, is 'at a distance' – neither light and colours, sounds, tastes, smells, nor feelings could be located in physical space. The notion of distance, of position in 'circumambient space', could only appear in a language which is, by this standard, loose and inaccurate; and with it would have to be introduced the rest of our ordinary discourse.

It is illuminating (up to a point) to say that, in the *Principles of Human Knowledge*, Berkeley is attempting to carry though consistently the more radical version, as I have just described it, of the argument of the *Essay*. In the *Principles* he does not say that God speaks to us in a visual language, thus contrasting what we see as signs with what we touch as things; he says that God's language of signs is 'sensible' – to each of the senses he reveals signs of what will be or might be revealed to any of the others, and what is revealed to them is a sign of yet further possible revelations. In this Berkeley pays the price of consistency by seeming (at least) to be gratuitously eccentric. His hesitation in the earlier book, his smuggling back (whether or not inadvertent) of ordinary language *via* 'touch' and the 'tangible object', gained for the *Essay* a readier hearing than the *Principles* found for many years. But some at least of this ready acceptance was due to its defects.

There is, however, at least one cardinal point on which the doctrine of the *Principles* diverges from anything to be found in the *Essay*. It is important to emphasize this, since the divergence in fact consists in a different use of the very same words. The critical sentence is this – 'Ideas are not without the mind'.

From the use of this sentence in the *Essay*, it appears that Berkeley intends by it merely to point a contrast between ideas and objects. Objects, he says, are 'without the mind', that is, they have definite positions in space and actually are at certain distances from observers and from each other. With 'ideas', however, this is not so. If I describe only the pattern of 'light and colours' that, at a particular moment, makes up my visual field, I do not mention anything that can be located in a definite place; my note-book is two feet away, but the diamond-shaped expanse of white that is in my visual field when I look at it cannot be said to be two feet away. Similarly we do not assign definite positions to sounds and tastes and smells, but only to the things that make the sounds, have the tastes, and emit the smells. And thus 'ideas are not without the mind'; they are not, as objects are, definitely located at certain distances from ourselves and each other.

In the *Principles*, however, Berkeley attaches a different sense to these words. When he says here, as he does, of all ideas that they 'have not any subsistence without a mind', he is not merely contending that ideas, the 'immediate objects' of perception, are not located in physical space: he is putting forward the very different contention that they *exist* when and only when they are *actually perceived*. Ideas, he here says, are 'not without the mind' in the sense that, unless some mind is actually perceiving certain ideas, there cannot be said to be any such ideas. Just as there cannot be unfelt pains, there cannot be unperceived ideas. There is nothing in the *Essay* to suggest this opinion. It is not there argued, for example, that the sounds that I hear would not have existed at all unless I or somebody else were actually hearing them; they are said to be 'not without the mind' only in the sense that they have no position in space, are not 'outside' as physical objects are. In the later book, with no change of terminology, it is maintained that we cannot speak of ideas that are not actually perceived; 'their being is to be perceived or known' – in this sense too they are 'not without the mind'.

It is of the greatest importance for the argument of the *Principles* that Berkeley adopts this opinion about ideas; we shall have to look carefully into his reasons for doing so, and into the consequences that follow. The change appears in some ways to be the more remarkable in that, in the *Principles*, Berkeley is less inclined than he was in the *Essay* to suggest that ordinary language is somehow wrong, and is apt to suggest instead that he is merely clarifying the *meaning* of ordinary words and sentences. He contends, in fact, that what I called above the 'more radical' version of his doctrine is not really radical at all, but is simply a clear account of common speech with its common assumptions. Even the suggestion that the 'ideas' we perceive exist when and only when they are perceived is not, he maintains, a novel or paradoxical suggestion;

THE PROPER OBJECTS OF TOUCH

we should, he believes, see at once that this is so, if only we would ask ourselves with sufficient care what is really meant by our words. He is convinced that failure to do this is apt to result, not only in confusion of thought about perception, but also in scepticism, atheism, and vice. For these, he believes, must inevitably ensue upon 'materialism'; and 'materialism' he regards as the insidious but self-contradictory outcome of serious mistakes. If this be so, it is indeed a matter of importance that our ideas should be made as clear as possible.

4

BERKELEY'S ACCOUNT OF LANGUAGE

WITH the *Principles of Human Knowledge* Berkeley seriously launches his projected campaign. In the *Essay* his aims, as we have seen, were precise and limited; he was concerned with no more than a detail of his grand design. But in 'Part I' of the *Principles*, and in the volumes intended to follow it but never actually written, he proposed to survey the whole field of philosophical inquiry, to solve or show the means of solving all the difficulties, and so to make open again the congested road of philosophical, moral, and scientific progress. Accordingly he prefixed to his first volume a general discussion of the nature of philosophy, of language, and of the fundamental blunders which, he believed, were at the root of the confusions and perplexities in learned minds.

This *Introduction* is in many ways his most original and lively contribution to philosophy. An early draft, differing at one or two points from his final version, survives in manuscript and has been recently published. This draft bears marginal dates showing that it was written in November and December of 1708 – shortly before the publication of the *Essay*, on which he must have been working concurrently with the *Principles*. This fact tends to support the idea that he knew of, and accepted, the inconsistency of the earlier with the later work; and it is very likely, if this were so, that he had in mind the pursuit of some tactical aim. For Berkeley felt himself to be a pioneer. He expected to find himself in conflict with the entrenched prejudices of the learned world, and his confidence of the support of 'the vulgar' was not, or at least soon ceased to be, very strong. He expected his campaign to be long and arduous; and so he was willing to lighten his task, if possible, by insinuating his views rather than proclaiming them, by leading up to the truth through preliminary half-truths, and by winning acceptance for his principles without any premature revelation of their consequences.

*

In the first few paragraphs of his *Introduction* Berkeley enunciates with vigour and clarity a view of the nature of philosophical inquiry which would be widely accepted today, and which is in fact sometimes taken to be wholly modern. He argues that a large number (at least) of the philosophical difficulties in which we find ourselves entangled are really *our own fault*, problems of our own making. Locke and many others had been apt to reflect that men are, after all, of narrowly limited capacities; they should not be surprised if some matters seem to baffle their comprehension, but should be thankful that their powers are adequate for all the purposes of daily life. Berkeley's attitude, if less humble than this, is also less resigned and complacent. 'Perhaps', he says, 'we may be too partial to our selves in placing the fault originally in our faculties, and not rather in the wrong use we make of them. ... Upon the whole, I am inclined to think that the greater part, if not all, of those difficulties which have hitherto amused philosophers, and blocked up the way to knowledge, are entirely owing to our selves. That we have first raised a dust, and then complain, we cannot see.'

He goes on to contend, still anticipating contemporary views, that the dust we raise is the dust of linguistic confusion. We mismanage our own language and it trips us up; we spin puzzles out of it that call, not so much for answers or solutions, as for diagnosis and removal. If we can come to see clearly how the problems seemed to arise, they will vanish, cease to be puzzling – not solved but rather dissipated, cleared away. A plain and important corollary of this view is that many of the so-called doctrines maintained, disputed, or rejected by philosophers turn out on inspection to be neither true nor false nor even problematic doctrines, but rather to be meaningless – not doctrines at all, but mere concatenations of misused words. One of Berkeley's favourite controversial moves is to urge that his opponents mean nothing by what they say – that their views are not even false but simply nonsensical. Often he seems to think of his task not as that of *replacing* one set of doctrines by another, but as that of *eliminating* certain unnecessary perplexities; not of contradicting mistakes, but of 'laying the dust'.

But there is a further subtlety in Berkeley's argument. He is not merely concerned with ordinary verbal confusions; for the phenomenon of verbal misunderstanding was, and no doubt always will be, familiar enough. He saw that there was a quite different and philosophically more insidious way of lapsing into linguistic errors. Philosophers, like other men, are liable to mismanage their own language and to misunderstand the language of others, but they are also exposed to a special risk; they may hold a mistaken theory about language itself. The case of Locke was at this point in Berkeley's mind. Locke had been well aware of the risks of confusion in the use of words; and he devoted a large section of his *Essay Concerning Human Understanding* to the discussion of language. He was there concerned, in particular, with the questions what it is for a word to have meaning, and what it is to understand a word or a sentence. But unluckily, so Berkeley contends, his account of these matters was radically mistaken: and so he was out of the frying-pan into the fire.

This is what lies behind a point which sometimes seems baffling to Berkeley's readers. He contends, in his *Introduction*, that there are no 'abstract ideas'; and he sometimes says, in his main text, that some word is evidently supposed to stand for an 'abstract idea' and so must be meaningless. Now it seems to some people, naturally perhaps, that to deny that there are any abstract ideas amounts to denying that any general terms are meaningful. Surely Berkeley cannot mean to deny this? But if he does not, why does he object only to *some* words, on the curious-looking ground that they are supposed to stand for abstract ideas?

The structure of the argument is in fact as follows. When Berkeley says that there are no 'abstract ideas', he is intending to reject a particular theory (a theory which he attributes to Locke) about the meaning of general words. He is not saying, so far, that any particular word is or is not meaningless, but only that a certain philosopher's account of what it is for a word to have meaning is mistaken. But, he maintains, there are some words, particularly words used by philosophers and other theorists, which *could* not be meaningful unless this mistaken theory were true. Locke's theory, he says in effect, is not merely mistaken; it is disastrously mistaken. For it leads men to think that certain words have meaning (since according to Locke's theory they could have meaning), which in fact neither have nor could have any meaning. Thus, when he condemns some word on the ground that it is supposed to stand for an 'abstract idea', he means to convey that this word could be thought to have a meaning only if Locke's theory of language were taken to be true; but since that theory is mistaken, the word in question must be meaningless. He is concerned to reject a certain theory about language as mistaken, and *also* certain words as meaningless – words countenanced and given currency by the mistaken theory, and used by its dupes though (he implies) by nobody else.

Berkeley speaks of this doctrine of 'abstract ideas' as if it were widely accepted among philosophers, and no doubt this was the case. He refers to 'the Schoolmen those great masters of abstraction'; but the only writer whose words he actually quotes is Locke. This is natural enough, in view of the great and deserved influence of Locke's writings at that time; but it has often been objected that the view which Berkeley attributes to Locke and demolishes is not, in fact, a view which Locke ever held. It can perhaps be argued that this is so; but Locke is protected, if at all, only by the extreme vagueness and obscurity of his language. If Locke did not mean what Berkeley says that he meant, it is an extremely difficult problem to decide what he did mean. For the fact is that Locke neither stated nor held any one clear theory at all; and Berkeley attributes to him one fairly precise doctrine which conforms with much, at least, that he actually said.

It is an important feature of Locke's doctrine that he insists that we ourselves construct, or in his own word 'frame',
abstract ideas; they are, so to speak, not raw material, but
products. Suppose I see, for example, a red book, a red flower,
and a red coat. I can then, according to Locke, ignore, or in a
sense mentally separate off, all those respects in which these
objects are distinct from each other – their shape, their feel,
their positions, and so on – and so pick out, and 'frame an
idea' of, that in which they are all alike. I can see in these
three things, and so can 'abstract' from them, that one respect
in which they are alike; thus I 'frame an abstract idea', in this
case the abstract idea of Red. We are able to do this, Locke
says, because as a matter of fact things do resemble each
other in many fairly obvious respects; but we are not obliged
to pick out any particular points of resemblance in preference
to others. No doubt things resemble each other in countless
ways which we never refer to and perhaps hardly notice; what
points of resemblance we attend to, and hence what abstract
ideas we actually frame, is in Locke's view at least to some
extent a matter of choice.

When we have abstracted and 'framed' our idea of Red, we
can if we wish, Locke proceeds, assign to it a name. The word
'red', which clearly is not the proper name of any particular
red object, is in effect regarded by Locke as the proper name
of the abstract idea. (He speaks as if we first frame the abstract
idea, and then we name it.) The 'immediate signification' of
the word is thus an idea in our own minds, something that
we have framed by abstraction. How then, if the word 'signifies' an idea in our minds, can we use it, as we do, to characterize particular objects in the world? Locke's answer to this
question is decidedly vague. He says that, for instance, the
adjective 'red' can be used to characterize particular red things
because they show 'a conformity to that abstract idea'; and by
this, presumably, he means to say that any red object fits, or
in some way 'matches', the abstract idea, because it is like the
things from which that idea was abstracted in the very respect
in which those things resembled each other – we see in any

red thing that same feature which we picked out in framing our abstract idea. Hence, when we characterize any object as red, we do so because it 'conforms' to that abstract idea of which we have made the word 'red' serve as a sign.

Now it may well seem that this account is, so far as it goes, straightforward. It is certainly the case that our ability to use general terms (and indeed our ability to use language at all) depends on the fact that objects, events, and situations do resemble each other more or less closely, in more or less obvious ways; anything absolutely unique, in every respect, would necessarily defy description – for we could not, *ex hypothesi*, say of what sort it was, what it was *like*. It is true too that we commonly teach the meaning of a word by indicating cases in which it is used, relying on the pupil eventually to get the idea of what it is in those cases which justifies its use, and hence to be able to use it for himself in other cases – other cases of, as we say, the 'same sort'. But it does not seem that Locke is merely observing that we *do* teach (or learn) the meanings of words in this way; he seems to intend what he says to be taken more seriously – to be taken, in fact, as the *explanation* of our ability to teach and to learn the use of general terms. To say that a man has framed and named an abstract idea is not simply Locke's way of saying that he understands a general term; it is Locke's answer to the question *how* he has managed to do so. And according to Locke, the essential step to take is that of 'framing an abstract idea'.

What then is it exactly to frame an abstract idea? And in particular, what is it that we 'frame'? What have we got, so to speak, when we have completed the work of abstracting?

Unfortunately, on this central point it is impossible to elicit from Locke a clear answer. By the term 'idea' he confessedly means almost anything one cares to choose; he says that term stands for 'whatsoever is the object of the understanding when a man thinks'; that it means the same as 'phantasm, notion, species'; and also that it stands for objects of perception generally. His remarks about abstract ideas in particular are scarcely less baffling. An abstract idea is said to be 'representative of many particular things'; he says that it is particular 'in its existence' though general in its signification – and also, most perplexing of all, that 'it is something imperfect, that cannot exist'. Locke can hardly mean by this that abstract *ideas* cannot exist; for the main burden of his account is that they can and do. He must rather mean – and this is an important point – that no *object* that exists could be at all like an abstract idea. There are certainly good reasons why he should say this. Any particular red thing, for example, must have, as well as its colour, some shape or size; but in the abstract idea of Red there is to be included no idea of shape or size, but *only* the idea of that particular colour. There could not exist an object that was red and nothing else whatever; but there can (according to Locke) be an abstract idea of Red and of nothing else at all.

But none of this really enables us to get at Locke's meaning. It does not help us very much to be told that abstract ideas, though 'particular in their existence', are not at all like actual objects: this is too wholly negative to be enlightening. What *are* abstract ideas? What is it to frame and to have an idea of this sort? It is evidently something more than merely to have learned the meaning of a word – but what more? What is this explanation that Locke is offering? Locke supplies no explicit answer to these questions; none can be extracted from his text, and he seems hardly to have realized that any answer would be required.

Berkeley, however, does not choose to let Locke escape into a thicket of vagueness; he proceeds to ask what Locke must be *supposed* to have meant. Now there is at least one clear sense in which we may be said to 'frame ideas' – a sense, too, which is from time to time recognized by Locke. Namely, we can *imagine*. This word 'imagine' itself has several uses. We may imagine how Napoleon felt on the eve of Waterloo, what it would be like to be inside a diving-suit, or how we might behave if suddenly left a fortune. But also we may, in a rather different sense, imagine a centaur, a winged horse, or an octopus; I may try to 'see in my mind's eye' how a black swan would look, or a car with mechanical legs instead of wheels; or I may try to 'visualize' the face of an absent friend. It is with this second sort of imagining – seeing in the mind's eye, visualizing – that we are here concerned. Berkeley assumes that, if Locke meant anything at all, he must have meant by 'framing ideas' this sort of imagining; this is at least something that might be meant by his words, and it is also something that we certainly can do.

But if this is what Locke means by 'framing' ideas, the rest of his account at once becomes vulnerable. For can we really frame the ideas that he says we must frame, if we are to understand the meanings of words? There are limits to what can be imagined. Certainly we can imagine all sorts of extraordinary and (in one sense) impossible things – for example 'a man with two heads or the upper parts of a man joined to the body of a horse.' But suppose that I try to frame the abstract idea of Man. I am, according to Locke's instructions, to disregard all those particular respects in which one man may differ from another – shape, features, colour of hair and skin, and so on; and I am to pick out, to incorporate in my idea, *only* that respect in which all men are alike, that which entitles them all to be classed as men. What then do I see in the mind's eyes, what idea have I framed by this process of abstraction? The obvious answer is, none at all. It is impossible to *imagine* a merely generic man, a man of no particular size and shape, of no definite colour and no definite features. 'The idea of man that I frame to myself, must be either of a white, or a black, or a tawny, a straight, or a crooked, a tall, or a low, or a middle-sized man. I cannot by any effort of thought conceive the abstract idea above described.' If, as is 'agreed on all hands', and by Locke himself, there could not actually be a man with no characteristics whatever except that of *being a man*, it is also impossible to imagine such a man, to 'frame the idea' of him. Even more clearly, although we understand well enough the meaning of the word 'slow', it is impossible to imagine, frame the idea of, Slowness. I can imagine a ship or some other object moving slowly; but if I omit, as irrelevant to the meaning of the word 'slow', the image of the ship or whatever the object may be, there is left to the mind's eye not Slowness, but nothing at all. Slowness cannot be 'abstracted' from slow-moving things, if by 'abstracting' we mean 'imagining separately'. Lastly, Berkeley deals what he calls in the *Commentaries* 'the killing blow'. Locke sometimes tells us, in his instructions for abstracting, not to *omit* from our abstract idea features in which those things that 'conform' to it differ, but to *include* in the idea every feature that any of them has. This, he admits, can be done only with difficulty. 'For example, does it not require some pains and skill to form the general idea of a triangle (which is yet none of the most abstract comprehensive and difficult) for it must be neither oblique nor rectangle, neither equilateral, equicrural, nor scalenon, but *all and none* of these at once. In effect, it is something imperfect that cannot exist, an idea wherein some parts of several different and inconsistent ideas are put together.' This, surely, must be decisive. 'If any man has the faculty of framing in his mind such an idea of a triangle as is here described, it is in vain to pretend to dispute him out of it, nor would I go about it. All I desire is, that the reader would fully and certainly inform himself whether he has such an idea or no. And this, methinks, can be no hard task for anyone to perform. What more easy than for anyone to look a little into his own thoughts, and there try whether he has, or can attain to have, an idea that shall correspond with the description that is here given of the general idea of a triangle, which is, *neither oblique, nor rectangle, equilateral, equicrural, nor scalenon, but all and none of these at once?*' (I. 13). It is difficult to see how Locke could parry this 'killing blow', without altering his account out of all recognition.

There are however some faults on Berkeley's side; he has allowed his critical zeal to run away with him. In his eagerness to expose the absurdity of abstract images, with any or no particular characteristics, he exaggerates the extent to which definite characteristics must be or can be attributed to imagery. It has often been pointed out that visual images may as a matter of fact be vague and schematic, wavering and incomplete, shifting and indefinite. When we imagine, say, a well-known face, how often can we claim to find in it every detail, exact and definite, of feature or of expression? But there is also a more serious point than this. Suppose I am trying to imagine, to visualize, an aeroplane flying through a cloud. Clearly, it would be absurd for someone to question me about the aeroplane's wing-span, or its weight, or its speed. I might perhaps say that I was imagining a large aeroplane travelling very fast; but it would be entirely inappropriate to insist that it must have a definite size and speed; it would be ridiculous to ask for the figures. I could, of course, invent answers to such questions or give answers at random; but there is no way in which, having visualized my aeroplane, I could then set about *discovering* the answers. Imagined aeroplanes cannot be measured, weighed, and timed – though they can, of course, be assigned imaginary sizes, weights, and speeds.

Thus, although Berkeley is certainly right in saying that there could not actually *be* a house (for example) of no definite character or dimensions, it does not follow from this, as he thought it did, that the 'idea' of a house – taking this to mean a visualized, imagined house – must be in all respects equally determinate. A real house must necessarily (for otherwise it would not be a real house at all) be capable of being measured, photographed, charted, and thoroughly inspected; whereas no sense whatever can be attached to the notion of measuring (etc.) merely imagined houses. We may invent, but we cannot take, their measurements.

Berkeley's attack, however, survives such criticism. For while it is not true that, if I imagine something moving, its movement must be of some definite sort and speed, he is quite right in maintaining that I cannot imagine 'movement' entirely apart from anything that moves. And according to Berkeley's account of Locke's theory, that theory supposes that I can do exactly this. It is supposed that there is an abstract idea of Movement and of *nothing else whatever* – of nothing that moves, of no sort of movement rather than any other, but of Movement simply. Likewise there is said to be an abstract idea of Red and of nothing else whatever – of nothing that is red, not even a vague surface or shape, but just Red by itself. Now if the 'ideas' here in question are indeed supposed to be things *imagined* – and if not we are left in the dark as to what is meant – the theory is patently untenable. It is wholly impossible to 'frame' an *image* instantiating one and only one property. Or, to take Locke's alternative version, we cannot actually imagine anything with all of several inconsistent properties. If I visualize an isosceles triangle, it is indeed out of place to ask for its dimensions or to ask whether it is really exactly isosceles; but it would be even more absurd to say that it both is and is not isosceles, that it is both large and small, that it both is and is not rectangular at the apex. These remarks are logically self-contradictory; and this is to say that they could not be a correct description of anything, not even of something merely imagined. Imagining may be much less like seeing than Berkeley ever recognized, but for all that it cannot defy the rules of logic. Words that are contradictorily put together cannot be converted into correct descriptions merely by supposing that they describe unusual things.

*

So far, then, Berkeley has argued merely destructively. He has read into Locke's opaque account a theory of meaning which relies on the assertion that there are abstract ideas, but which so characterizes these alleged ideas as to make it plain that there could not be any such things. Berkeley now sees that two further tasks are required of him. First, he must provide an outline, at any rate, of an alternative treament of the meaning of words – the demolished structure must be replaced by a better one. And second, he must try to explain how acute and sensible men could ever have come to embrace so extraordinary a doctrine as this of 'abstract ideas' has turned out to be. He must 'consider the source of this prevailing notion', which he has shown to be decidedly 'remote from common sense'.

'By observing how ideas become general, we may the better judge how words are made so' (1. 12). Berkeley does not object to the assertion that there are general ideas, but only to the very different assertion that there are *abstract* ideas as described by Locke, and 'framed' according to his recipes for abstraction. In his view, what can be called a general idea 'considered in it self is particular'; its generality consists not in its own nature, but in the *use* that is made of it. Suppose, for example, that a teacher of geometry is demonstrating the method of bisecting a line; he draws, perhaps, a line in chalk, six inches long, on a blackboard. His demonstration of course holds good not only for this line in particular nor yet for any other particular lines, but simply for *any* straight line. Now it was for just this reason that theorists had supposed the geometer's discourse to be about the 'abstract idea' of a line, and not about an actual line or lines at all. But Berkeley finds no difficulty in the admission that the geometer is really referring, as he seems to be, to the actual line that he has drawn on the blackboard; there is no need at all to suppose that he is speaking of anything else. But how, if so, can we say, as we wish to say, that he is teaching his pupils something about lines in general, showing the method of bisecting any line? If we say that he is speaking of this particular line, surely what he says can have no generality. Berkeley's answer is the obvious answer: he is referring to this particular line, but this line is being *used as an example*; '... as it is there used, it represents all particular lines whatsoever.' In this proceeding there is no mystery. Nothing that the geometer says depends for its truth on the features of this particular line – on its being six inches long and drawn in chalk on this particular blackboard: he deliberately avoids all mention of such peculiarities, and says only things that are true of all lines, of any line, and of this one among them. This particular line *can* 'represent all particular lines whatsoever' because it has (or for purposes of illustration can be *supposed* to have), besides its own peculiar features, the features that any line must have; and on this occasion it does represent all particular lines, in as much as the teacher uses it for that purpose. Of course he need not have done so; he might have drawn this very line and gone on to speak of its particular dimensions and composition. When we call it an 'example', we are saying nothing about *it* but are indicating the use that the teacher makes of it. We would not perhaps say, as Berkeley does, that a line thus used as an example is a 'general line'; but we may agree with him that a general discourse about lines may refer to a particular line used as an example, and need not be conceived to be about some entity quite other than actual lines, an 'abstract line' or the 'abstract idea' of Line.

An example, then, is a particular thing used in a certain way for a certain purpose. Berkeley suggests, quite rightly, that here lies a clue to the proper understanding of general terms. He cannot say, as Locke had said, that 'a word becomes general by being made the sign of a general idea'; for (to postpone his further objections to this remark) he has argued that there is nothing, no 'idea', that is intrinsically general. Instead he concentrates on the idea of *use*. We say, for example, that 'Tom' is a proper name, but that 'telephone' is a general term. Locke would have sought to account for this difference by saying that 'Tom' is the name of a particular person, but that 'telephone' is the name of an 'abstract' entity. That is, he had attempted to locate the distinction in the different natures of the things named. Berkeley locates it elsewhere, in the use of the words. By the name 'Tom' we can refer to a particular person or persons; by the word 'telephone' we can refer to any telephone. It is the essential feature of a proper name that there are particular people (animals, towns, etc.) whose name it is; it is the essential feature of a general term that it can be applied to any object (event, situation, etc.) of a certain sort. To put it in Berkeley's own way, a proper name 'denotes' a particular thing or things, while a general term 'denotes indifferently' any things of a certain sort. To say that the word 'line' can be used of any line does not imply that it is the name of an 'abstract idea'; it implies, in fact, that 'line' is not a *name* at all. Berkeley has seized on the enormously important point that to say that a word is general is not to say what sort of entity it names, but is rather to say how it is used in discourse about ordinary things. This may seem an obvious point enough, but it has been overlooked quite startlingly often. And plainly the consequences of neglecting it must be serious; for it is obvious that very few words can be construed as proper names of ordinary things; and hence philosophers are drawn into bewildering discussions of the nature of those *non*-ordinary things that other words are assumed to name. Herein lies the main source of Locke's perplexities; and it must be counted as a major achievement by Berkeley that he was able to shake off a mistake so recently made by his eminent pre-decessor and (apparently) so perennially tempting to philos-ophers.

Nor did Berkeley stumble upon this point by accident or without appreciating its importance. He sees quite clearly that it was Locke's assumptions about language which led him into his strange account of abstract ideas, and he cor-rectly identifies the fundamental mistake. ' 'Tis thought that every name hath, or ought to have, one only precise and settled signification, which inclines men to think there are certain abstract, determinate ideas, which constitute the true and only immediate signification of each general name. And that it is by the mediation of these abstract ideas, that a general name comes to signify any particular thing.' Now there is, of course, little reason to object to the idea that every word has, or ought to have 'one only precise and settled signification', *if* by this is meant that each word has or ought to have one 'precise and settled' meaning. But Locke and very many other philosophers have gone on to assume, or to state, that to have one precise meaning is to be the name of one determinate entity. They have taken the 'signification' of a word to be that thing (or idea) which it names. As soon as this is accepted tangles are inevitable. Consider the word 'triangle'. This word is applicable, of course, to triangles of any shape or size, drawn in ink or chalk or pencil, cut out of paper or made with wire; and so it seems inevitable that that single, determinate thing which is (it is assumed) the nominee, the 'immediate signification' of the word, must either exhibit all the characteristics that every conceivable triangle could have, or else must have none of the particular features in respect of which any one triangle may differ from others. Unless it has *all* or *none* of these distinctive features, it cannot fulfil its supposed role of 'mediating' between the word and any particular triangle; but then, as Berkeley so forcefully points out, it makes no sense to speak of anything as being triangular but *neither* equilateral, isosceles, nor scalene, and it is equally absurd to say that it is *all* of these. It is in fact impossible to devise a coherent account of these supposed mediators, the things or ideas which general terms are supposed to name. The only way to escape from the confusion is to recognize that no such things are required. General terms are *not* the proper names of anything; there is (it is really tautologous to say) no *one* entity which a general term 'signifies'. Of course this is not to deny that a general term may have one meaning; it is only to insist that this is not the same as to be the name of one particular thing. The word 'Englishman' has one meaning, however many and various Englishmen may be. ' 'Tis one thing for to keep a name constantly to the same definition, and another to make it stand every where for the same idea : the one is necessary, the other useless and impracticable.'

But Berkeley has not yet completed his indictment; he discovers in Locke's doctrine yet further mistakes of scarcely less importance. Locke (and again many others before and since) had held 'that language has no other end but the communicating our ideas.' In this Berkeley rightly finds much to criticize.

For one thing, this account strongly suggests that the only use of language is to convey information, that a speaker's or writer's aims are completely achieved if he is *understood*. But this is a very one-sided view. At best, it is adequate only to the case of sentences in the indicative mood. But we use words also to ask questions or to give orders : and here we are not seeking merely to 'communicate ideas'. One who asks a question wishes, not merely to be understood, but to be answered; and one who gives an order wishes to be obeyed. But the notion of 'communicating ideas' is also inadequate to many cases in which the words used have, as interrogative and imperative sentences have not, the grammatical form of ordinary statements. A lecturer on Roman history may perhaps be concerned only to 'communicate ideas'; but the same is certainly not always true of an advocate in court or a politician at a meeting. They may use nothing but grammatically indicative sentences, but their 'end' in doing so will often be to arouse in their audience, not 'ideas', but emotions, attitudes, or frames of mind. Besides the communicating of ideas, 'there are other ends, as the raising of some passion, the exciting to, or deterring from an action, the putting the mind in some particular disposition; to which the former is in many cases barely subservient, and sometimes entirely omitted, when these can be obtained without it, as I think doth not infrequently happen in the familiar use of language.' The less we bother about the orator's meaning, the more violently do we react to his eloquence. And 'may we not, for example, be affected with the promise of a *good thing*, though we have not an idea of what it is?' (I. 20).

Berkeley finds too that Locke's assumption misleads in subtler ways. The account of significant words as 'signs of ideas', combined with the notion that language is always used to communicate ideas, is apt to suggest a misleading picture. It suggests that the speaker has a certain series, or 'train', of ideas; that he speaks a series of words composed of the 'signs' of these ideas; and that the hearing of these signs causes the same train of ideas to arise in the mind of his hearers. Thus are his ideas 'communicated'. But this, Berkeley rightly contends, is an inappropriate account of the matter. It suggests that the speaker and the hearers of a meaningful utterance are always thinking of, always 'have in mind', the meanings of the words spoken and heard. But the notion that each word is associated with its own 'idea', that its meaning is actually borne in mind, is more appropriate to such a special case as the reading of a difficult passage in a foreign language than to the case of common discourse in one's own tongue – 'in reading and discoursing, names being for the most part used as letters are in *algebra*, in which though a particular quantity be marked by each letter, yet to proceed right it is not requisite that in every step each letter suggest to your thoughts, that particular quantity it was appointed to stand for.'

Apart from this, there are two special dangers in the notion that each word used 'stands for an idea' in the speaker's or the writer's mind: in two ways, it tends to beget the same perplexities found already in Locke's doctrine of 'abstract ideas'. We have seen how Locke's account of the meaning of words led him to ask the unanswerable question, what sort of entity it is that a general term *names*. We can now see that his account of significant utterance, and of understanding, must lead him to raise the same disastrous question. He suggests that, when we understand a sentence, we have that set or series of ideas of which the words used are the signs; should it not, then, be possible for us to consider each word *separately*, and to pick out separately that idea which it signifies? But Berkeley rightly objects to the notion that words can be thus *isolated* from the contexts in which they occur. In another passage he gives an example. If I tell someone to meet me 'at such a *time*, in such a *place*, he shall never stay to deliberate on the meanings of those words.' The sentences I speak are perfectly intelligible to him. But if I go on, as Locke implies I might rightly go on, to ask him what particular ideas were signified to him by the words 'time' and 'place', then 'it will perhaps gravel even a philosopher' to answer me. The fact is that, though we understand well enough sentences in which the words 'time' and 'place' are used, we can find no satisfactory way of giving the meanings of these words by themselves, extracted from the sentences in which they commonly occur. If, without considering any particular sentences, we try to 'frame an idea' of Time and Place, we are soon 'lost and embrangled in inextricable difficulties.' For another reason too (which Berkeley does not mention in his published version) it is a mistake to suggest that each word in a sentence 'stands for' its own appropriate idea. This suggests that all the words in a sentence function in the same way – each 'stands for' something. But this is a fatal supposition. It ignores the vital distinction between that part of a statement which really does 'stand for' something, and that part which has the very different role of saying something *about* that which the first part 'stands for.' Consider (to use Berkeley's example) the statement 'Melampus is an animal'. The name 'Melampus' does indeed stand for something; it is the name of a particular animal. But the phrase 'is an animal' does not stand for something else; it is used to say something about Melampus. ' "Animal" does not in that proposition stand for any idea at all.' It is used to describe what the word 'Melampus' stands for. Berkeley is clearly right in his suggestion that, if we ignore this distinction and insist on asking what 'is an animal' and other such phrases *stand for*, we can hardly avoid giving incomprehensible answers. And in fact an anthology of the repeated attempts to find a good answer to this impossible question would fill many large volumes.

*

Three matters remain to be discussed.

There is firstly a rather troublesome question of terminology. When Locke speaks of the 'ideas' for which words stand, or which they raise in the mind, it is clear (however much else is obscure) that he means to distinguish ideas from objects. An idea, whatever it may be, is something 'in the mind' and an object is not. Locke holds, in fact, that language has reference to the world, not directly, but in some way through the ideas in human minds. He admits that 'men often suppose their words to stand for the reality of things', but this, he goes on to say, is really a mistake. Reference to 'the reality of things' can only be indirect, by way of our ideas.

Now Berkeley is in fact eager to deny this. He explicitly disputes the notion that words have meaning by the 'mediation' of ideas, and objects to the 'interposition' of ideas between the words and the world of which we speak. At the same time, perplexingly enough, he often speaks as if words do signify ideas, and seems sometimes to disagree only about the way in which they do so. This is, however, only an apparent inconsistency. It is true that Berkeley, in his *Introduction*, proposes no sense for the word 'idea' except, more or less, that of 'image' – which is the sense he attributes to Locke. But it is clear that he himself uses it in quite another way. He says, for example, that the word 'line' refers to many *ideas* of the same sort, and in the same paragraph that it is the sign of all particular *lines*. And of the name 'Melampus' he says, in almost successive sentences, that it denotes an 'idea' and is the name of a 'particular thing'. The explanation of this does not fully emerge until we come to the main text of the *Principles*. There we find that one of his main concerns is to reject Locke's distinction between ideas and objects, and to hold that (in effect) objects *are* simply ideas. Whatever we may come to think of this apparently paradoxical view, it is enough to establish that Berkeley is not guilty of allowing ideas to slip back as 'intermediaries' between language and the world. The main burden of his case is that the language in which we speak of the physical world refers directly to what we see and feel, taste, hear, and smell. Indeed he regards this, rightly, as one of his most important principles.

The second point is this. Berkeley's sense of the confusions, trivialities, and perplexities, generated by misuse and misunderstanding of language, was so keen that he ends by actually offering the advice that we should try to 'lay aside' and dispense with words altogether. 'It cannot', he says, 'be denied that words are of excellent use. ... But at the same time it must be owned that most parts of knowledge have been strangely perplexed and darkened by the abuse of words, and general ways of speech wherein they are delivered.' In his first edition he had added 'that it may almost be made a question whether language has contributed more to the hindrance or advancement of the sciences.' Later, presumably, he omitted this as going too far; and indeed it is a fantastic exaggeration.

Certainly verbal tangles are tiresome and not uncommon; but if there had been no language either to be used or abused, each inquirer in any field would have been obliged to start from a position of total ignorance, doing all the work for himself. In such conditions, clearly, we could look for no advancement in any science: nor, indeed, for any science at all. Anything that is useful can be misused; but language as a means of communication is so enormously useful that the unavoidable risks must be cheerfully accepted.

Of course, what Berkeley invites his readers, and himself resolves, to 'lay aside' is, as he himself says, 'the *abuse* of words', and 'controversies *purely* verbal'. He would have us constantly consider what facts, situations, events, experiences we are talking about, so that we shall not let our words work loose, so to speak, from the actual contexts in which they are used. But his notion of dispensing with words altogether is not, it seems, merely a wild exaggeration of this sound advice; it appears to be founded upon a definite mistake, which prevented him from seeing how hopelessly bereft and at a loss we should be if we took him at his word. Suppose, he says, that I take my ideas 'bare and naked into my view': then, not only shall I avoid all risk of merely verbal error – I shall avoid mistakes altogether. For 'the objects I consider, I clearly and adequately know'. I cannot make mistakes about my own ideas. Now so long as I merely 'take into my view', or (as he also says) attentively 'perceive' my own ideas, I shall indeed make no mistakes. But this is not because I then know anything for certain; it is rather because, so long as I *only* 'consider' or 'perceive', there is nothing in the case which could be either mistaken or not mistaken. It is only when I say (or think) something *about* what I perceive that I can be mistaken; but unless I say or think something, I cannot *know* anything either. If I confine myself to the mere contemplation or perception of ideas, I avoid the possibility of saying or believing something false only because I do not take the risk of saying or believing anything at all. To abandon speech and thought in favour of 'attentive perception' indeed eliminates the risk of mistake; but it eliminates knowledge as well. What we can do correctly we can do wrongly; but if we avoid the risk of going wrong by doing nothing, we do *nothing* – we do not turn ourselves into infallible performers.

This, I believe, undermines Berkeley's main reason for advocating the complete abandonment of language. And if risks must be accepted in any case, it is clear that we shall have but little compensation for the appalling inconveniences involved in the attempt to think without words. There is no reason to suppose that thought without words is impossible; but there is every reason to suppose that it must be arduous and somewhat rudimentary. Let us then ignore Berkeley's misguided injunction to dispense with language, and instead lay to heart his salutary warnings against the 'abuse' and 'deception' of words.

Finally, we must try to make somewhat clearer than Berkeley does the general importance in his doctrines of the *Introduction*. Why exactly did he think it so essential to dispose of 'abstract ideas', before embarking on his discussion of the 'principles of human knowledge'? At present this question can be answered only in rough and general terms, but some answer can usefully be offered.

In the first place, he thought (rightly) that this confused body of doctrine worked against, rather than for, clarity and precision in the use of words. The whole notion of an 'abstract idea' is so obscure that, when we are told that even some common word stands for such an idea, we may suddenly come to feel that we do not at all understand what before had seemed (and had indeed been) quite clear. 'The plainest things in the world, those we are most intimately acquainted with, and perfectly know, when they are considered in an abstract way, appear strangely difficult and incomprehensible' (p. 97). With what are we more familiar than with time? We can tell the time, make and keep appointments, talk without difficulty of the past and the future, and use without discomfort such words as 'then' and 'now', 'before' and 'after'. But as soon as we try, as we are told we ought to try, to frame and consider the 'abstract idea' of Time, we find ourselves quite at a loss; 'till at length, having wander'd through many intricate mazes, we find our selves just where we were, or, which is worse, sit down in a forlorn scepticism.' In this and a thousand other instances, Berkeley holds with justice that fewer perplexities would have arisen if philosophers had not committed those mistakes enshrined in the doctrine of 'abstract ideas'. 'We have first raised a dust, and then complain, we cannot see.'

Secondly, Berkeley believed, again with justice, that the doctrine of 'abstract ideas' opened a door that should at all costs be kept bolted. We become aware by our senses, he holds, of a variety of 'particular ideas'; we are aware also of our minds and their 'operations'; and we use words in order to speak about that of which we are thus aware. Now any word, he contends, which really has a meaning – which really has some use in our language – must refer, and can only refer, in one way or another, to something that human beings actually experience. For how else could we know what words mean, or learn their meaning? If I attempt to speak of something of a sort which neither I nor anyone else has ever experienced nor ever could have experienced, the words that I utter must be unintelligible. I cannot pretend to know, nor can I explain, what sort of thing it is that my words refer to; that is to say, I do not know the meaning of my words – I am, indeed, using words that can have no meaning.

In principle, Locke had been sympathetic to some such opinion. He held that all our ideas come 'from experience', and has always been regarded as a pioneer of 'empiricism' in philosophy. But Berkeley argues – and in this he is certainly right – that Locke did not follow his own axioms faithfully. (One might alternatively, as so often with Locke, maintain that he did perhaps observe his own axioms, but that if so these were intolerably vague.) The most serious offence that Locke committed was that he allowed himself to speak of 'matter', or 'material substance', admitting that these expressions do not and cannot denote any object of anyone's experi-

ence, and yet *not* concluding that for this very reason they
must and can only be meaningless, empty words. Nor does the
evil stop with these expressions themselves; for, since every
material object is regarded by Locke as really *being* a piece or
specimen of 'matter', he comes to believe that even those
familiar statements we make about common objects of everyday experience really refer to something inaccessible, in principle, to observation. In this way almost everything we say is
made to seem mysterious and perplexing; it seems that we are
constantly speaking of 'something, we know not what'. The
fatal step Berkeley diagnoses as follows – by asserting the
existence of 'abstract ideas', Locke concealed from himself the
fundamental point that our words can have reference only to
what we do actually experience. And this was a disaster. For
once we allow that a word, which in no way refers to what we
actually experience, may be significant because it stands for
something else, where are we to draw the line? We know well
enough what experiences human beings can and do have; but
what bounds could be set to their claims to have 'abstract
ideas'? What outlandish and fantastic verbiage might not be
proliferated by this fatal blunder? The word 'matter' is, in
Berkeley's opinion, the most pernicious impostor which bat-
tens on the doctrine of abstraction, but he finds others also of
importance. Mathematicians pretend to treat of 'infinitesimals', scientists of 'forces', 'virtues', and 'essences'; even
every common noun, according to Locke, refers to something
incapable of being observed. And the door is thus everywhere
open for a flood of misunderstandings and unnecessary problems. The rejection of 'abstract ideas' was intended to be the
bolting and barring of this door. If we can only shake off this
mistaken doctrine, we shall see that words cannot be used
significantly to speak of anything that is not found in our experience; and thus we shall at least be in a good position, not
only to avoid the use of nonsensical words, but also to understand rightly our customary discourse.

*

It would, I believe, be difficult to exaggerate the importance and the originality of Berkeley's *Introduction*. Hume, a philosopher of not less power than Berkeley himself, was not unaware of its merits: he described the rejection of 'abstract ideas' as 'one of the greatest and most valuable discoveries that has been made of late years in the republic of letters'. But in general this part of Berkeley's work was ignored or, if not ignored, then imperfectly understood and undervalued. The common assumption seems to have been that an almost minor disagreement between Locke and Berkeley was the issue here at stake – can we, or can we not, 'frame abstract ideas'? And then it has been, as it plausibly can be, maintained that Berkeley discharges his ammunition against a position which Locke did not definitely occupy, and that much of what he says is in consequence beside the point. It has even been suggested with distressing frequency that, as a result of misinterpreting Locke, Berkeley simply missed the real problems entirely. Nothing could be further from the truth.

To appreciate the value of Berkeley's argument, it is essential to see that the superficially prominent question 'Can we, in accordance with Locke's instructions, frame abstract ideas?' is in itself of little importance. It does not matter much that Berkeley says 'No' to this, nor does it matter that he gives to Locke's words a definite sense that perhaps Locke never intended. The essential thing is his contention that the assumptions about meaning, which led Locke to propound his doctrine, are wrong. Locke asks what it is of which general words are names; and the crux of Berkeley's contention is, not that he answers this question wrongly, but that the *question itself* is wholly wrong. For it is already implied in the form of Locke's question that any word must stand for, be the name of, something; and this assumption, which Locke never questioned, is precisely what Berkeley rejects.[5]

The effects of making this assumption are, as Berkeley well saw, widely diffused. It is not only that we become involved in intolerable confusions in the attempt to say what words, which are not in fact names, can be supposed to be the names of –

though tangles of exactly this kind have occupied time and energy enough, both before and long after Berkeley's own day. There is also the more general point that we may be thus led to feel baffled and perplexed even in fields with which we are perfectly familiar. The scientists of Berkeley's time, for example, were apt to lament their ignorance of the true nature of *motion* and *force*. They were of course familiar enough with the phenomenon of movement, and were even well able to calculate and predict how objects would move and how they would react to 'impressed forces'. But it seemed to them that in these multifarious phenomena they had not found the true *meanings* of the words 'motion' and 'force'. They felt that it was their business to discover, not that and how things move, but that one thing – they hardly knew what sort of thing – which really *was* Motion; they sought for that one mysterious stuff that *was* Force. Naturally enough, they could not solve these problems. But, as Berkeley saw, there are actually no such problems as these. A man who knows what these scientists knew quite well already knows what force and what motion are; the refusal to be satisfied with this is due merely to the notion that there must be some *one thing* – an 'essence', an 'idea', or some such entity – that is really named by the words 'force' and 'motion'. And this is a special case of the general mistake of assuming that all words are really names. Instead of appreciating that to speak of motion is to speak about how things move, the theorists supposed that, when they spoke of motion, they were referring to some single (but strangely elusive) thing, present (but seemingly concealed) whenever anything moved. And thus, though they well knew that and how things moved, they were afflicted with the quite needless feeling that they were in a state of incurable ignorance. Again – to take a non-Berkeleian example – 'the mind' has often proved similarly elusive. We are on the whole sufficiently adept at discussing, describing, and assessing the characters and intellects, tastes, propensities, motives, purposes, and feelings of ourselves and of other people; the human mind is something of which we all have some first-hand knowledge, and usually a great deal of second-hand knowledge as well. But if we assume, as theorists have assumed, that there is some one thing to which the expression 'the mind' refers, we shall soon come to see that we know of no such one thing, and hence – it will seem – we know nothing of the mind itself. Here too the application of Berkeley's principles would be salutary. Endless labour might have been avoided if philosophers had really taken notice of his observation that 'indeed we are apt to think every noun substantive stands for a distinct idea, that may be separated from all others: which hath occasioned infinite mistakes' (P. 116).

The related blunder of failing, on the ground that 'all words stand for ideas', to distinguish between expressions used to refer and those used to describe, is one of those interwoven mistakes that have generated the ancient problem of Universals. To examine this would be beside our present purpose. I mention it, however, because it is this problem, for which Berkeley so ably indicates a cure, which he is often said to have 'missed'.

And now we may embark upon the main text of the *Principles*. Berkeley asks us constantly to bear in mind that significant words can only have reference to what we do or could actually experience; but we must not suppose that every word is used to stand for, to name, one particular idea. And our words refer directly to what we experience, not (as Locke thought) only indirectly, *via* private and non-material mediators. Finally, we must constantly remind ourselves of the contexts in which our words have their uses; if we cannot dispense with words altogether, at least we can avoid deception by careful attention to their actual meanings.

5

BERKELEY'S THEORY OF THE MATERIAL WORLD

THE philosophy of the *Principles of Human Knowledge* has been described as 'a triumph of simplification'. This is indeed what Berkeley intended it to be, and there is no reason to doubt that he was satisfied with the results. But, as is so often the case in philosophy, the more closely we look at his doctrines the less simple they appear; the distant view seems clearly and sharply drawn, but many complexities emerge as we come closer. Or we might compare Berkeley's theory with an iceberg: an elegant, translucent shape appears above the surface, but it is continuous with a far larger volume that lurks and looms below. In the present chapter I shall describe the top of the iceberg. The outline of Berkeley's positive doctrine can be drawn, as he himself draws it, very briefly. Then we must consider what it was that he was contradicting; his arguments cannot be understood until it is clear what he was arguing against. And in the chapters that follow we must try to bring to light the many intricacies that lie below the surface. Berkeley, it seems clear, was not aware of these. In spite of his brilliant criticism of his predecessors, he was so much at home in a certain philosophical tradition as really to be unaware of its influence. We shall have many questions to ask that he either did not ask at all, or at least answered without much reflection.

*

Berkeley strikes at the outset a note of high but apparently unconscious dogmatism. 'It is evident', he writes, 'to anyone who takes a survey of the objects of human knowledge, that they are either ideas actually imprinted on the senses, or else such as are perceived by attending to the passions and operations of the mind, or lastly ideas formed by help of memory and imagination, either compounding, dividing, or barely repre-senting those originally perceived in the aforesaid ways. By sight I have the ideas of light and colours with their several degrees and variations. By touch I perceive, for example, hard and soft, heat and cold, motion and resistance, and of all these more or less either as to quantity or degree. Smelling fur-nishes me with odours; the palate with tastes, and hearing conveys sounds to the mind in all their variety of tone and composition. And as several of these are observed to accom-pany each other, they come to be marked by one name, and so to be reputed as one thing. Thus, for example, a certain colour, taste, smell, figure and consistence having been ob-served to go together, are accounted one distinct thing, signi-fied by the name *apple*. Other collections of ideas constitute a stone, a tree, a book, and the like sensible things; which, as they are pleasing or disagreeable, excite the passions of love, hatred, joy, grief, and so forth.' (p. 1)

Now, Berkeley continues, quite apart from all these 'ideas or objects of knowledge', there is 'something which knows or perceives them, and exercises divers operations, as willing, imagining, remembering, about them. This perceiving, active being I call mind, spirit, soul, or my self.' These words do not denote any ideas, but refer to something entirely different and distinct, 'wherein they exist, or, which is the same thing, whereby they are perceived; for the existence of an idea con-sists in being perceived'. (p. 2)

This last remark is, Berkeley thinks, quite obviously true. No one supposes that thoughts, or 'passions', or 'ideas formed by the imagination' can exist in complete independence of any mind. If a thought occurs at all, or any process of thought, there must be somebody whose thought it is, who is actually thinking. An image which crosses my mind, or which I call up, plainly does not survive my imagining it; when I cease to imagine, the image is *ipso facto* annihilated. Berkeley finds it no less evident that 'the sensations or ideas imprinted on the sense' cannot be supposed to exist except 'in a mind perceiving them'. What after all, he asks, does the term 'exist' *mean* when 'applied to sensible things'? 'The table I write on, I say, exists, that is, I see and feel it. . . . There was an odour, that is, it was smelled; a colour or figure, and it was perceived by sight or touch. This is all that I can understand by these and the like expressions.' But what we call *things* – an apple for example – are only collections of ideas; when we speak of an apple, we refer to a certain set of colours, tastes, smells, and shapes; and these are all ideas. But since the existence of ideas consists in their being perceived, it follows that the existence of things, i.e. collections of ideas, consists also in their being perceived. 'Their *esse* is *percipi*, nor is it possible they should have any existence, out of the minds or thinking things which perceive them.' This Berkeley takes to be one of those truths 'so near and obvious to the mind, that a man need only open his eyes to see them.'

It now follows, Berkeley claims, that 'there is not any other substance than *spirit*, or that which perceives.' It is commonly (and, he thinks, rightly) supposed that colours, shapes, smells, and so on – that is, 'sensible qualities' – must inhere or exist in something; qualities are thought not to be 'self-subsistent'. And if we ask in what qualities exist, we have to answer 'Substance.' So far, so good. But, according to Berkeley, we are apt to go badly wrong when we have reached this point. For we are, it seems, prone to think of substance as an unthinking, material *substratum*, or 'support', of qualities. But if sensible qualities are in fact ideas, this notion must seem very ridiculous. For everyone must really admit that an idea can exist only in a mind; which is to say that mind, or 'spirit', is the only possible substance. That 'wherein colour, figure, and the like qualities exist, must perceive them'; and that which perceives ideas is mind, soul, or spirit.

Berkeley turns aside at this point (P. 8) to consider certain likely objections and prejudices against his views. But let us for the present continue with plain exposition, to which he returns in P. 25. Here he claims that all our 'ideas, sensations, or the things which we perceive . . . are visibly inactive, there is nothing of power or agency included in them.' We do not perceive 'power or activity' in ideas; therefore there is none, for our ideas just *are* what we *do* perceive. Now, from the way in which ideas succeed each other in our minds, with endless variety but also with orderliness, it must be concluded that they have some controlling cause. But a cause, being active, cannot be an idea; it must therefore be a substance. But the only substance is spirit; hence, the cause of our ideas must be 'an incorporeal active substance or spirit'.

Berkeley finds that, of some of his ideas, he can suppose that his own mind is the cause. 'It is no more than willing, and straightway this or that idea arises in my fancy.' This, however, does not take him far; for he finds that 'the ideas actually perceived by sense have not a like dependence on my will'. I can, within limits, decide what to look at or listen to; but if I look out of my window in broad daylight, I cannot then decide what to *see*. The world outside is simply there to be seen, and I cannot choose but see it so long as I look. Such ideas as I then have are not 'creatures of my will'. 'There is therefore some other will or spirit that produces them.'

This spirit, Berkeley concludes, can only be God. If we consider the 'steadiness, order, and coherence', and also the 'admirable connexion', of the ideas of sense, we must confess that our experience 'sufficiently testifies the wisdom and benevolence of its Author'. Berkeley finds that men have a strange tendency to overlook this; but he thinks that anyone who considers the point without prejudice must find it entirely conclusive and inescapable.

*

We now have before us a bare but complete outline of Berkeley's view of the world. Almost the whole of the rest of the *Principles* consists in the elaboration, defence, and elucidation of the doctrines already stated. There are, he says, two and only two classes of things – there are ideas, and there are spirits. Among spirits there is one infinite spirit, God; and there are many finite spirits, men being among them. There is nothing active in the Universe but Mind. Finite minds have some small power to cause ideas; but when we observe the world about us, we are for ever being affected with the ideas that God's mind perceives, and which by God's will finite spirits also perceive. God gives us ideas by certain rules and in a certain order, so that we may know what to expect and how to conduct ourselves. If we study these rules attentively we may learn, not how one object or event produces another, but rather what plans they are that God carries out in conveying to finite spirits the ideas they perceive. Ideas are all particular and determinate; none is 'abstract'; and to say of any idea that it *exists* is to say that, by some mind or spirit, it is *perceived*. 'Some truths there are so near and obvious to the mind, that a man need only open his eyes to see them. Such I take this important one to be, to wit, that all the choir of heaven and furniture of the earth, in a word all those bodies which compose the mighty frame of the world, have not any subsistence without a mind, that their being is to be perceived or known; that consequently so long as they are not actually perceived by me, or do not exist in my mind or that of any other created spirit, they must either have no existence at all, or else subsist in the mind of some eternal spirit: it being perfectly unintelligible and involving all the absurdity of abstraction, to attribute to any single part of them an existence independent of a spirit.'

*

It is of course difficult – most of Berkeley's contemporaries found it impossible – to resist the impression that this is mere eloquent eccentricity and paradox. We are, as we think, familiar enough with minds; and we find it natural to speak of ideas in these minds. But what about *things*? It would seem that Berkeley has left them out altogether. Are we always mistaken when we claim to see stones and to kick them? Is there nothing at all but our own ideas? And surely it is the fire that boils the kettle, not the 'will of a spirit'. Either we, it may be thought, or Berkeley must be utterly mistaken;

both parties cannot be right. And surely Berkeley has, as Kant said that he had, 'degraded bodies to mere illusion'.

However, the issue is not so simple as this. It soon becomes clear that not only is Berkeley well aware that he *may* convey to his readers this startling impression – he is also immensely anxious not to. He devotes the greatest efforts to the attempt to show that he is in no way a 'sceptic'; that he propounds no paradoxes; that his only concern is to set down, clearly and without ornament, the natural views of any sensible man who has not been confused and corrupted by philosophy. He is not, he would persuade us, devising a novel theory. If only we will clear the air of the 'learned dust' and get the false doctrines out of the way, we shall all see the world exactly as he sees it. If we feel discomfort in accepting his statements, either we have misunderstood their purport, or we are still in the grip of untenable theories. It is true that Berkeley's language is sometimes unorthodox; but only, he says, because common language is so often misleading. In any case he believes (and that he believed this is of the first importance) that his doctrines cannot be denied unless we are ready to accept, as the only alternative, opinions far more obviously strange and mistaken. Let us ask, then, what those theories and opinions were, by rejecting which Berkeley arrived at his own standpoint.

Probably the first objection to Berkeley that comes to mind is this – that, though there may be and no doubt are 'ideas in the mind', there certainly are also objects *not* in the mind. Ideas perhaps 'have not any subsistence without a mind', but why should we take the same to be true of *things*? Berkeley presents this natural objection to his case in the form which it would have been given by Locke – almost, in fact, in Locke's own words.

'But say you, though the ideas themselves do not exist without the mind, yet there may be things like them whereof they are copies or resemblances, which things exist without the mind, in an unthinking substance. ... Some there are who make a distinction betwixt *primary* and *secondary* qualities:

by the former, they mean extension, figure, motion, rest, solidity or impenetrability and number: by the latter they denote all other sensible qualities, as colours, sounds, tastes, and so forth. The ideas we have of these they acknowledge not to be the resemblances of any thing existing without the mind or unperceived; but they will have our ideas of primary qualities to be patterns or images of things which exist without the mind, in an unthinking substance which they call *matter*' (P. 8, 9).

In these words Berkeley sets up his main target. The doctrine outlined was, in one version or another, exceedingly ancient; but it had recently been revived and refurbished by Locke, and had acquired immense prestige from its apparent harmony with the methods and assumptions of the newly and greatly flourishing physical sciences. Berkeley's vehement objections to it are somewhat complex. He thinks it philosophically wrong and absurd; but he regards it also as the main prop of vice and atheism; and further, in an almost personal way, he dislikes it. Matter, which he often and naturally calls 'unthinking', he sometimes and more insultingly calls 'stupid'. He is clearly made most uncomfortable by the view that what there really *is* in the world is, as Locke held, an inert, featureless, 'stupid' something, of which we know nothing except that it exists and is named 'matter'. Berkeley would detest so brutish a world as this, even if the assertion of its existence had not appeared to him to bristle with gross mistakes and disastrous consequences.

The doctrine as codified by Locke may be summarized as follows.[6] Observation of the world in which we live consists essentially, according to Locke, in having *ideas*. These ideas are the 'immediate objects' of the mind, and its *only* immediate objects. Ideas, in Locke as in Berkeley, are 'in the mind'; if there were no minds there would be no ideas. Furthermore, in Locke as in Berkeley, ideas have causes. But at this point sharp disagreement arises. For Locke does not share Berkeley's view that a cause, or at any rate a *real* cause, must be and can only be the will of a spirit; accepting the doctrines of contemporary science, he supposed that the occurrence of ideas in our minds could be attributed to the operation of purely physical causes. God, he allows, decides what causes are to have what effects; we cannot explain *why* the cutting of my finger causes me pain, except by saying that God has 'annexed' those sensations to that event; but, allowing this, Locke sees no objection to the view that one event is the cause of another. In Locke's world there are, then, physical objects wholly independent of ('external' to) any mind; and these objects cause observers (in suitable conditions) to have ideas. Now the power of an object to cause an observer to have an idea is what Locke says that he means by a *quality* of that object. Hence he concludes – and this is an important step – that the ideas we have by observation are ideas of *qualities*. 'External objects', he says, 'furnish the mind with the ideas of sensible qualities.'

Locke next propounds (though he was not the first to do so) a distinction between two sorts of qualities, which he calls *primary* and *secondary*. His arguments for this distinction are, unfortunately, confused. Partly – and this is the argument he states at length – he thinks that our ideas of secondary qualities (colours, tastes, smells, warmths, and sounds) are so very variable and fluctuating that we can find no one such quality to be assigned as *the* quality of the object. Things look different colours in different lights and from different points of view, they taste different to different percipients, water feels warm or cold depending on the temperature of the hands with which we feel it; and so on. But there is no reason to suppose that the object itself varies in this extreme fashion; the ideas we have vary, as our own physical state or the conditions of observation vary, but the object itself does not vary in this way. Hence, Locke concludes, we must admit that colours (etc.) are 'only in the mind'. The object has indeed the power to produce ideas of colour, but these are so various that we can attribute no one colour to the object itself. In addition to these considerations, it is clear enough that Locke also had in mind scientific explanations of colour-vision and the rest; and these apparently tended to the same conclusion. The scientific doctrine was that 'particles' or 'corpuscles' were reflected or emitted from the object, which by 'impact' upon the nervous system *caused* the idea of colour to arise in the mind. To these particles were assigned certain metrical properties – speed, weight, shape, and so on – but in the scientific account of colour-vision it was unnecessary to state that the particles, or anything else, were actually coloured. The question of actual colour was supposed not to come up until the particles caused this idea to arise in the mind. From this source also, then, Locke drew the conclusion that in the physical world there really was nothing at all that was actually coloured, though there were objects having the power to produce ideas of colour; and analogously for the other secondary qualities.

Now clearly, if this sort of 'corpuscular' explanation is to be carried through, it must be possible to assign to objects themselves those properties without which their alleged causal action could not be described. A novel feature of the sciences in and just before Locke's day was the enormously fruitful application of mathematics; natural laws had begun to be stated, with wonderful convenience and success, in the form of numerical functions; and in the work of Newton this comparatively recent technique appeared to have been carried almost to final perfection. It was thus no accident that, in the scientific account of perception, the properties mentioned were invariably metrical – those to which numbers could be assigned by measurement, and thereby mathematical techniques brought to bear.[7] And thus we find in Locke's list of *primary* qualities – the qualities that physical objects actually have – size, shape, speed, and number; with solidity thrown in, no doubt to allow for the supposed action of particles by 'impact'. Locke also appears to have appreciated that, however objects may *seem* (to different observers or in different conditions) to vary in size or shape or speed, or however various they may *look* in these respects, we can by measurement assign to them definite sizes and shapes and speeds. And so he concluded that the sort of 'argument from variability' which he used to place secondary qualities 'in the mind' could not be applied to the case of primary qualities. However things may seem to us, we can discover what their primary qualities really are.

And so the position in which Locke found himself was this. There is a world of physical ('external') objects; and these have power to cause ideas to arise in the minds of observers. Some of these ideas, namely ideas of primary qualities, are 'copies' or 'resemblances' of the objects themselves; in this case the objects actually have the qualities which our ideas incline us to assign to them. But in the case of ideas of secondary qualities, there is nothing actually in the objects themselves in the least like the ideas that we have. There is indeed the power to cause us to have these ideas, but the ideas are totally unlike their causes. The particles which cause ideas of colour are not actually coloured, and no more is anything else.

There is one more important feature in Locke's picture of the world. In his view, when we observe an object we perceive its qualities; when we speak about an object we say what qualities it has. Now there must, Locke assumes, be something, not itself a quality, in which qualities inhere; for qualities cannot 'subsist *sine re substante*'. But here we seem to run into a two-fold difficulty. First, if what we have ideas of, what we perceive, is and can only be some sensible quality, it seems to follow that what *has* qualities is necessarily and for ever imperceptible. It seems logically impossible that we should perceive the *possessor* of qualities, since to perceive simply is to perceive the qualities themselves; and anything we might come to perceive in the future could only be another sensible quality. But second, we cannot even *say* what it is that has qualities. Certainly it seems at first sight that we can do this; can I not say that, for instance, my shoes are brown? But, Locke points out, if I ask what I mean by 'shoes', I can only say they are things having certain qualities; and at once I encounter again the question what it *is* that has these qualities. In fact, all I am saying when I say that my shoes are brown is that some things having the typical qualities of shoes have also the quality of being brown. And this is wholly inescapable; for to say anything at all about what *has* all these qualities can only be to ascribe to it a further quality, and this does not get us any nearer to saying what it *is*. Indeed, all we can say about the possessor of qualities – about what there *is* as distinct from what qualities are possessed – is that it is *something* which supports qualities, or in which they inhere. We cannot dispense with this something, for qualities must be possessed by, or inhere in, something which is itself not just another quality; but we can neither perceive this something nor say what it is. It is logically beyond the reach of perception and of language. We may invent a name and call it 'matter' or 'material substance', but all that we mean by this is 'something we know not what'.

And now we have the essentials of Locke's view before us. The stuff of the physical world, what there really *is*, is this substance or 'matter' of which we know nothing except that it exists. In this substance there inhere certain primary qualities (with which the sciences deal); and it has, in virtue of possessing these qualities, the power to cause some ideas which are 'copies' of its qualities, and also other ideas (of colour etc.) which are totally different. The only empirical data available to observers are the ideas produced in their minds in this way.

*

It will, I believe, become apparent that this doctrine of Locke's is indeed, as Berkeley maintained, confused and even untenable in principle. But it would be a mistake to deny that it has a certain plausibility. Locke knew and admired many of the leading scientists of his day; he was clearly concerned to make his philosophy harmonize with their views and their discoveries, and in fact he made it a main part of his plan to state, in simple and ordinary language, a theory that would in no way perplex or hinder the work of such 'master builders' as Boyle and Newton. In this aim at least he seems to have been curiously successful. His account of 'matter' appeared for many years to accord well enough with scientific assumptions; and his analysis of perception is often propounded today by unwary scientists.

Views similar to Locke's seem naturally to suggest themselves to those whose main interest lies in scientific theories. It is natural to think that the properties assigned in scientific theory to 'corpuscles' (or whatever the entities may be in terms of which the current theories are stated), are the properties which the 'external world' really has; and to argue from this that the numerous other properties which, on the basis of ordinary observation, we commonly ascribe to ordinary objects, are somehow illusory – things seem (perhaps because of the nature of our sense-organs) to have such qualities as colour and smell, but science shows that the real 'external objects' cannot be supposed to have such qualities as these. Connected with this is the persistent tendency to represent the 'immediate objects' of common observation as 'in our minds', almost as it were in our heads, and the 'external world' as a mysterious realm whose nature we can discover only, if at all, by risky inference or elaborate construction. Views of this sort, of which Locke was a pioneer, have never been without their devotees. And it is an important merit of Berkeley's philosophy that he seeks, not merely to reject and ridicule these opinions, but also to present an account of the sciences that will not appear to make such opinions plausible. His objections to Locke are many and various. Some are fundamental, others are on points of detail; some are effective, indeed lethal, others miss the mark. We can consider them most conveniently, not in Berkeley's order, but collected and arranged from the various passages in which they occur.

There are, first of all, certain arguments against Locke's distinction between primary and secondary qualities.

(1) It is easy to bring an *ad hominem* argument against Locke's position. In seeking to show that secondary qualities are 'only in the mind', Locke relies on the fact that, as the observer's state or the conditions vary, objects look, feel, etc. different – now red, now black; now warm, now cool; and so

on. But the same thing is equally true of the primary qualities. In a mist things look bigger than they do in plain daylight; in an unusually dry, clear atmosphere distant objects
look closer than they do when the air is less clear; a distant
aeroplane seems to move much more slowly than it would
seem to do if it were close at hand; from some points of view
an oval table may look round. If this sort of variability is
taken, in the one case, to prove that the qualities in question
are 'in the mind', it must be taken to prove the same thing in
the other case also.

Locke would presumably reply to this objection by pointing out that, although things may in some conditions *look*
bigger or closer or slower-moving than they look in others,
this does not show that size or distance or speed is 'only in the
mind'. For size and distance and speed can be determined by
measurement; and then, however variously things may look,
we can say what their size or distance or speed in fact *is*. Now
this is perfectly correct; but once again we may argue *ad
hominem*. If the fact that it is possible to distinguish how
things look or seem from how they actually are, for instance
to distinguish apparent from actual size, entitles us to say
that a quality is *in* an object, then by parity of reasoning
secondary qualities may be really *in* objects. For here too,
however variously things may look or seem, we can often discover and decide how they really are. If a piece of paper looks
red in a strong red light and green in a green one, and if it
looks white when held near a plain glass window at mid-day,
then undoubtedly that piece of paper is white. That it should
look very different in different lights, so far from preventing
our saying what colour it *is*, is exactly what we should expect
of a piece of white paper. Certainly, different statements of
its colour cannot all be true. If I say 'It is white', and you at
the same time say of the same piece of paper 'It is red', at least
one of us must be mistaken. But if I say 'It *looks* red', and you
then say 'It looks green', we may both be right; and furthermore we may both agree that it has not really changed its
colour and is in fact white. The distinction (or distinctions)

between appearance and reality can certainly be drawn in the field of primary qualities, but so it can with secondary qualities also. There is a difference in the *methods* of drawing the distinction. In some cases we measure or count, in others we look again in standard, ordinary, normal conditions – in daylight for example. These are indeed important differences, particularly to the scientist who seeks numerical values; but they do not justify Locke's conclusion at all. The suggestion that objects look so bewilderingly various in colour that we cannot in any instance say what colour they are, is simply not true.

Berkeley draws from this objection the opposite conclusion to ours. Instead of maintaining that Locke's argument fails to show even that *secondary* qualities are 'in the mind', he maintains that Locke's argument must be taken to show that *primary* qualities also are 'in the mind'. Further discussion of this must be postponed. But at least we can agree with Berkeley so far as to say that, *if* Locke succeeds in relegating secondary qualities to the mind, then primary qualities must be located there also. The distinction as he seeks to make it cannot be upheld. 'In short, let anyone consider those arguments, which are thought manifestly to prove that colours and tastes exist only in the mind, and he shall find they may with equal force, be brought to prove the same thing of extension, figure, and motion' (P. 15).

(2) Berkeley's second argument against Locke's distinction is less effective. Locke had maintained that external objects are (for example) solid and extended, but are not really (for example) coloured. The former qualities are in the objects themselves, the latter is only 'in the mind'. Berkeley contends that this is inconceivable, on the ground that colour and extension are 'inseparably united'; any object which is solid and extended must have some colour. His idea seems to be that to say that an extended object has no colour is like saying that a three-sided rectilinear figure is not a triangle; just as a three-sided figure must have three angles, an extended figure must have some colour. But his case is in fact not at all so

clear as this. There is certainly no good reason for supposing that physical objects, roses for instance, actually *are* extended but without colour; but this supposition is surely just false, and not, as Berkeley maintains, nonsensical. It is not only that some objects, such as window-panes, can properly be described as colourless; for it might be maintained, not wholly without reason, that anything which is at all visible is thereby, perhaps in some slightly extended sense, also coloured. (Berkeley, I think, would certainly have maintained this.) It is rather that we can well understand the suggestion that there might be *totally* invisible objects. Tales about invisible men do not strike us as *meaningless*, even if we think it unlikely or physically impossible that there are, or ever will be, invisible men; we can at least understand the supposition that one might, in broad daylight, bump into a solid and extended body, and yet be able to see nothing at all. No doubt there is *some* absurdity in Locke's suggestion that physical objects are not, though they invariably seem to be, coloured; but it is not that the notion of extended but colourless objects is actually inconceivable.

(3) The next point is of more fundamental importance. Berkeley states with considerable force an objection to Locke which has been constantly repeated ever since, and which is indeed wholly conclusive. Locke asserts that there are, besides the ideas which we actually perceive, external objects which cause these ideas to arise. But how, Berkeley asks, is it possible for him to *know* this? He cannot claim to have discovered it by observation, since in Locke's own view the objects of observation are always, necessarily, and only ideas; we cannot, he argues, actually perceive external objects, but are aware only of the ideas they cause. If, then, we do not perceive external objects, do we know of their existence by inference? No, for any such inference would be invalid. It is admitted that ideas may occur (for example in dreams or hallucinations) 'though no bodies exist without, resembling them' – it is not *necessary* that ideas be caused by objects. Even if we accept the view that they must be caused somehow, we

are not justified in proceeding, as Locke proceeds, to describe the nature of their causes in detail. How could it be known that the cause of certain ideas is an (imperceptible) external object, really having some qualities of which the ideas are 'resemblances'? To decide that a portrait is a good likeness of a man, I must look both at the portrait and at the man. If the man is, like Locke's external objects, not to be seen, I can decide nothing at all. I cannot say that the portrait is in any way like the man; indeed, for all I can discover, the picture might not be a portrait at all. 'In short, if there were [in Locke's sense] external bodies, it is impossible we should ever come to know it; and if there were not, we might have the very same reasons to think there were that we have now' (P. 20). So long as we continue to have ideas, it can make no difference to us at all whether there are or are not external objects; our actual experience would be quite unchanged even by their total annihilation. We have then no reason to suppose that there are such objects; they are entirely superfluous.

Here, I think, is the crucial point of Berkeley's disagreement with Locke. It appeared to him that Locke's picture of the world embodied an absurd and quite needless *duplication*. There are, first of all, the things that we actually perceive, which Locke calls 'ideas'; and then, Locke adds, there are behind or beyond the ideas completely unobservable counterparts, which he regards as the real physical objects. But Berkeley condemns this addition as simply unnecessary. If by asserting the existence of ideas we have already brought in everything that we actually perceive, then nothing more is required. What could be the point of supposing a second set of things behind the scenes, things that we never perceive? We could not possibly know that there were any such things, and it could make no difference at all to us if there were not. The only result of Locke's manoeuvre is the disastrous one, that he makes it seem always questionable whether there are or are not physical objects; he makes it seem that nothing that we perceive can settle this question, for the real physical objects, he says, are not perceptible. But can we not make this absurd question impossible, and also avoid the quite superfluous duplication of entities, by simply leaving out of the picture Locke's 'external bodies'? Their inclusion does nothing but harm; by cancelling them out we can surely lose nothing whatever, except a fertile source of pointless perplexities.

(4) And even if, Berkeley adds, we suppose that there are in Locke's sense 'external bodies', they could not do what Locke requires of them. They are supposed by him to be the *causes* of the ideas that we have. But it is, according to Berkeley, absurd to attribute causal activity to inanimate things. For 'in truth, there is no other agent or efficient cause than *spirit*.' This will be discussed in the following chapter.

(5) Finally, we must seek to clarify Berkeley's disagreement with Locke about 'matter' or 'material substance'. The central point of Berkeley's argument is that the expression 'material substance' is *meaningless*, an empty noise. Locke, who held that our ideas are of qualities, had of course admitted that we do not 'perceive' substance, that it is indeed 'something we know not what'; but he thought that we must none the less accept this something, as being the essential 'support' of qualities. But Berkeley points out (P. 17) that even this is not intelligible. For what is meant here by the word 'support'? Presumably substance does not support qualities as the foundations support a building, nor yet as a bread-winner supports his dependants; but we cannot give any *other* sense to 'support' unless we know what sort of thing it is that does the supporting. We cannot pretend to understand the *relation* between substance and qualities, so long as one of its terms, namely substance, admittedly eludes our comprehension. But plainly we shall never comprehend the alleged mystery of substance, since by definition it cannot be characterized in any way. What it *is* cannot be known, and could not even be *said*; it is, in the scholastic phrase, *nec quid nec quantum nec quale*, and that is as much as we can do for it. It has (P. 68) 'a definition entirely made up of negatives . . . and how nearly this comes to the description of a non-entity, I desire may be considered.' We can indeed say what matter is

not; and 'you may, if so it shall seem good, use the word *matter* in the same sense, that other men use *nothing*, and so make those terms convertible in your style. For after all, this is what appears to me to be the result of that definition, the parts whereof when I consider with attention . . . I do not find that there is any kind of effect or impression made on my mind, different from what is excited by the term *nothing*' (p. 80). We might just as well say 'nothing' as 'something we know not what'.

Curiously enough, in urging all these points Berkeley is hardly saying more than Locke had himself already admitted. Locke had confessed with complete candour that neither he nor anyone else could explain what matter was, or what the expression 'material substance' meant. But at the same time he seemed to find a 'necessity of thought' obliging him to assert the existence of this unknowable, 'bare' support of qualities. Some of his critics accused him of diluting substance so far that in effect it vanished from his philosophy altogether; but this Locke justly denied. However tenuous and unsatisfactory his notion of substance might be, he had repeatedly said that it was indispensable. And indeed, given his other assumptions, he was perfectly right. If it is true, as Locke maintains, that we can perceive *nothing but* qualities, and also that there must be something which 'supports' these qualities, it follows that there must be something which we cannot perceive. However much Locke may have deplored his imperceptible *something*, he could not avoid asserting its existence.

But for Berkeley, the seemingly inevitable emergence of the phrase 'material substance', about which everyone admitted himself to be baffled, was not a curiosity to be accepted with resignation, but a sign that something had gone radically wrong. He does not, however, explain very satisfactorily how and where the error crept in. He is inclined to think that the emptiness of the phrase 'material substance' was simply not recognized. Influenced by the doctrine of 'abstract ideas', theorists came to think that they could frame a 'most abstract idea' of Entity, or some such thing, even though no such idea was actually perceivable; they supposed, in fact, that words could be given sense even though they had reference to nothing in human experience. He devotes his main energies to arguing that this is not the case. But even so, there is more to be said. For Locke, whatever might be true of other writers, was uncomfortably aware that 'substance' was, in a way, an empty phrase. Why, in spite of this, did he feel obliged to use it?

It is clear enough that he was not influenced by empirical evidence; for he insisted that, whatever we do or even might perceive, we do not and never could perceive substance. He was influenced, then, by *a priori* arguments. And it is clear that the most important of these was the argument, already mentioned, that since we perceive nothing but qualities, the essential *substratum* or 'support' of qualities must be an unobservable (and indescribable) *something* – we can say no more than this, but we cannot say less. But now we must inspect the premises of this argument; why should it be said that 'we perceive nothing but qualities'?

This is itself a sufficiently extraordinary contention. It is no doubt true that we do perceive qualities – we see the colour of the grass, we feel the roughness of gravel. But there would seem to be no warrant for the suggestion that we perceive *only* qualities; on the contrary, in seeing the colour of the grass we see the grass itself. In fact, to perceive the qualities of any object is *necessarily* also to perceive the object itself. When I see the colour of the roses, what has this quality does not elude my observation; the roses have it, the roses at which I am looking.

Locke appears to have been led away from these simple considerations by the following argument. If I am asked what a rose *is*, I may say it is a flower having such and such characteristics; if I am then asked what a flower is, I may try to list the defining attributes of a flower. At each stage I can always be asked for the meaning of any noun, 'rose' or 'flower' or whatever it may be; and I must try to explain its meaning by describing what it is to which that noun applies. 'When we speak of any sort of substance, we say it is a thing having such or such qualities.' Now it may seem that I shall not have explained my meaning fully, until I have offered in place of *every* such noun a descriptive (adjectival) phrase that gives its meaning. But here there seems to be a difficulty. For if in this way I replace every noun by an adjectival phrase, what will become of the grammar of my remarks? No grammatical statement can consist wholly of adjectives; there must be some substantival word for all these adjectives to qualify. No ordinary noun, however, will serve my purpose; for I could at once be asked to explain *its* meaning, and then it too will dissolve into adjectives. So in order to avoid the use of an ordinary noun, I must have recourse to the expression 'something'. Indeed, I might have satisfied my questioner at once by saying, not 'A rose is a *flower* with such and such characteristics', and thus inviting the question 'What is a flower?' – but by saying 'A rose is *something* having such and such characteristics.'

But might he not have asked 'What then is something?'? And here we arrive at the final dilemma. For it seems that I must either reject his question as improper, on the dangerous-looking ground that the word 'something' (unlike all the other substantives) *has* no meaning; or else I must allow that his question is a proper one, but that neither I nor anyone else can answer it.

Locke's conclusion from all of this runs somewhat as follows. Consider such a statement as 'I see a rose'. Now if I analyse this statement – if, that is to say, I try to state fully what is meant by the words used – I must replace the substantive 'a rose' by an expression describing what it is that is so called, listing the qualities that anything must have if it is to be called a rose. But if we carry out such analyses in every case, we shall discover that the proper version of any statement of perception is 'I perceive *something* having such and such qualities'. Thus, what distinguishes any statement of perception from any other is, not the *substantive* in it – for this is in every case 'something' – but the *adjectives*. But this surely is to say that what we actually perceive is always certain qualities – what the adjectives stand for; that 'common subject', *something*, which they qualify, is never actually to be found in what we perceive. But we cannot deny that something has all the qualities that we perceive; 'because we cannot conceive how they should subsist alone, nor one in another, we suppose them existing in, and supported by, some common subject; which support we denote by the name substance, though it be certain we have no clear or distinct idea of that thing we suppose a support.' If someone asks 'What is substance?', it must be confessed that we cannot give him an answer.

Perhaps it will now be clear where Locke has gone wrong. His mistake, I think, can best be described by saying that he interprets as a baffling fact about the world what is really a quite straightforward fact about language. It is both true and obvious that, if we decide to replace every common noun by an expression of the form 'something having qualities A, B, and C', then all such substantives will vanish from our language, leaving only the expression 'something'. If this recipe is consistently followed, 'something' will appear as the subject of every subject-predicate sentence, and all other expressions will appear as descriptive phrases; and 'something', with appropriate adjectives, will always appear as object in sentences of the form 'I perceive ...' But, plainly, we do not discover anything about the world by deciding to use language in this way; we cannot bring to light empirical facts by examining or reforming the way in which we speak. Locke must be mistaken then in deriving, from the fact that 'something' can be made to emerge as the only substantive, the conclusion that there *exists* some 'common subject' to be called 'substance'.

Furthermore, Locke derives his supposed existential conclusion by misconstruing the sense of the expression 'something'. It is true that this word has no *descriptive meaning* (though not of course true that it is meaningless). If I say that there is something in the cupboard, I do not tell you what is in the cupboard, what sort of thing it is, as I would have done if I had said there was a mouse, or a piece of cheese, or a decanter, in the cupboard. But then this is precisely the use of the expression 'something'. It is used exactly when we do *not* wish to specify what in particular; it is a device for avoiding the explicit mention of anything. And this is why it served Locke's purpose; for if all ordinary nouns are to be turned into descriptive phrases, we must find some expression, grammatically substantival, which does not, as ordinary nouns do, refer to things of some definite sort; we must avoid the use of a substantive with descriptive meaning, in order to find some substantive that need not and cannot be converted into a descriptive phrase. But Locke, instead of regarding the expression 'something' as a device for avoiding explicit reference to anything, construes it as if it does have some explicit reference. But then, naturally enough, he finds that he cannot say what it refers to. If, when I say 'There is something in the cupboard', I am interpreted, not as avoiding, but as making mention of what is in the cupboard, it will have to be held that what I refer to has the curious property of completely baffling description; what I allegedly refer to in this word without descriptive meaning must be, it will seem, a characterless, indescribable thing. But this perplexity vanishes as soon as we construe 'something' in the natural way, not as referring to an indescribable entity, but as avoiding mention of anything at all. The use of the expression 'something having such and such qualities' does not show, as Locke thinks it does, that 'the substance is supposed always something besides' the qualities, 'though we know not what it is'. It is not that we do not *know* what has the qualities; for roses (truistically) have the qualities of roses; it is rather that, in using the expression 'something', we do not *say* what has the qualities. And not saying what has the qualities does not entail saying that 'substance' has them, nor yet admitting that we do not know what has them.

Locke's 'substance', then, is a kind of hallucination; it is what we are supposed to be mentioning, when in fact we are not mentioning anything at all. It is like what the person saw who 'saw a man that wasn't there'. 'And how nearly this comes to the description of a non-entity, I desire may be considered.'

*

Let us briefly sum up what it is that Berkeley denies. Locke had asserted the existence of 'matter', 'material substance', a *something* of which nothing could be either said or known; Berkeley dismisses this as nonsensical. Locke had also maintained that real, 'external' objects are not themselves what we perceive, but are the *causes* of the things we perceive. Berkeley denies that such things could ever be causes; and points out that, in any case, we could know nothing of their nature, nor could we even know of their existence. What is the use of this second, shadowy world, alleged to lie somehow behind or beneath the things that we touch and see, hear, taste, or smell? We have no need of this extra world; we cannot sensibly suppose its existence; and nothing but disaster will follow if we do.

So far, I imagine, we are all inclined to take Berkeley's side. There are indeed mistakes and inextricable tangles in Locke's doctrine. But is it correct to say that Locke *duplicated* the world – simply adding to the perceptible world another and redundant world that can never be perceived? We may soon come to feel that this cannot quite be correct; for when Berkeley rejects, as he does, Locke's imperceptible world, he appears to be left with something *less* than the world as we know it. Dispensing with 'matter' and Locke's 'external objects', he seeks to make do merely with *ideas*. Hence, apparently, he concludes that 'all the choir of heaven and furniture of the earth ... have not any subsistence without a mind, that their being is to be perceived or known.' He does not, as many other philosophers have done, maintain merely that we cannot know for certain that objects exist when they are not perceived; he regards it as demonstrably the case that they do not and cannot exist when not perceived – to say that they do, he contends, is self-contradictory. Nor does he argue, as others have done, that we may say that an object exists though not perceived, provided that we mean only that, in certain conditions, it would be perceived. He goes further than this; he holds that to say of an object that it exists can only be to say that it actually is perceived. And this induces a certain discomfort. In saying 'Matter and external objects do not exist', Berkeley claims that he is merely rejecting certain mistaken doctrines of Locke's. But when he goes on to say that the whole material world is 'in the mind', we may well feel that certain quite ordinary opinions have somehow become involved in Locke's downfall. Berkeley claims that they have not. This claim must be considered.

6

THE CHARACTER OF BERKELEY'S THEORY

W HEN Berkeley turns from rejecting the doctrines of Locke to stating his own views, the first impression that he makes upon his readers is that he is grossly in conflict with common sense. Not all of them find this disagreeable. W. B. Yeats, for example, was pleased to think that Berkeley had 'proved all things a dream'. But not many people would regard this as meritorious, nor would Berkeley himself have relished this account of his work. In this chapter we must make a beginning on the task of clearing up this situation. I shall try to show that neither party is wholly in the right. Berkeley is not, in the way that many of his readers suppose, *grossly* in conflict with ordinary views; but the view that there is no actual conflict at all, that it is *only* his language that is surprising, is not wholly tenable either. He has his own view of the world, and it is not a common one.

*

Suppose we begin with Yeats' idea that Berkeley 'proved all things a dream'. It is easy to see how this idea arises. In dreams we seem to see places and people, we seem to hear and to speak, but we do not actually do these things. The face that I see in a dream is not physically present, and there do not really occur the sounds that I dream of. We might naturally say that the items of and the events in my dream are 'only in my mind'; I do not when dreaming see or touch or hear real physical things. But does not Berkeley maintain that this is always the case? He denies the existence of 'external bodies' altogether; he says that there is no such thing as 'matter'; and he says of everything that it is 'in the mind'. What is this but to say that we are dreaming always?

But Berkeley takes the greatest pains to deny that he is saying anything like this. Certainly in dreaming, as also in imagining and remembering, he says that we are aware of ideas; and in waking life we are aware of ideas also. We may well be uncertain, and at present we must remain so, of the exact meaning of this word 'idea'. But at least we can agree that what Berkeley says does not amount to saying that there is *no difference* between dreaming and being awake, between seeing real things and having hallucinations. When we are perceiving real things, our ideas are 'strong, orderly, and coherent'; when we are merely imagining, they are 'less regular, vivid, and constant', and their occurrence is also dependent on our own wills; we can decide to stop having such ideas, but not the ideas that we have when we perceive real things. Presumably, if I have a hallucination, I cannot decide to stop having it; but I can still recognize it *as* a hallucination, by observing that the hallucinatory ideas are not 'coherent' with the ideas of others, or with my own on other occasions. *Of course* there are detectable differences between waking and dreaming, imagining and seeing visions. If there were not, how could we have come to attach differen*t meanings* to these words? It may be that Berkeley does not adequately say what these differences are; but he certainly recognized their existence. 'There is a *rerum natura*, and the distinction between realities and chimeras retains its full force' (p. 34). Suppose that there seems to you to be a cat in the chair; if you go up to it and see it more clearly, stroke it and feel its fur, and induce it to purr by tickling its chin, then there *really is* a cat in the chair. Your ideas have been 'strong, orderly, and coherent'. But if, when there seemed to you to be a cat in the chair, you went closer and no such thing was to be seen – no one else had seen a cat and no cat was anywhere about – then there was no cat in the chair. It was a 'chimera', or simply a mistake. Your ideas turned out not to be 'coherent' with your original impression that there was a cat.

Berkeley's account of these matters is really much less paradoxical than Locke's. According to Locke, the ideas that we have in ordinary waking life are distinguished from those of hallucinatory experiences by 'that steady correspondence they have with the distinct constitution of real beings.' But, in his view, the 'distinct constitution of real beings' is not accessible to observation. I cannot, then, ever be sure that I am not having a hallucination; for I cannot discover the only thing that would show me that I am not. But Berkeley is surely in the right in insisting that the difference between 'realities and chimeras' must be a *detectable* difference; if we represent the difference as consisting in something not open to observation, we make it seem wholly impossible to tell the difference. This is why Berkeley always maintained that no one could be less 'sceptical' than himself. He did not hold, as Locke did, that the existence of real physical things must be established by a dangerous *inference* from what we observe; he held that we do observe real things. 'That the things I see with mine eyes and touch with my hands do exist, really exist, I make not the least question. The only thing whose existence we deny, is that which philosophers call matter or corporeal substance. And in doing of this, there is no damage done to the rest of mankind, who, I dare say, will never miss it.' It is no use, then, producing evidence that we are not always dreaming; for Berkeley never suggests for a moment that we are.

But, it may be objected, the existence of 'matter or corporeal substance' is not the only thing that Berkeley denies. He also denies that anything we perceive exists when it is not perceived; he holds that '*esse*' is '*percipi*'. And here he is not in conflict merely with philosophers; he is also in conflict with 'the rest of mankind', who certainly do not believe that solid objects vanish whenever it happens that no one is perceiving them.

But then Berkeley does not believe this either. It would, he says, be absurd to suggest that 'things are every moment annihilated and created anew'. Sometimes, certainly, objects are totally destroyed and then remade; but there is no reason to think that this happens to my desk, whenever I look away from it and look at it again. Indeed, there is every reason to believe that all the contents of my room are still there, when neither I nor anyone else is in it; for I can be quite sure that no one has taken them away, and the mere absence of people from the room could not be supposed to have destroyed its contents. But, we may say, is not this to admit that things may exist though no one perceives them? And does it not follow that 'esse is percipi' is false?

At one point (P. 3) Berkeley offers the suggestion that, when he says that his table exists though his study is unoccupied, he means 'thereby that if I was in my study I might perceive it. . . .' More or less elaborate versions of this suggestion will be familiar to readers of more recent philosophy; but it certainly does not represent Berkeley's own view. He never mentions this idea again, but invariably relies on a different contention. He was, in fact, clearly convinced that, when we are speaking of 'sensible things', 'to exist' means 'to be perceived'. He regarded this indeed as his major discovery. And of course, if esse is percipi, then to say that if I were in my (at present unoccupied) study my table would be perceived, is to say that if certain conditions were satisfied my table would exist. But Berkeley regards this as quite inadequate. He knows that any plain man would insist that the furniture in an unoccupied room actually does exist, not merely that it would exist if the room were occupied; and he himself thinks that it would be merely absurd to question this. But then, he asks, what do we really mean when we say that the contents of my unoccupied room are not perceived? We mean that nobody is there to perceive them; no human being perceives the ideas that constitute my room and its contents. But it does not follow from this that they are not perceived at all, 'since there may be some other spirit that perceives them, though we do not. Wherever bodies are said to have no existence without the mind, I would not be understood to mean this or that particular mind, but all minds whatsoever' (P. 48). Indeed, it is not only that there may be some other spirit that perceives them; for 'sensible things do really exist: and if they really exist, they are necessarily perceived by an infinite mind: therefore there is an infinite mind, or God.' Once again, then, Berkeley is able to accept all the empirical facts that plain men may adduce; anything that there is reason to believe exists he is ready to recognize; for, though much is not perceived by men, there is nothing which God does not perceive.

*

We meet with a very similar result if we examine what he says about causation. We say, for example, that the heat of the fire causes the kettle to boil. But Berkeley holds that this is the wrong way to put it. For on inspection of his ideas he cannot find (just as Hume could not find) anything in them to be called 'power' or 'agency'. We feel, certainly, the heat of the fire; but we do not feel, or otherwise find, an additional something called 'the power to make kettles boil'. What we actually observe is this – that the fire is in fact hot, and that in fact if a kettle is put on it the water boils. When we say that the fire *makes* the kettle boil, we are saying more than we find; for all that we find is that in fact the kettle does boil. And not only so – we are saying something absurd. For only conscious beings, creatures able to form intentions and exercise their wills in carrying them out, can properly be said to make things happen; it is absurd to attribute real 'power or agency' to mere inanimate things. It is, then, quite improper to say that the fire *makes* the kettle boil. But it is no less clear that I do not myself make the ideas of boiling water ensue upon the ideas of heat in the fire. I have no such control over the course of events. These things, however, must be caused somehow; and Berkeley concludes that they are due to the activity of God. But God's 'operations are regular and uniform'; and so, when I see and feel, as I say, a hot fire, I can rightly take this to be a *sign* that, if a kettle is placed upon it, I shall in a short time find boiling water. It is, then, God who causes us to perceive all the 'ideas of sense'. But, although it would be an absurdity to say that any idea could make other ideas occur, we can very reasonably say that the occurrence of certain ideas is a sign that others will or may occur subsequently. 'Now the set rules and methods, wherein the mind we depend on excites in us the ideas of sense, are called the *Laws of Nature*: and these we learn by experience, which teaches us that such and such ideas are attended with such and such ideas in the ordinary course of things. This gives us a sort of foresight, which enables us to regulate our actions for the benefit of life.'

It is evident that in all of this Berkeley has nothing to say either about what actually occurs or about what may reasonably be expected to occur. He is not relying upon, and so could not be refuted by, empirical evidence. His case amounts to this – that where we ordinarily speak of *cause* and *effect*, we should speak instead of *sign* and *thing signified*; recognizing that, strictly speaking, it is God's will alone that makes natural events occur. To the objection that, on this view, the subtlety and complexity of so-called 'natural causes' would be merely superfluous, he is able to reply that they have value as signs. If God works according to set, discoverable rules, we must expect to find some complexity in the details of his operations, compatible with and even actually required by the simplicity of the rules themselves.

Perhaps we can now see more clearly in what way we may profitably come to grips with Berkeley. It is clear that, in a sense, he intends to pick no quarrel with the ordinary beliefs of ordinary men. He does not intend to startle or perplex us with an argument that we are all living in a dream. He does not pretend to have shown that we are all mistaken or unreasonable in thinking that solid, enduring things are solid and endure. Nor does he suggest that we are either wrong or unjustified in relying upon the 'laws of nature'. On the contrary, he claims to be defending such common opinions against philosophers who have, not always unwittingly, contradicted them. It is Locke, whose 'external bodies', real physical things, are supposed to be imperceptible, who really violates common sense. 'How sincere a pleasure is it to behold the natural beauties of the earth! ... How vivid and radiant is the lustre of the fixed stars! ... How magnificent and rich that negligent profusion, with which they appear to be scattered throughout the whole azure vault! ... Is not the whole system immense, beautiful, glorious beyond expression and beyond thought! What treatment then do those philosophers deserve, who would deprive these noble and delightful scenes of all reality? How should those principles be entertained that lead us to think all the visible beauty of the creation a false imaginary glare?'

But Berkeley does not really believe that Locke and other philosophers actually held the strange opinions that their doctrines imply. In ordinary life no doubt Locke knew very well the difference between waking and dreaming, between a real and an imaginary fire. His theories condemned the visible world as a 'false imaginary glare', but his conduct would have proved that he took the visible world no less seriously than other men. His mistakes were *theoretical* mistakes; he misdescribed, misrepresented the true state of things, and so generated apparent doubts and perplexities in cases in which neither he nor anyone else was actually doubtful or perplexed. He did not really, any more than Berkeley himself, expect the world to look any different, nor any different events to occur in it, from what would have been expected by any plain man. The use of such phrases as 'corporeal substance' and 'external bodies' was not a symptom of absurd or mistaken empirical beliefs, but of theoretical confusion. Accordingly we may think of Berkeley's intention as (in part) that of correcting and avoiding these confusions. By rigorous care and attention to the proper use of language, he hopes to describe quite familiar facts in a way that will *obviously* eliminate the confused and unnecessary puzzles that philosophers have generated. This is why it would be beside the point to look for empirical evidence against Berkeley; he intends to provide, *whatever* the facts of experience may be, an exact and illuminating way of describing them – a vocabulary offering no temptation at all to the spinning of philosophical, 'sceptical' webs.

But for various reasons, he thinks, it will not do simply to adhere to the common, accepted ways of speaking. Certainly if we did this we should avoid certain dangers; we should not be liable, as philosophers are liable, to lapse inadvertently into the use of meaningless words. For it is, to say the least, very unlikely that expressions with no meaning at all could survive, or even occur, in the common discourse of plain, practical men. But common language has, as Berkeley thinks, certain defects. Not that it is actually wrong; indeed, up to a point, 'common custom is the standard of propriety in language', and 'the common use of language would receive no manner of alteration or disturbance from the admission of our tenets'. But ordinary language is of course intended for use 'in the ordinary affairs of life', and here brevity, convenience, and intelligibility are of more importance than strict and absolute accuracy. The truth is that common ways of speech fit the facts, adequately for common purposes, but loosely all the same. They do not bring out, nor do we usually attend to, the precise nature of the facts to which we refer. And therefore Berkeley makes it his business to speak in a way that fits the facts really closely. In this way we may come to *understand*, and not merely to be familiar with, the common idioms; and we shall no longer be liable to be led astray.

But ordinary language, Berkeley believes, has one defect more serious than any so far mentioned; it fatally conceals the place of God in the universe. (On this point Berkeley has to affirm that almost everybody is in error; here he cannot plausibly contend that mistaken philosophical theories are alone to blame.) By saying that one natural event causes another, we conceal the fact that God's will alone is the true cause of both; in our use of such words as 'thing' and 'object', and also of particular words for particular things, we conceal the fact that the entire universe is dependent upon the mind of that 'infinite, omnipresent spirit', *'who works all in all*, and *by whom all things consist'*. It is easy to come to think that there might be all those things that there now are, and those natural laws that we discover, even though there were no God. We may think that the existence of material things does not entail the existence of any living, spiritual thing, and that the operation of natural causes is enough in itself to explain the course of events. But Berkeley holds that the 'monstrous systems' of 'every wretched sect of atheists' are not merely false; they are *demonstrably* false. If we uncover the facts that common language glosses over and obscures, we shall find that 'nothing can be more evident to anyone that is capable of the least reflexion, than the existence of God, or a spirit who is intimately present to our minds, producing in them all that variety of ideas or sensations, which continually affect us, on whom we have an absolute and entire dependence, in short, *in whom we live, and move, and have our being*. That the discovery of this great truth which lies so near and obvious to the mind, should be attained to by the reason of so very few, is a sad instance of the stupidity and inattention of men, who, though they are surrounded with such clear manifestations of the Deity, are yet so little affected by them, that they seem as it were blinded with excess of light' (P. 149). Here, then, is another feature of Berkeley's intentions; he wishes to speak in such a way that it shall be an obvious and a necessary truth that ordinary things and events are the work of God. And here he is obliged to recognize that, to many people, this does not appear either necessary or obvious.

*

This shows that it is not quite correct to say that, except on questions of terminology, Berkeley has no positive thesis of his own with which ordinary men could possibly disagree. Consider, for instance, the case of causation. It is true that Berkeley accepts, as other men do, what are commonly called the Laws of Nature. But he does not merely contend that instances of natural laws are often misdescribed; he contends that if we understand and describe them rightly, we shall realize a truth that otherwise we are apt to overlook – that every instance is a 'sign or effect of the Power of God'.

But the issues here are by no means clear-cut. It would be generally agreed that, if by 'making' an event occur we understand the deliberate, purposive *doing* of something, it would be an absurdity to say that a hot fire makes the kettle boil. A fire is not an 'agent' with purposes; a hot fire could not reasonably be said to have a stronger will, or more executive talent, than one less hot. But when we say that the fire's heat causes the kettle to boil, surely we are not guilty of the absurdity of attributing plans and purposes and actions to the fire. Very well then, Berkeley would say; provided you do not thus misconceive the situation, it does not much matter how you describe it; by all means use the word 'cause', provided you realize that what you call the cause is in reality only a sign of what you call the effect. Let us agree, at any rate, upon the fact that kettles placed on hot fires invariably do boil; other facts about heat and water are consistent with this; this is how things occur, and how we may reasonably expect them to occur.

And now, Berkeley thinks, we can consider without prejudice the *real* cause of these phenomena – what it is which really *makes* things happen as they do. This must be something capable of deliberate and purposive action; it must be an animate being, a spirit. But obviously not a *human* being. The efforts, decisions, and intentions of human beings play a very small part in the whole field of natural events. And if we consider even for a moment the immeasurable power and wisdom required for making the entire universe proceed as it does, we shall see that the 'spirit' who makes all these things happen is and can only be God. In this way, he believes, we score over all atheists 'the most cheap and easy triumph in the world'.

However, the atheists' reply to this reasoning is clear. Why should we suppose, they would ask, that natural events have any *real* cause at all, in Berkeley's sense of those words? Certainly, if everything that happens is made to happen – is a case of the intentional doing of something – then there certainly must be some very powerful and able person at work. But then natural events are not made to happen; they just do happen. We may say indeed that every event has a cause, and mean by this that every event is a case of some natural law. But if we ask why this is so, or why there should be the particular laws that there are, no answer can be given. We can say only how things actually do occur; we can try to discover, in Berkeley's terms, what events are reliable signs of what others. There is no reason whatever to suppose that there is, in any other sense, a *real cause* of any natural phenomenon.

It appears, then, that here we have a direct conflict. Berkeley sees, in every instance of natural causation, the hand of God: his opponent (who really need not be an atheist) does not. But the conflict is of a peculiar kind. For, clearly enough, neither opinion entails any empirical beliefs that the other disallows; Berkeley and his opponent may both accept and expect the very same events. In fact, Berkeley is careful to ensure that his statements about God have *no* definite and characteristic empirical consequences. He says indeed that 'impious and profane persons ... exclude all freedom, intelligence, and design from the formation of things', from events which in fact 'display the goodness and wisdom' of a 'governing spirit'; but he admits that we cannot hope fully to understand the design behind the works of God, and thus allows himself to attribute to God's design events in which no design at all is actually apparent. The true foundation of his view is, I believe, the conviction that to hold that events merely *occur*, without any purpose and volition behind them or anything analogous with purpose and volition, is to say something which is really quite *unintelligible*; and what can the 'atheist' do but reply that it is not – that the unintelligibility lies, if anywhere, in Berkeley's remarks and not in his own? It would seem that Berkeley took very seriously what we may be tempted to interpret as a kind of metaphor – the idea, in particular, that that of which we have experience is the 'rational discourse' of a 'governing spirit', that every object and every event is an intelligently used, intelligible *sign* set before us by the will of an 'infinite mind'. In a sense, his views can be understood as a protest against the scientific, 'corpuscularian' view of the world. The idea that we inhabit a

blankly unthinking, 'inert' and 'stupid', universe, and hence
that facts are in the end to be merely accepted; that there
comes a point at which explanations can no longer be given
because it no longer even makes sense to ask for explanations
– this idea he not only detested, but genuinely found incomprehensible, 'repugnant' (as he said) in more senses than one.
His opponent might well protest that, in attributing all that
occurs to 'the Power of God', he is himself not offering any
real explanation; for we understand neither how God exerts
his power nor why he should exert it in one way rather than
another; how is this better than no explanation at all? But
Berkeley, and many others of similar temper, would be un-
moved by this objection. The fact that we (admittedly) cannot comprehend the designs of the divine Intelligence, and
that its 'rational discourse' often seems to be a riddle, would
seem much less important than the idea that there *is* an
intelligent power everywhere at work; for in this case, whatever the mystery may be, it will not be the blank lack of intelligibility of a totally mindless universe. It would be, perhaps, absurd to attempt to decide whether Berkeley's under-
lying view of the universe, or that of his 'corpuscularian'
opponents, is right; we can hardly do more than display the
divergence, and point out that no method of decision appears
to be available. If each side finds unintelligible what the other
side embraces without demur, no argument will carry conviction to both.

But what about Berkeley's further doctrine that '*esse*' is
'*percipi*', and that (hence) there must be an 'omnipresent
spirit' in whose mind all 'sensible things' exist? The argument here is rather more complex. It is clear that Berkeley
felt to be incomprehensible the idea that material things
might exist in complete independence of any mind, just as he
found it impossible to envisage events as simply occurring,
unplanned, unthinkingly, unwilled. But in this case he seems
to have believed that his contention could be *proved*, not
merely by appeal to the (disputable) unintelligibility of its
contradictory, but also by deduction from very commonly

held opinions both of philosophers and plain men. He was sure that he could prove that *'esse'* is *'percipi'*, and hence that we must either admit the existence of the universe in the mind of God, or deny the existence of everything not actually perceived by human beings. The second alternative clearly is not acceptable; and so, he believed, the first must be accepted. In observation we do not encounter a world of independent, block-like objects, 'material' things in Locke's sense of that word; rather we are made aware of the mind of God. We say that there are trees and mountains, planets and stars, and of course it is true that there are these things; but these are themselves 'ideas', the communicable contents, of a benevolent, omniscient, and omnipotent Mind.

This contention of Berkeley's, naturally enough, led many of his readers to believe that he was advocating, or at least was in sympathy with, the doctrine of Malebranche that 'we see all things in God'. There was reason enough in this assumption to make it intensely irritating to Berkeley; he wished to have no such ally. Malebranche was a Frenchman, a generation older than Berkeley; he was a priest, and a philosopher whom no one would hesitate to regard (as Berkeley is often not regarded) as a metaphysician. The *Philosophical Commentaries* contain several references to him, none at all sympathetic ('Scripture and possibility are the onely proofs with Malbranch add to these wt. he calls a great propension to think so.') Berkeley must have been influenced by him in some degree, but there are also grounds for his evident antipathy. For Malebranche was completely without one characteristic which is most marked in Berkeley; he felt no desire whatever to 'recall Men to Common Sense', and did not feel any discomfort in contradicting even the very commonest beliefs. Berkeley combined with his curious metaphysical convictions a strong distaste for flagrant departures from plain common sense; though undoubtedly he held many beliefs which ordinary men found (and find) astonishing, he would not himself willingly controvert the beliefs of ordinary men. He even attempts to maintain that no one could disagree

with him who had not been misled by the subtleties of 'speculative men'; like many other philosophers, he would like to
be regarded as himself not a philosopher at all. Of Malebranche this is by no means true.

Starting from the sharp Cartesian distinction between mind
and matter, Malebranche had argued that there could not
really be any such interaction between the two as is implied in
saying that men perceive objects; we have the impression that
this does occur, but our senses are radically deceptive and
misleading, and we should pay to their promptings as little
heed as we can. 'Your room is in itself absolutely invisible.'
Ideas are the only possible objects of awareness; and since the
human mind cannot be supposed to 'illumine itself', its awareness of these ideas must consist in some sort of unification
with God. 'For all our clear ideas are in God so far as their
intelligible reality is concerned. It is in God alone that we see
them; in the universal Reason alone which illumines all in-
telligences.' In order to establish the existence of the totally
imperceptible material world, we must look to certain passages
in Scripture where its existence seems to be implied.

All this was by no means to Berkeley's taste. He observes
with justice that Malebranche 'builds upon most general and
abstract notions', and this is itself enough to arouse his hostility. The appeal to Scripture he regards as absurd and quite
unnecessary; the creation of an utterly imperceptible world
is a strange caprice to attribute to an intelligent Deity, and in
any case our senses are *not* radically deceptive – for we certainly do perceive the actual world. That we and it are wholly
dependent on God's mind is a sentiment with which he
agrees; but then Malebranche's account of this dependence
'is I must confess to me incomprehensible'. What we perceive,
though God causes us to perceive it and perceives it himself,
is perceived by us in a perfectly ordinary sense; and there is
not a quite different world which we do not perceive at all.

However, though the role of God in Berkeley's philosophy
is comparatively more pedestrian than in that of Malebranche, and is indeed put forward as the only means of

avoiding gross conflict with ordinary views, it is not wholly perspicuous. An American correspondent of Berkeley's expressed particular concern on this point. Berkeley himself says, as one would think he must say, that 'God perceives not anything by sense as we do'. But does this not imply that the ideas in God's mind are not *the same* as the 'ideas of sense' in my own? If so, is there not for each idea that I perceive by sense a duplicate idea perceived otherwise by God? And does this not amount to saying that there is a real world existing in God's mind, of which my own ideas are 'copies or resemblances'? And does this not bear a perilous resemblance to the exploded doctrines of Locke? In a rather perfunctory reply, Berkeley says that he does not object to saying that ideas in God's mind are 'archetypes' of ours; but this admission is not without difficulty. For we wish to say, and Berkeley usually seems to agree, that *what we perceive* exists when we do not perceive it; and this seems incompatible with the view that there exists (in God's mind) an 'archetype' of what we perceive. On the other hand, could we possibly say that what we see with our eyes is itself perceived by God, who has no eyes? Then too there is something very strange in the notion of perception of everything simultaneously, from every point of view; but this is what Berkeley attributes to God. It might be said that we cannot expect to understand such things completely. But then Berkeley puts forward his views as being true, and it is fair to ask what exactly these views are. Even the apparent difficulty in them is serious; for can it really be the case that, whenever we speak of the existence of unperceived things, we are accepting a doctrine so difficult to understand? Finally, is Berkeley consistent with his own principles in taking the word 'God' to be *intelligible*? He may indeed say that God is a 'spirit', that we are 'spirits' ourselves, and hence understand in some degree what God is. But God is certainly not a 'spirit' for whose existence we have any similar evidence to that which we have for the existence of 'finite spirits', nor surely is he a spirit of a similar sort.

*

The general character of Berkeley's doctrine is, then, briefly as follows. Firstly, it is not offered as *contradicting* any of our ordinary beliefs about the world and about events in the world, but rather as enabling us to *describe* the world in a clear and philosophically illuminating terminology. But secondly, Berkeley claims that the use of this improved vocabulary makes it obvious that all that exists and all that occurs is 'in the mind of God' and dependent on God's will. He seeks to recall us from strange 'speculative' theories to common sense – and thereby to recall us to Theism also. In the chapters that follow I shall seek to show that this second (metaphysical) contention is, not false, but not necessary either; and in more detail, that even if we accept it and waive its difficulties, it will not do quite so much as Berkeley requires. Without this appeal to the will and the perception of God, his theory would be (at least in his own view) plainly untenable; but even with it, I shall argue that he fails to achieve that agreement with common sense (and common language) which, with one half of his mind, he so ardently desired. Though he does not indeed flatly *deny* the beliefs of ordinary men, these beliefs cannot in fact be restated in his own allegedly improved way of speaking: so that, without the need of any perilous argument about his theory's metaphysical foundations, we can show that Berkeley in any case does not succeed in his aim of 'recalling men to Common Sense'.

7

THE IMMEDIATE PERCEPTION
OF IDEAS

In the pages that follow I shall first try to elucidate Berkeley's use of the term 'idea'. Berkeley himself is at no great pains to do this. It is as if he had become so well accustomed to the word that he had almost forgotten that it was not, as he himself used it, a familiar and established expression in ordinary English; he appears to take for granted that his readers will find no difficulties here. But certainly Berkeley's use of the term 'idea' is *not* a use generally established in ordinary discourse; and this is a most important fact. We do not customarily say that we see and hear 'ideas', still less, as Berkeley would have us say, 'our own ideas'. It must be admitted, then, that we do not at once see what is meant when we are said to 'perceive ideas' – and further, are said to perceive nothing else.

This of course means that we are not, without considerable further inquiry, able to assess the force of Berkeley's arguments. When a writer uses expressions with which we are familiar, we are able to see well enough whether some of the things that he says do or do not follow from others; we can detect any inconsistencies and ambiguities. Indeed, the ability to assess his words in these ways (if we try hard enough) is an important part of what it *is* to be familiar with the terms he employs. Certainly our logical acumen may fail us; we may fail to notice mistakes and ambiguities, as for that matter we may easily fail to notice if he gradually deviates from the usages of ordinary speech. But if we are really familiar with the terms used, at least we are equipped to be competent critics of his case. If, on the other hand, he uses non-ordinary expressions, or uses ordinary expressions in unusual ways, we hardly know how to begin. If we are said to perceive ideas, is it or is it not legitimate to speak of ideas as *sensations*? If it is proper to speak of them as sensations, can it also be right to speak of them as *sensible qualities*, or as *sensible objects*? Is it or is it not a necessary truth that ideas are *in the mind*? Until we have made ourselves fully familiar with this new use of 'idea', we cannot begin to answer these questions.

It is important to realize that the introduction of new terms is by no means a simple affair. A word may be thought of as a piece in a jig-saw puzzle; it has its own separate identity, but it also fits on in its own particular way to a variety of other pieces that surround it. And if we want to introduce a new piece, it is not simply a matter of taking up a new bit of wood and making it into some arbitrary shape – we have to make sure that there is *room* for a new piece, and if there is room that the new piece *fits*. It would be, perhaps, going too far to suggest that philosophers should never intro-duce new ways of speaking of their own; for it is of course conceivable that ordinary language may not provide the means of saying what they wish to say. But at least they should make quite sure that this is so before they indulge in neolog-isms. For the neologist is exposed to serious risks; it may be that the word he introduces cannot be used in the way he demands – that it simply will not fit in; it may be that he will fail to make clear exactly how his new word is to be used; and it may be that he himself and his readers will fall into confusion through lack of familiarity with his ways of speak-ing.

In this chapter our scrutiny of the word 'idea' will not be taken very far. We shall be concerned with the question why Berkeley says that we perceive 'ideas' – or rather, with the even more restricted question why he is *not* content with our ordinary statements of what we perceive.

*

'What do we perceive besides our own ideas or sensations?' (p. 4). Berkeley presents this question as merely rhetorical; he assumes that the answer is *obviously* 'Nothing'. Indeed, he asserts in his very first sentence that it is 'evident to any one' that we perceive ideas. On one point at least he is certainly mistaken; this is not 'evident'. Curiously enough, Berkeley himself does not regard his answer to this question as evident, either in the earlier *Essay* or in the later *Three Dialogues*. He there offers arguments in its support, apparently anticipating doubts or disagreement. And of course his assertion requires to be supported by argument; it is not a mere truism that anyone would accept. It at any rate seems evident to most of us that we perceive physical objects – houses, trees, and flowers, plates and tables, and so on; also things, not exactly physical objects, such as rainbows, reflections, flames, and beams of light; also winds, and showers of rain, and peals of thunder. We should probably not feel inclined to give any one answer to the question 'What do we perceive?', just as we would not give any single answer to the question 'What do we read?' But Berkeley's answer 'Ideas', so far from seeming obviously right, seems on the contrary obviously wrong. For the term 'idea' has, and had in his day, an ordinary use in which it would certainly not be said that the objects of perception are ideas; it would rather be usual to *contrast* what a man perceives with the ideas he has, the things in the world with the ideas in his mind. The use of 'idea' which Berkeley here adopts without question is the invention of philosophers; it is not the ordinary use of the word, and hence at the outset of a philosophical argument nothing about it should be taken as evident or obvious.

The doctrine that we perceive ideas was, as we have seen, maintained by Locke; and Berkeley would also have found it regarded as a commonplace in the writings of Descartes and Malebranche. It may be that he thought there was no need to explain or defend a doctrine on which there appeared to be so much agreement; but, if so, he was mistaken. For the agreement did not in fact extend beyond the words; it is clear enough that Berkeley and his three predecessors did not interpret these words in the same way, nor did they subscribe to them for the same reasons. It is quite likely that they would not have agreed at all except in the opinion that ordinary answers to the question 'What do we perceive?' are inadequate. Locke, for example, appears to have been influenced mainly by his picture of perception as a *causal transaction* between 'external objects' and the mind; what was really 'present to' the mind, and so really perceived by it, was the effect of an elaborate chain of physical causes. But the 'external object' was not the effect, the last item, in this causal chain; it was, on the contrary, the first item, the real cause. Hence, the 'immediate objects' of perception are not external objects, but ideas produced in the mind by the operation of external causes. But Berkeley's opinion is very different from this. He certainly holds that ideas are causally produced, but not by 'external bodies' that we do not perceive. In fact, he would not have thought it *untrue* to say that we do perceive material things. His objection to this view is not that it is false; the trouble is, as he thinks, that it is inexact, not sufficiently strict or accurate. When he says that we perceive ideas, he does not think that he is answering *truly* a question to which the plain man's answer is false, but that he, where the plain man speaks loosely, is speaking *strictly*. This is, of course, consistent with his general claim to be clarifying, not contradicting, the views of ordinary men.

An example from the *Essay* will recall what it is that Berkeley has in mind. Suppose that I say, in the ordinary idiom, that I hear a coach in the distance. Berkeley holds that this is an adequate but loose way of speaking, which an exact inquirer would wish to analyse further, For, strictly speaking, what I actually *hear* is a sound; and this sound, as a result of my past experience, *suggests* to me that there is a coach in the distance. Past experience is in these cases a reliable guide, so that no practical disadvantages result from my mentioning the coach in saying what I hear; but this may be misleading in theory, and in any case it is not accurate. The sound is all that I actually hear, and in strictness this ought to be kept distinct from what is suggested, or 'signified', by the sound. In the *Essay* Berkeley holds that what is suggested is the

existence of a certain 'tangible object'; but in the *Principles*
this is abandoned. He there holds that the ideas, the 'immediate objects', of each sense suggest only the obtainability
of *other ideas*, or that there are (in God's mind) other ideas.
When we refer to any *object*, we are referring to a certain
collection of ideas, perception of any of which suggests the
existence and perceivability of all the others. Thus, when I
say what object it is that I perceive, I am referring to a collection of ideas not all of which I am at the time perceiving –
most of them are merely *suggested* by the ideas that I actually
perceive. But if I am to speak strictly, I ought not to refer in
saying what I perceive to ideas which at the time I do *not*
actually perceive; hence, I ought not to say that I perceive the
object, but only those ideas from the object-constituting collection which I now actually perceive.

Let us leave aside for a moment the merits and demerits of
this line of thought, and concentrate on the question, whether
Berkeley is right in his view that to speak as he recommends
is to speak *strictly* – is to correct the 'looseness' of the customary use of words.

It is not difficult to see how one might come to question the
propriety of customary speech. Suppose I say, for example,
that I see a book. Now a book is quite an elaborate affair. It
has a cover, often hard and rather stiff to the touch, pages
inside, flexible and liable to tear and covered with print; it is
of a certain moderate weight, and often has a characteristic
smell. But when I see (as I say) this book, lying closed on the
table, I cannot see the inside of it; I have not yet felt its covers,
turned its pages, sniffed at it, or weighed it in my hand. But
now suppose that on investigation the object at which I am
looking turns out to be made of painted wood, to be hollow,
with a hinged lid, and to smell of tobacco; it would then be
clear that this object is not a book at all, but a cigarette-box
cleverly made and painted to resemble a book. Surely, then,
in saying that I saw a book, I was going much too far. I was
simply *taking for granted* that I could, if I investigated
further, find pages and print, covers and all the other char-

acteristics of a book; this was merely assumed, and not actually seen. But in a strict use of the verb 'to see', we ought to say that we see only what we actually *see*, eliminating entirely the assumptions that we normally make. Even if there was in fact a book and not a cigarette-box on the table, I ought not to have said that I *saw* the book; to say this would be to go beyond the actual evidence, even though what I take for granted is in fact the case. According to Berkeley, what I actually saw was a certain 'diversity of light and colours': this suggested to me, led me to assume, that I could if I liked feel the weight and texture of a book, turn over and read its pages, and sniff its aroma; but whether I am led rightly or wrongly in making these assumptions, it is only the light and colours that I actually *see*. It is not that my claim to see a book may be mistaken, though of course this is so; it is rather that, mistaken or not, it goes too far. Even if no mistakes were ever made, Berkeley would still maintain that, *strictly speaking*, I did not see a book.

An analogue from ordinary life to this line of reasoning reveals a certain similarity but an interesting difference. Consider the case of a barrister's criticism of a witness. The witnes is asked what he saw. He answers 'I saw that villain Smith rifling my desk.' To this the barrister would no doubt object – he does not want to hear the witness's opinion of Smith's general probity, nor can the dishonesty of his conduct on this occasion be assumed. Will the witness please confine himself to saying what he actually *saw*? He now answers, perhaps, 'Well, I saw Smith with his back to me by my desk, and he was looking at some papers.' Could the witness see what those papers were? Well, he felt sure they were his (the witness's) private letters. But could he see that at the time? No, he could not. So that all that the witness actually saw was Smith standing by his (the witness's) desk, looking at some papers or other? Yes, that was all that the witness actually saw.

The point of the barrister's questioning here is clear – he is seeking to make the witness distinguish between what he actually saw, and what on that basis he merely took for granted.

It is not necessarily (no doubt it would be in fact) implied that the witness's first impressions were mistaken. It might have been the case that Smith was in fact rifling the desk, intending to make some dishonest use of private letters; but still the witness did not actually *see* this. He jumped to conclusions; and even if he was right, he ought not, when asked to say in evidence what he saw, to mention what he took for granted but did not actually see.

And this brings us to the point. The objection that the witness was not confining himself to stating what he *actually saw* was, in fact, the objection that he was saying more than he was *entitled to say*. Perhaps Smith was rifling the desk; but the glimpse that the witness got does not entitle him to say so. To return now to Berkeley's argument. I say that I see a book on the table. Berkeley objects that I do not actually *see* this; in saying that I see a book I am making various assumptions. But before we conclude that I am not, for this reason, saying what I actually see, it is now clear that there is a further question to be asked – namely, am I *justified* in making the assumptions that I make? Am I *entitled* to say that I see a book? In order to show that my statement was not acceptable as a report of what I actually saw, it is not enough to show merely that I was taking certain things for granted; it is necessary to show also that I was not justified in taking them for granted, that on the evidence I was not entitled to say what I said. And this makes an important difference. In some cases I might say that I see a book, and it be rightly held that I am not entitled to say this. Perhaps the light is very bad, it is not very likely that there should be a book where I say there is, and so on. It might be held that what I actually *saw* was a dim dark shape on a slightly darker background; I certainly ought not to have assumed, and asserted, that it was a book. But suppose that the book is only a yard away, the light is excellent, and I am in my own room. Then surely I can say with assurance that I see a book. I am, no doubt, taking for granted that what I say that I see can be opened, has covers and pages and print; but in these conditions I am perfectly entitled to do so. Indeed, if in a case of this sort I were told not to say that I see a book, but to report instead what I *actually see*, I should have no idea what was required of me. It is apparently implied that I was saying too much; but in the excellent conditions of observation that obtain, it would be utterly unreasonable to say less. Berkeley would wish me to say that I see, say, a diamond-shaped expanse of red on a shiny brown background. But this is a very special sort of report, appropriate to discourse with oculists, for instance, or painters. There is no reason to say that this would be the *only* correct report of what I actually see. For in order to report correctly what I actually see, it is sufficient for me to confine my statement to what, on the basis of sight on the present occasion, I am entitled to say; and in good conditions of observation, I am certainly entitled to say that I see a book. It is necessary, indeed, that what I say I see should actually be there; if there were in fact no book on the table then I did not see a book, even if I had every possible excuse for supposing that I did. But the suggestion that, even if there is a book on the table, it is in *no* circumstances correct to say that I actually see it, is simply a mistake.

The fact is that there is no *general* answer to the question 'What do we actually see?' For circumstances differ. It is true that such a question is ordinarily used as a request to confine our remarks to what, on the evidence before us, we are entitled to say; but what this is can only be decided for particular cases. When conditions of observation are exceptionally bad, a Berkeleian report about 'light and colours' may well be all that can be offered; but when conditions are good and the chances of mistake are negligible, it would normally be wrong to make a report so tentative as this. Berkeley suggests that, in making such reports, we ought to take for granted *nothing whatever*; but this is much too stringent. So long as we take for granted no more than we are reasonably entitled to do, we are correctly reporting what we actually see; at least, though we may be *mistaken*, we are not claiming *too much*.

There is another point of some importance. It is tempting,

but it is also a mistake, to suppose that, in saying what we actually see, we ought not to make use of or in any way rely upon any of our senses except that of sight. It might be argued, for instance, that a book is fairly hard to the touch, of a certain weight in the hand, and so on; if an object did not (to speak roughly) have the right sort of *feel*, we might refuse to say that it was a book. But if so, in saying that I see a book, I am not only making without question assumptions about what on further investigation I could *see*, but also about what I could *feel*. And surely these last assumptions, at any rate, ought not to be made in reporting what I actually see. In saying that I see a book, I am not merely taking a good deal for granted; I am taking for granted certain results of investigation by senses *other than sight*; and surely this cannot be correct.

However, a little reflection shows that though perhaps surprising this is entirely correct. Suppose that I hear, as I should say, a dog barking under my window. Certainly, it will not be true to say that I hear a dog, unless there *is* a dog barking under my window; and I would not say that there is a dog under my window, if on going to look out I saw no dog nor any place where a dog might be concealed. Thus, in saying that I hear the dog barking, I am taking for granted that the result of looking out of my window would be that I should *see* a dog – or at least not see that there was no dog. Ought I then, strictly, to say that I hear a noise, and merely take for granted that this noise is made by a dog?

But if there is in fact a dog barking under my window, then I hear a noise which is in fact made by this dog. And to say that I hear the noise made by the dog is no better than, nor indeed is it at all different from, saying that I hear the dog. I might of course say that I hear the noise, without mentioning what I take to be making it; I might cautiously refrain from making any assumptions about the source of this noise. But to say only that I hear the noise is to be more *cautious*, not more *correct*, than one who says that he hears the dog. If I say that I hear the dog, I am mentioning what my sense of hearing leads me to believe is actually there. I may be *mistaken* about this; but I am not speaking *incorrectly*. To make no assumptions about what makes the noises that I hear is to be specially cautious in saying what I hear; but correct speech does not require us always to be as cautious as possible.

Berkeley, it is evident, had the idea that it is a rule of correct, strict speech that to each of the senses should be assigned its 'proper objects'; that each sense should be confined, as it were, in its own compartment; that each of the five main verbs of perception should have its own private set of accusatives. But our language embodies no such rule; to suppose that it does is a natural, but serious, misunderstanding. We do not normally use the word 'see', for example, in order to say only what 'visual experiences' we have, but rather in saying what is *there to be seen*; if I say that I see a car in the drive, I am saying what my 'visual experiences' lead me to believe – namely, that *there is* a car in the drive. (I am claiming, indeed, to *know* that there is a car in the drive; for if it turned out that there was not, I should withdraw my claim that I saw a car; nor could I properly say 'I see a car in the drive, but I am not sure that any car is there'.) Similarly, if I say 'I hear a car in the drive', I claim to know (by hearing) that *there is* a car in the drive. What concerns me is not my 'visual' or 'auditory experiences', but the *fact*, if it is a fact, that there is a car in the drive. Seeing and hearing (and tasting and smelling and touching) are alternative ways of getting to know such facts as this; and accordingly a car in the drive can be said indifferently to be seen or heard, smelled or touched. It is the facts, and not the 'experiences', in which we are interested; and our ways of speech naturally conform to our interests.

It is worth remembering too that it is quite correct to say that I see something, even if I could not possibly *know* that I see it on the basis of my present 'visual experience' alone. I could say, for instance, 'I can just see my house from here', even if the house is several miles away, and no one without other sources of information could possibly know that my house is to be seen. I must indeed know that what I can see *is* my house; but it does not matter *how* I know this. It may be that I only realized that I could see my house by using a telescope, or after elaborate study of maps or photographs. In deciding what we see we are not restricted simply to *looking*; we can properly make use of any kind of evidence or aids – telescopes, testimony, maps, encyclopaedias, guide books, and so on.

We can now say more about the question 'What did you actually *see*?' Suppose that I saw Smith standing by my desk, looking at some papers. And suppose that later I get to know (perhaps from the testimony of others) that he was at the time going through my desk with dishonest intent. If I now *know* this, then, notwithstanding the fact that I did not know it at the time when I saw him, it would be perfectly proper for me to say 'I saw Smith rifling my desk' – I might quite reasonably add 'But unfortunately I didn't realize at the time what he was doing'. But thereupon I am sharply instructed to confine myself to saying what I actually *saw*. Why? Because in saying 'I saw Smith rifling my desk', I am claiming to know (though not to have known at the time) that he *was* rifling my desk. But this is something that I did not get to know merely by seeing Smith on that occasion; I have obtained further evidence since. And what is wanted from me in the witness box is a statement which, on the basis only of what I *then* saw, I am entitled to make. I must not, in giving my evidence about that incident, make use of the evidence of other witnesses, nor in general of what I got to know in other ways. Thus it emerges that the question 'What did you actually *see*?' is by no means the same as the question 'What did you see?' In answering the second question, I can quite properly make use of anything I know about what was going on; I can properly say 'I saw Smith rifling my desk', even if at the time I did not know that he was doing that, and perhaps did not even suspect him of any such thing, but only discovered afterwards that that was what he was doing. But in answering the question 'What did you actually *see*?', I have to leave out of account what I got to know in other ways or on other occasions, and try to say only what, on *that* occasion, the use of my eyes entitled me to say. Thus, if Berkeley is, as I have argued, mistaken about the correct way of answering the question 'What did you actually *see*?', he is very much more wrong if he suggests (as he does) that his is also the only correct answer to the question 'What did you see?' Even in the first case it is not necessary, in all circumstances, to reduce our answer to some remark about 'light and colours'; and in the second case this is clearly not necessary at all. For certainly in saying what I see (or saw) I am proceeding perfectly correctly if I enlist the help of any of my senses, or of other people, or even of dictionaries, telescopes, or cameras. The suggestion that, in speaking strictly, I should merely describe my 'visual experiences', the contents of my visual field, is enormously wide of the mark.

*

I do not wish to exaggerate the importance of these considerations. Certainly I do not think that they wholly destroy the force and value of Berkeley's arguments. But these arguments do at least require to be restated. He asserts that we perceive *ideas*. Part of the meaning of this (the part with which we have been concerned) is that the 'proper' objects of the sense of sight are peculiar, or *private*, to the sense of sight; and similarly for each of the other senses. We commonly say that we see, for instance, books, and also that we touch or smell them; books, that is, are not objects private to the sense of sight, nor to any one of the senses. The suggestion that therefore we should *not* say that we see books, but in answering the question 'What do we see?' should take nothing for granted about, nor in any way refer to, what we might discover by our other senses or by any other means, is offered by Berkeley as an injunction to speak 'strictly', 'properly', 'exactly'. But to say this is to imply that there is a rule of language (commonly disregarded) enjoining the use of the verbs 'see' etc. in this way. But there is actually no such rule.

One may quite naturally come to think that there is; indeed, many philosophers seem to have followed Berkeley on this point. But the actual use of the verbs 'see' etc. is quite other than that which Berkeley recommends as 'proper'. It is also well worth pointing out that an answer to the question 'What did you see?' is not shown to be wrong by the fact that it might be unacceptable as an answer to the question 'What did you actually *see*?' For these are very different questions, so that *of course* they require to be answered differently.

In saying, then, that we 'perceive ideas', Berkeley is not, as he believes, answering strictly a question to which the ordinary man's answer is loose and inaccurate. But he can without much difficulty change his ground. He can say (as indeed he often does) not that we perceive or actually perceive ideas, but that we *immediately* perceive them. And since this expression has no ordinary use at all, he can proceed with an entirely free hand to lay down what its use shall be. And his argument would then run as follows. I say, for instance, that I see a book. Let it be admitted that this is a perfectly *correct* thing to say. But there is still in this situation something (not the book) which is *immediately* seen. For, whether or not any further investigations would confirm the claim that I see a book, whatever I know or believe about what I see, and whatever I might see, touch, or smell if I came closer, there is *now* in my visual field a certain coloured shape, or pattern of colours. This is what I *immediately* see; and furthermore, this gives me *the* essential reason for my claim that I see a book. If I came closer I would see different coloured shapes, different in visual texture and perhaps in hue; I might have certain feelings in my hands; but these are all different from, and additional to, the pattern of colours which at first I immediately saw. This is more 'fundamental' than the book itself, in the sense that, although I might immediately see this pattern of colours and yet no book be there, I could not see the book nor indeed *anything at all* unless such coloured shapes occurred in my visual field. Accordingly there is something more fundamental than what is ordinarily (let us admit, correctly) called 'seeing', 'hearing', etc. There is this *immediate* perception of coloured shapes, sounds, aromas, tastes – that is, of the 'ideas' appropriate to each of the senses. The simple assertion 'I see a book' conceals, so Berkeley would argue, the complexity of the case. For the situation which it (correctly) describes is one in which there is, *immediately* perceived, a certain pattern of colours, and in which it is unthinkingly taken for granted that there *could* be (immediately) perceived other ideas of sight, touch, and of smell. Unless enough of these different ideas are in fact obtainable, the claim that I see a book would have to be retracted. This claim depends on the support of many diverse tests; it is indeed a matter of purely contingent fact that we can learn to make such claims, and that we often find them to be well founded. If the enormous variety and complexity of the things *immediately* perceived were not, as it might not have been, orderly and predictable, we could not rightly have made the statements of perception that we ordinarily make; we could not even have learned to understand the words in which those statements are made.

*

In saying, then, that we 'perceive ideas', Berkeley is attempting to isolate a factor which is, he claims, less complex and more 'fundamental' than ordinary perception of chairs and tables. I could not see a table without 'immediately perceiving an idea of sight', just as I could not score a bull without firing a gun; but I might immediately perceive an idea of sight even though there were no physical object that I saw, as I might fire a gun even though I score no hit on any target. Firing guns is the essential foundation of scoring bulls; and the immediate perception of ideas is the essential foundation of all perception. But 'I saw a table' is not for this reason an *improper* answer to the question 'What did you see?', any more than 'I scored a bull' is an improper answer to the question 'What did you do?' In both answers much that might be said goes without saying; a philosopher may reasonably think it *illuminating* to be more specific (and verbose), but he is not thereby correcting any *mistakes*.

Berkeley's argument up to this point leads him to make the following list of 'ideas', things 'immediately perceived' – of hearing, sounds; of sight, 'diversity of light and colours'; of smell, odours; of taste, tastes; and of touch, a variety of sensations. Together these make up 'the ideas of sense'; and these, it appears, are the basic elements into which he proposes to analyse the complex structure of ordinary perception, and from which (he claims) that structure can be illuminatingly reconstructed.

8

IDEAS AND SENSATIONS

OUR attempt to see clearly what Berkeley means by 'ideas' is not yet by any means concluded. There is another point of the greatest importance, which again Berkeley takes to be entirely obvious, but which is certainly not obvious at all. Ideas, he repeatedly insists, exist 'only in the mind'; they exist only when they are actually perceived; 'Their being is to be perceived or known.' This too, at the very outset of his argument, he declares to be 'evident', the contrary 'plainly repugnant'. He seems to think that his assertion stands in no need of explanation or defence.

But in fact his confident pronouncements on this point have given, understandably, a great deal of trouble. It has been thought that Berkeley is either simply begging the question, or else he is seriously confused, or possibly both. The trouble is that, since he usually deems it unnecessary to argue in defence of his opinion, it is difficult to see what his grounds for it actually were; and the apparent grounds seem to be entirely inadequate.

It often looks as though Berkeley bases his view simply on appeal to the meaning of the word 'idea'. 'Certainly no *idea* ... can exist otherwise than in a mind perceiving it' (P. 33). Does not the word 'idea' just *mean* something mental, something that has no existence outside, independently of, the mind? But it is really obvious that Berkeley cannot rely on a point of this kind. There are indeed two uses of the word 'idea' that would locate ideas 'in the mind'; but Berkeley's own use is different from both of these. There is first the ordinary, colloquial use. If I say that my ideas on astronomy are confused and rudimentary, I am indicating the state of my knowledge and understanding – about astronomy my *mind* is very far from clear. Ideas in this sense are 'not without the mind', in that to speak of somebody's ideas *is* (to put it vaguely) to say something about his mind – about what he thinks or believes, fancies or understands or supposes. But of course Berkeley does not use the word 'idea' in this way. In his terms ideas are said to be things that we *perceive*, and thus have nothing whatever to do with our states or qualities of *mind*. Hence, from the fact that ideas in the ordinary sense could reasonably be said to be 'in the mind', it does not follow that the same either must or can be said of ideas, in his *non-*ordinary sense.

Secondly, there is Locke's use of 'idea'. This is terribly confused and confusing, but does at least make it seem 'evident' that ideas exist only in the mind. For they are said, in Locke's analysis of perception, to be entities actually produced in the mind by the causal agency of 'external bodies'. Locke's 'ideas' are mental entities by definition. But Berkeley, whether he realized it or not, did not use the word 'idea' as Locke did; and hence what is obviously true in Locke's use of that word may be not only not obvious, but actually false, in Berkeley's idiom.

It might be urged that, not only is Berkeley not entitled to appeal to either of these different usages in support of the view that ideas exist 'only in the mind', he will actually derive a quite false conclusion if he does. If, instead of concentrating upon the meaning of the word 'idea', he had reminded himself of what he has said that ideas are, he would have had to draw quite the opposite conclusion. For instance, he says that the 'ideas of hearing' are sounds. Do sounds, then, exist only 'in the mind'? Obviously not. When I hear a sound, I do not suppose that there would have been no sound if I had not heard it, nor yet if no one had heard it at all. We can say that a meteor which fell in a desert must have made a very loud noise when it landed, whether or not there was anyone or anything within earshot at the time; and an old house at night is certainly full of noises which, as a rule, nobody hears.

Next we must notice the remarkable fact that Berkeley

from the beginning treats the words 'idea' and 'sensation' as synonyms. He refers indifferently to 'ideas or sensations'. This raises the suspicion of a serious confusion. Certainly, if ideas are sensations, we might defensibly say that they exist 'only in the mind'. For there only *is* a sensation if someone *has* a sensation. It would be absurd to say to a dentist: 'There is a disagreeable ache in my right lower molars, but I don't feel anything.' If I do not now feel anything, perhaps I *had* an ache in my teeth; but I do not now have an 'unfelt ache'.

Now some of the things that Berkeley says, apart from the doctrine that ideas are 'only in the mind', are consistent with the views that ideas are sensations. We say that we have or that we feel, that we get or are given, sensations. For example, 'Flying always gives me a painful sensation in the chest'; 'If you touch that fence you'll get a sort of prickly sensation all up your arm.' And sensations may be said to have *owners*. I can say '*My* sensations were very unpleasant', or 'Your sensations can't have been so violent as mine, or you'd have had to let go'. Berkeley often employs two idioms which seem to be analogous with these. He often speaks of '*our own* ideas', your ideas and mine. And he often says that we are 'affected with' ideas, as one might say that we are given (or sometimes, afflicted with) sensations.

But now we must recognize the unpleasant fact that hardly anything else that he says seems consistent with this view. Consider, for instance, the 'ideas of sight' – according to Berkeley, light and colours. Is it proper to say that these ideas are sensations? It seems obviously not. We do not *have*, or *feel* or *get*, light and colours; on the contrary, as Berkeley frequently says, we *see* them. Furthermore, when we see light and colours, or for that matter anything else, we usually have no sensations at all. If the light is glaring or dazzling, or our eyes are delicate, or we are straining our eyes, we may have in our eyes sensations of discomfort, sometimes of actual pain; but this is not the usual case. Usually, when for instance I look out of the window, I do not get any sensations at all. I *see* the trees in the garden, but I *feel* nothing. The same is true of hearing; and moreover it is hard to see how, for instance, the ideas of hearing could be spoken of as 'our own' ideas. When I hear the sound of the front door being unbolted, I do not call it *my* sound. What could be meant by my calling it so? Simply, perhaps, that I hear it? But then other people hear it also. And what is the point of saying that I perceive only my own ideas, if all that this means is that I hear only the sounds that I hear? This is the bleakest of mere tautologies. But if it be meant that I *alone* hear the sounds that I hear, this is certainly quite untrue. One is often a member of an audience.

There is one group of Berkeley's ideas which would be naturally called 'sensations'. But that this is so serves only to emphasize the oddity (at least) of so calling the others. These are what he calls the 'ideas of touch' – of 'heat and cold', 'motion and resistance', and the rest. It is true that when we touch something hot we have (if our bodies are normally sensitive) a certain sensation in that part of our body with which we touch it. One might say 'I like the sensation of rapid movement', or 'It felt as if something were pressing against my ribs'. It seems perhaps rather odd that Berkeley should connect all these sensations with touching; sensations of 'heat and cold', for instance, are not obtained only by touching things. But it is at any rate true that, in touching things, we do very often (not necessarily) have sensations. But here the sensations are not of course *what* we touch; they are what we *have*, *when* we touch things. But the other ideas are supposed to be *what* we perceive, not what we have or get or feel *when* we perceive.

It is sometimes said that it is really pointless to insist that, in the ordinary use of 'sensation', we usually have no sensations when we see and hear, though we usually do have sensations when we touch. For Berkeley, it is said, must have known this perfectly well. Clearly, he slightly *extends* or alters the use of 'sensation', so that in this new sense it *is* the case that in seeing and hearing we have sensations. This point is however not very impressive. For even if we recognize an extended use of 'sensation' such that we do have sensations whenever we perceive, it still looks like a serious mistake to regard these sensations as *what* we perceive. For what I have *when* I perceive is no more *what* I perceive, than what I do when I kick a football is what I kick.

It would, I think, be impossible to deny that Berkeley is in some degree guilty of this confusion.[8] Certainly he was not the first to fall into it. Indeed, it could be maintained that just this confusion is actually embedded in the whole terminology of 'ideas', and that Berkeley almost automatically fell into it by accepting, or inheriting, this terminology. From the first it was never wholly clear whether 'having ideas' was meant to be a kind of mental or sensory happening, involved in or a necessary condition of perceiving, or whether it was supposed itself to *be* perceiving – namely perceiving ideas. The first interpretation leads to the conclusion that ideas are sensations: and if the second interpretation is then slipped in, we seem to have the paradoxical consequence that the things we perceive actually *are* all sensations. As Reid pointed out, we are led to say, not only that the pain I feel when I stick a pin into my finger is a sensation, but also that the pin itself is a sensation or set of sensations. But this looks obviously wrong; and Reid contended with some force that no one would ever have said so strange a thing if philosophers had not used, and made a muddle of, their technical term 'idea'. By saying that I perceive only ideas, and then regarding these ideas as *my own sensations*, I seem to confine myself in a wholly private world – a world, furthermore, in which there are no things but only *feelings*. It would be true enough that nothing in such a world would 'have any subsistence without a mind'; but this is only because such a world is so exiguously furnished.

But we have not, I think, defeated Berkeley's whole case by these considerations. It is true that the terminology of 'ideas' is unfortunate and liable to mislead; and it is also true, in my opinion, that Berkeley should have avoided referring to ideas as *sensations*. But the doctrine that '*esse* is *percipi*' is not the consequence merely of simple confusions. If he had not been confused at all, Berkeley could not, I think, have treated this strange doctrine as an *obvious* truth; he would surely have felt obliged to make clear the reasoning which led him to say so surprising a thing. (His denials that it *is* surprising look very like bluff.) But he has some reasons, by no means obviously bad ones. We must now try to make clear what those reasons were.

*

There is one fairly elaborate passage in which Berkeley attempts to prove that 'sensible things' exist 'only in the mind'. This is not in the *Principles*, but in the first of the *Three Dialogues between Hylas and Philonous*. These were first published in May 1713, in London, during Berkeley's first visit to England. His intention in writing this book was to remedy, if possible, the apparently complete failure of the *Principles*. The text of the *Principles* had assumed a general familiarity with philosophy, and had contained a certain amount of polemic against particular philosophical views. Was it perhaps for this reason that it had failed to make any impression on the general public? Accordingly in the second work he attempts to restate the doctrine of the *Principles*, omitting the more technical points of controversy, explaining some things that before he had taken for granted, and generally adopting a more 'popular' style. In the *Principles*, Berkeley had taken it as agreed in the learned world that what Locke called 'secondary qualities' are 'only in the mind'; he had therefore contented himself with maintaining that the arguments by which this was supposed to be proved apply equally to the case of the 'primary qualities'. 'Where the secondary qualities are, there are the primary also' – if the latter are 'in the mind', so are the former. But in the Dialogues, not assuming prior acceptance of Locke's arguments, he undertakes to *prove* that secondary qualities are 'in the mind', and thereafter to prove the same thing of the others also. In fact he attempts to prove this generally for all 'sensible things'. Hylas, representing

Berkeley's opponent, asserts confidently that 'to *exist* is one thing, and to be *perceived* is another.' This Berkeley sets himself to disprove.

For this purpose he uses arguments of two different kinds. In some cases he tries to show by direct argument that some of what we call 'sensible qualities' actually are *sensations*; in others, he uses the 'argument from illusion' in an attempt to show that certain qualities are not 'in' objects and so (he assumes) must be 'in the mind'. It is fortunately not necessary for us to examine these arguments in detail. It must be admitted that Berkeley handles them with much less than his usual ability; but it is also easy to see that he does not need the support of such broken reeds, and is quite mistaken in having anything to do with them.

The first group of arguments relies on the point that many qualities of things are often said to be 'pleasant' or 'disagreeable', sometimes even 'painful'. We say that a fire is pleasantly warm; that if one gets too close it feels painfully hot; the vinegar is disagreeably bitter. Berkeley quite wrongly proceeds to *identify* the pleasant or painful heat of a fire with the pleasant or painful *feelings* that people have in its proximity, the bitterness of vinegar with the disagreeable sensations of one who tastes it; and he concludes that these 'sensible qualities' *are* 'sensations'. But this is obviously a confusion. The fire's 'quality' of being pleasantly warm is not a sensation, but rather what a fire is said to have which does, or would, occasion pleasant feelings of warmth in normally sensitive people who do not get too close to it.

The second group of arguments trades on the fact that objects sometimes seem different to different observers or in different conditions. Colours look darker in candle-light; sweet things seem bitter 'to a distempered palate'; warm water feels quite cool if one's hands are unusually hot; and so on. Points of this sort appear always to have fascinated philosophers, but it is difficult to see why this should be so. For if the conditions, or the observer's sense-organs, are abnormal, *of course* things will seem to be other than they really are. Of course a

colour-blind man makes mistakes about colours; of course, to
a man whose palate is 'distempered', something that is actually sweet may taste bitter; and obviously an unusual light
will alter the look of things. Such cases are very familiar, and
not in the least disconcerting.

Berkeley, however, offers these familiar facts as a proof that
no 'sensible qualities' are really 'in' objects. For firstly, he suggests that, because things sometimes appear to have qualities
which they really have not, it is always impossible to say what
qualities they really have. 'I own myself entirely satisfied, that
they are all equally apparent.' But this is nonsense. To normal
observers in ordinary daylight things *look* the colours that
they really *are*; sizes and weights and speeds can be accurately
measured; sugar *is* sweet because it tastes so to normal people.
The very fact that we say that people sometimes make *mistakes* implies that we know perfectly well how to decide what
qualities things really have. But secondly, Berkeley makes a
most curious assumption. He asserts in the course of his argument that if some property were 'really inherent' in an object, the object would necessarily *appear* to have that property
in all circumstances. This extraordinary assumption, which
entirely disregards the importance of the *conditions in which*
objects are observed and of the question *by whom* they are
observed, needs only to be stated clearly to be seen to be
absurd. (It amounts to saying that if an object were *really*
blue, it would necessarily *look* blue under a strong red light,
through coloured glasses, or to a colour-blind man; and nothing could be more absurd than this suggestion.) It is only fair
to say, however, that more than one modern philosopher has
either stated this as his own opinion, or represented it as the
opinion of ordinary men. It might also be suggested that,
unless this fantastic assumption is made, the 'argument from
illusion' cannot get started; for unless we begin by supposing
that things *cannot* appear to be otherwise than they are, why
should we be at all put out by the obvious fact that they can
and do?

But there is a yet more serious blunder in Berkeley's argument; for it appears that the arguments in his second group, even if they had not been wholly fallacious, would have had no tendency to establish the required conclusion – that 'sensible things' exist only 'in the mind'. If he had contrived to show that certain 'sensible qualities' *are* sensations, this would indeed have served his purpose; for we might all agree without demur that sensations are 'in the mind', exist when and only when they are felt. But his argument about colour, for instance, seems quite unlike this. For even suppose it were agreed that I can never see with the naked eye the real colour of, the colour that is 'in', my suit; and that I cannot in any other way ever claim that I see its real colour. Would this have any tendency to show that what I *do* see is 'in the mind', exists only when it is seen? Clearly it would not. All that would be established would be that I cannot decide what colour the suit really is. Or suppose we agree that clouds are not really red, though they sometimes *look* red, that their apparent red colour is not 'in' the clouds. This does not tend in the very least to show that what I see when I look at the morning sky is 'in the mind', exists when and only when it is seen. How then did Berkeley come to suppose that these arguments, even if they had been cogent, would have lent any support to his case?

Partly, I think, he was misled by his (inherited) terminology – by the phrases 'in the object' and 'in the mind'. One is tempted to argue that if some quality is not 'in the object', is not a 'real property' of the object, then it follows that the quality must be 'in the mind'. For where else could it be? If it is not in the one place it must be in the other. But the phrases 'in the object' and 'in the mind' do not refer to two different *places*. A quality is said to be 'in the object', if the object really has that quality; something is said to be 'in the mind', if it exists when and only when it is perceived – as there only *are* aches in my teeth if I feel my teeth aching. If this is remembered it becomes obvious that what is not 'in the object' need not for that reason be 'in the mind'. If a book looks red but is actually not red, the quality that it appears to have is not 'in the object'; but there is no reason to conclude that it exists when and only when someone sees it.

I think that Berkeley also failed to notice the important distinction between such phrases as 'It looks . . .' and 'It looks to me now . . .' Suppose that he were right in suggesting that we cannot distinguish between, for example, 'real' and 'apparent' colour — that we can never say what colour an object *is*, but only what colour it *looks*. This would not be enough to prove his conclusion. For to say 'This piece of velvet looks dark red by candle light' does not imply that the speaker or anyone else is actually looking, by candle light, at the velvet; it is only to say how the velvet *does* look, *if* and when anyone looks at it by candle light. On the other hand, such a statement as 'It looks to me now crimson from here' can only be made when the speaker is actually looking; he is saying how something looks to himself, at the time of speaking and in the conditions then obtaining. To show that sensible qualities are 'only in the mind', then, Berkeley should have attempted to establish that each of us can say *only* how things seem *to himself*; if this were so, no statement (in the present tense) about the 'sensible qualities' of an object could be made, unless that object were actually under observation at the time; and any such statement would also mention some person *to whom* the sensible quality 'appeared', 'in whose mind' it was.

But this case would need to be supported by arguments far more radical than those that Berkeley employs. If I say 'It looks *to me now* crimson', my reason for including the words 'to me now' is that perhaps it does not look crimson to others, and perhaps will not look crimson to me at other times. I need not include these words at all, if there is good reason for supposing that it looks to others just as it looks to me, or invariably looks like this in these conditions. Thus, in order to show generally that the only statements of colour a man can make are statements of how an object looks to himself at the time, it would be necessary to show that objects do not (or probably do not) look to others as they look to him, and even that at other times they will not look to him as they now do.

Nothing short of this would force upon us the invariable use of the phrases 'It looks *to me now* . . .', 'It now feels *to me* . . .', etc.

But in most of his arguments Berkeley makes no attempt to prove so much as this. He says, for instance, that cloth which looks grey to the naked eye looks black, white, and brown under a microscope. But this enables us to say that, to the naked eye, the cloth *looks grey*; it does not at all oblige us to say only that it looks grey to some particular person at some particular time. No reason is offered for supposing that it looks different to some people from how it looks to others. Berkeley has missed an important distinction. There are two quite distinct ways in which things may appear to someone otherwise than as they are – the *conditions* may be peculiar, or his *senses* may be abnormal (or, of course, both). Many of the cases which Berkeley cites are cases of abnormal *conditions* – candle light, scrutiny through microscopes, and so on. But these are arguments from the wrong box. For in order to convince me that the way things appear to me may be *peculiar* to me and perhaps quite different for others, it is not enough to point out that, as the *conditions* of observation vary, things look, sound, feel, etc. different. For by a change of light, or distance, or point of view, we are all equally affected. A white rose looks to me red in a strong red light; but in those conditions it also looks red to almost everyone else. Hence, I am offered no inducement to say only 'It looks red to me now'; there is no reason to think that there is anything peculiar about how it looks *to me*. I can say, quite generally, 'in a strong red light a white rose looks red'; and I need not specify to whom it does, or on what particular occasions. I can also, of course, say this whether or not anyone is actually looking at the rose at the time. In order to show that each of us can only say how things appear *to himself*, at the time of observing and speaking, it would be necessary to show that even in the *same* conditions (normal or abnormal) an object does not, or often does not, appear the same to all or to most observers of it. It would be necessary to cast doubt on the general reliability of the human senses – to suggest that to other people even in these same conditions, things perhaps do not appear as they do to me; and that perhaps at other times, in these same conditions, they will not appear to me as they now do. Nothing short of this has any tendency to show that the way things appear depends upon their being observed by a particular person, or that one can only say how things appear to one's self, when one is actually observing them.

But now Berkeley seems to be in a fatal dilemma. For if the human senses were in general unreliable, and each person could say only how things appear to himself, would it be possible for (say) colour-words to come into general use and be generally understood? How could I teach someone, or be taught, to understand words for colours, unless we could be sure that things which look alike in colour to me also look alike to him and to people in general? For it would be as if each person had his own private, erratic, and peculiar type of colour-blindness; and if so, he could at best only have his own *private* use of colour-words. If this were the case, Berkeley's own arguments could not be so stated as to be generally intelligible. But if he does *not* seek to show that this is the case, he will not succeed in establishing his contention that 'sensible qualities' are 'only in the mind'. This contention could only be established by arguments which, if valid, are thereby shown to be unintelligible. We could say to him 'If your arguments are valid, I cannot understand what *you* mean by such words as "red" or "sweet" or "loud"; I know only what *I* mean mean by them; and our meanings may for all we know be completely different. But in fact your arguments must be mistaken, for I *understand* you perfectly well.'

*

It seems, then, that all Berkeley's arduous argumentation on this topic is a failure. He has argued, wrongly, that some qualities are sensations; he has argued, also wrongly, that in the other cases we can never decide what qualities an object

really has. Furthermore, even if this second group of arguments were valid, they would not prove his conclusion. He
would have to argue further that objects appear to us so vastly
Protean, our senses are so utterly unpredictable and unreliable, that each of us can say only how things seem to him
at the point and moment of utterance. This is of course not
true; Berkeley does not even try to prove it, nor could he have
proved it if he had tried. But now it is time to come to his
rescue.

For we can now see why, as I mentioned earlier, he does
not in the least degree *need* the support of these very bad
arguments; it is quite unnecessary, and indeed a mistake, for
him to appeal to the actual or supposed 'illusions' of perception. The conclusion that he purports to establish by this in-
effective appeal can be derived quite easily from his own
definition of his own terms.

The passage in which this emerges most clearly is brief, but
entirely adequate for his purpose. It is, in the opening of the
Three Dialogues, agreed between Hylas and Philonous that
'by *sensible things* I mean those only which are perceived by
sense, and that in truth the senses perceive nothing which
they do not perceive immediately: for they make no inferences.' Sensible things, then, are those things that we perceive
immediately; and *immediate* perception is to be distinguished
by the absence of any *inferences*. This is obscure; but we can
work out what Berkeley means.

It is clear that Berkeley cannot really mean to say that *the
senses* make no inferences. For this would not be worth saying. *People* make inferences. To say that my senses make inferences would be as nonsensical as to say that my vocal
chords make promises. But it is only worth saying that something does not make inferences, if at least it makes sense to
suggest that it does. Berkeley must, then, if what he says is
worth saying at all, have in mind certain inferences which
people do not make. Nor is it difficult to see what he has in
mind. Suppose that a noise breaks out, and I say 'I can hear a
dog barking in the road'. In saying this, Berkeley urges, I

have made an inference – indeed more than one. First, from the particular nature of the sounds that I hear I have inferred that they are made by a barking dog; and second, I have inferred that the barking dog is in the road. It would be well, however, to amend this slightly. For it is hardly correct to say that in such a case I make *inferences*; I do not think out what I say in the way that this suggests. I do not say to myself 'I hear a noise of such and such a kind; noises of this kind are made by barking dogs; therefore, I hear a dog.' The fact is that, on hearing this familiar sort of noise, I usually take for granted without thinking at all that it is made by a dog barking in the road. (I would only begin to think the matter out if I were asked 'How do you know?' or 'Are you sure of that?') And in such ordinary cases, of course, we are usually right, however little we think before we speak.

It follows that the statement 'I can hear a dog barking in the road' is not a statement of *immediate* perception. In making it I make inferences, take things for granted. What then do we perceive immediately? Clearly, the proper way to deal with this question is to ask 'What sort of statements of perception can be made in which nothing is taken for granted?' For the senses 'make no inferences'; that is to say, ideas or 'sensible things' are those the perception of which could be recorded in statements, the making of which involves taking nothing for granted.

The exact nature of these statements will be further discussed in the following chapter. But two points can usefully be made now – first, that Berkeley is quite mistaken in calling his 'ideas' or 'sensible things' sensible *qualities*; and second, that there is some justification for his calling them *sensations*. He is in the same sense justified in saying that 'ideas' are 'not without the mind'.

His 'arguments from illusion' are all misdirected, indeed quite contrary to the proper course of his argument. For he uses them, in a highly uncritical manner inherited from Locke, apparently to show that we *cannot in fact* ever say what qualities an object really has, though in general he is always concerned to defend our ordinary convictions from such paradoxical attacks, and would hasten to deride a philosopher who might argue, for instance, that I never really know the colour of my own socks. His mistake seems to have been that, finding in Locke arguments to prove that some sensible qualities are 'in the mind', he at once assumed that these same arguments could be used to show that his own 'sensible things' are 'in the mind'. But the fact is that what he calls 'sensible things' are not the same as what he (and Locke) called 'sensible qualities'. This can be easily seen. 'Primary' qualities are in any case not *sensible* qualities, since we ascribe them to objects by *measuring; a fortiori* they are not 'sensible things'. But neither are 'secondary' qualities; when, for instance, I taste a glass of wine and say 'It is bitter', I am at least taking for granted that it would taste so to all or most normal people who might taste it. I am not, as I must be in making a statement of 'immediate perception', merely saying that it tastes bitter *to me now*, making no assumptions about the experiences of others; indeed, to use this latter sort of phrase is precisely to *refrain* from attributing a definite quality to the wine. Thus, Berkeley need never have attempted to show that we *cannot* attribute definite qualities to objects; he is wholly on the wrong tack in attempting to show this. All that he need have said is that statements in which we attribute definite qualities to objects are not statements of 'immediate perception'; in making them we are not speaking, in his terms, of 'sensible things'. We are speaking in a way which he elsewhere describes as not 'strict'; but he need not maintain, nor does he usually maintain, that we *cannot* speak loosely – God so orders the world that we can, and we most conveniently do. He need only have pointed out that to say, for example, 'I see a red flower' *is*, by his standards, to speak loosely; for it involves assumptions, it is not confined strictly to the 'idea of sight' that the speaker has.

He is, however, on stronger ground in speaking of his 'sensible things' as *sensations*. This looked seriously wrong so long as he seemed to be identifying 'sensible things' with 'sensible qualities'; for there could be no sort of justification for calling sensible *qualities* sensations. But if 'sensible things' are not sensible qualities, this objection is beside the point. And in fact we can now see that statements about 'sensible things', records of the 'immediate perception' of ideas, have many points of resemblance with those statements in which we describe our sensations. Two points in particular are worth noticing. From the statement. 'There is a pain in my ankle', it follows that I *now feel* the pain (or rather, these are two ways of saying the same thing). From such a statement as 'There is something which now looks to me crimson', it similarly follows that I now perceive what I refer to. The statement 'There is a pain in my ankle' could not be shown to be false by appeal to the sensations of *other people*; and the observations of other people are similarly irrelevant to the statement 'There is something which now looks to me crimson.' I am, as it were, the authority on my own sensations, and also on my own 'sensible things' – on the question how things now appear *to me*. In both these respects, then, statements of 'immediate perception' resemble statements about sensations. To this extent Berkeley is justified in saying that ideas or 'sensible things' *are* sensations; in the sense in which we should be ready to say that sensations 'exist only in the mind', we may say that ideas also 'exist only in the mind'; and we can say that we immediately perceive 'our own' ideas, just as we say that we feel our own sensations.

Berkeley persistently obscures all these points in his favour. He constantly uses the word 'perceive', where the phrase he should use is his own technical term '*immediately* perceive'; he almost invariably cites as examples of 'ideas' things which do not in fact conform with his own use of that word – such as sounds, colours, sizes, and the rest; and he sometimes attempts to establish his case by using arguments which he has no need whatever to use, and which in fact run quite contrary to the true course of his views. That we *perceive* only our own ideas, is false; but that we *immediately* perceive only our own ideas, is a necessary truth. That sensible *qualities* are sensations is false; but that *sensible things* are sensations is again a (curiously worded) necessary truth. Berkeley would have saved himself and us from much labour if he had not so often disguised the necessary truths of his theory as seemingly obvious falsehoods in ordinary language.

9

PERCEPTION AND EXISTENCE

WE are now in a position to deal adequately with the question 'What are ideas?'⁹ We can deal with this question because we now see how it should be dealt with. This, precisely because the term 'idea' as Berkeley uses it is not in common use, was not and could not have been *obvious*; it is also, for different reasons, complicated. Plainly one could not have simply *pointed out* an idea, not only because ideas are 'in the mind', not public, physical objects – for pain is like this too, and yet we could in a sense 'show' someone what pain is, for example by kicking him on the shins. The reason is that ideas cannot be *picked out*; one could not arrange for someone to have an idea, and so get him to pick it out from other things; for this needs no arranging, he is already having ideas all the time. But simply to say 'You are having ideas all the time' would be no use; for this might mean almost anything – that he is awake, or thinking, or conscious, or alive, and so on. Nor would it have been sufficient to say simply 'Ideas are sensible things', or 'Ideas are what we immediately perceive.' For these phrases, 'sensible things' and 'immediately perceive', are drawn from the same specialized vocabulary in which the term 'idea' itself occurs, and hence could not be used to explain that word to someone who does not yet know how this specialized vocabulary is to be used. What we can do, however, is to explain what sort of statement it is that Berkeley calls a statement of 'immediate perception'; for this is to say what sort of statement it is that records the perception of an 'idea'. The question 'What are ideas?' thus assumes the form 'What is a statement of immediate perception?' And this is a question with which we are now equipped to deal.

It is a statement in the making of which we 'make no inferences', or (as we have suggested it would be better to say) take nothing for granted, make no assumptions. This suggests a method by which we can get at the exact character of such statements. An inference *may* be mistaken; even if it was reasonable to make it or even if it *is* not mistaken, it *could* be mistaken. Similarly if I take something for granted, reasonably or even correctly, what I take for granted might not be so. My own experiences may not bear out what I say at first; further investigation, the use of other senses, or other people's reports of their observations, may show me that what I had assumed is not in fact the case. If, on the other hand, in making my statement I commit myself to *no* assumptions about the outcome of any further investigations, whether my own or other people's, then obviously such investigations *could* not establish that what I said was false. Thus, a statement of immediate perception, in making which the speaker commits himself to no assumptions, will be one which could not be shown to be false in these ways.

The last three words, 'in these ways', are important. For a statement of this sort could be shown to be false in other ways. The fact is that no statement can really be made, in making which *nothing whatever* is taken for granted. This ideal (not of course a desirable one) could be achieved only by saying nothing, or at any rate by saying nothing which one could claim to be true. For, whatever one says, in putting forward what one says as being true there is at least one thing that must be taken for granted – namely that one is using the words correctly. If I have an 'idea' and say what 'idea' I have, then, even if I say or imply or assume nothing more, there is still one way in which I could have gone wrong – I could have misdescribed the idea that I had, used the wrong words. We may say if we like that this is a 'mistake of language' and not a 'mistake of fact'. But a false statement is not less false because one who makes it commits only a mistake of language. If there is a dictaphone on my desk and I say, intending to refer to it, 'There is a telephone on my desk', then (assuming that there is no telephone) what I say is false. Perhaps I carelessly uttered the wrong word and did not actually believe that there was on my desk what is ordinarily called a telephone; still, what I said was untrue, even if what I meant to say was not. Thus, even a statement in which I commit myself to no assumptions whatever about the outcome of further investigations could be shown to be false – I might, in a variety of ways, come to be convinced that I had misused the words that I spoke.

However, Berkeley would not mind admitting that even a statement of 'immediate perception' could in this way turn out to be false. It is not only that the chances of mistake in such a case are usually negligible; it is rather that he is not primarily interested in the possibilities of making mistakes. Some philosophers, for a variety of reasons, have been mainly concerned with this question; sometimes, searching for something that we can *know for certain*, they have attempted to find some statement or class of statements which *could* not be false; and statements of 'immediate perception' have often been taken to satisfy this requirement. They do not in fact do so; but Berkeley, who never suggests that any such requirement needs to be satisfied, would not be at all put out. For it never occurred to him to question that quite ordinary statements, in however many ways they could be false, are very often known for certain to be true. He would have thought it merely ridiculous to say that such statements as 'Dogs have four legs' or 'Today is Sunday' can never be known for certain to be true; and hence he feels no inclination to look for a special class of statements that we can know for certain. He is concerned with statements of immediate perception, not because he thinks that they alone can be known to be certainly true, but because he thinks that they are the only really accurate, exact statements of perception. Our more ordinary statements are unacceptable to him, not because he thinks them doubtful or questionable, but because he thinks them 'loose'. In making them we are not confining ourselves strictly to what we do immediately perceive, but are making assumptions about what could be immediately perceived but in fact is not. And he regards this as a deviation, not into uncertainty, but into imprecision in the use of words. For this reason he would not at all object to admitting that, even in making statements of immediate perception, we cannot help assuming that we are correctly describing our ideas; for, clearly, to make this assumption is not, by his standards, to lapse into imprecision. For so long as we are, at any rate, *trying* to describe only those ideas that we immediately perceive, we are making the right *kind* of statement; we are speaking in the exact and accurate idiom, even if what we say happens to be false.

*

Now what sort of statements will those be which, by Berkeley's standards, are strict and accurate? It is essential to be absolutely clear on this point, for it is on this that Berkeley's whole general case depends. Berkeley himself did not see that any special care was needed here. He seems to have assumed that his use of 'idea' and related technical terms must be clear to the reader without special explanation, and indeed many of his readers have proceeded as if it were perfectly clear. But this is a serious mistake. As we have already shown reason to believe, Berkeley's use of his technical terms was very far from being clear even to himself; and unless we try to repair this deficiency, we shall be arguing in a hopeless fog. We can usefully work our way towards a proper answer by examining a series of approximations to it.

Consider first the ordinary statement 'I hear a car'. It is obvious enough that this will not do, for in all sorts of ways it could turn out to be false. To mention only the most obvious way – it might be that when I look to see whether a car is actually there, I find no car (but for instance a motor cycle, or even a wireless or a gramophone). The sound that I heard led me to make certain assumptions, which further investigation might show to have been mistaken.

Suppose then that I say only what *sound* I hear – for example, 'I hear a sort of purring (engine-like) noise'. This is the sort of statement which Berkeley implies would be correct, when he says that sounds are 'ideas', the 'proper objects' of hearing. But as it stands, and taken in the ordinary sense, it does not satisfy his demands. For it too could in certain conditions turn out to be false. Suppose that, having a horror of very loud noises, I put wads of cotton-wool in my ears before setting out on a trip in an aeroplane; and suppose that on reaching the airport I forget that I have done this. Engines roar deafeningly all around me, but, having forgotten about my ear-plugs, I say 'I always thought these things made a terrible racket; but in fact I hear a mild sort of purring noise.' In this case I am of course mistaken. The noise that I call 'purring' is in fact, as everyone else hears only too well, deafeningly loud; I have gone wrong through forgetting about the wads in my ears. Of course the noise sounds *to me* mild and purring, but it actually is exceedingly loud. To make the statement 'I hear a mild sort of purring noise' is to claim that *there is* a noise of that sort to be heard; if there is not, the statement must be regarded as a mistake. In Berkeley's own terms, it embodies an *inference*; and this could (though often it would not) be shown to be mistaken by further inquiry.

Then what about saying 'I hear what *sounds to me* like a purring noise'? I do not assume in saying this that the noise actually is of this kind; to others it may sound loud. But whatever they say, however it sounds to them, even if I discover forgotten wads of cotton-wool in my ears, or even if I have suddenly become rather deaf, it now *sounds to me* like a purring noise. Surely in saying this I am on firm ground; surely I am stating, without any assumptions, a basic and incontestable fact.

But no; there remains at least one serious possibility of error. Perhaps I actually hear *nothing*. Perhaps my fellow-travellers at the airport look at me in astonishment, and point out that in fact no aeroplane's engine is running and a complete silence reigns. This is of course quite possible. It might be, for example, that in plugging my ears with the forgotten wads of cotton-wool I somehow set up a local irritation in my ears, as a result of which I begin to suffer from 'noises in the head' (as deaf people often do). I seem to hear noises, when in fact there are no noises to be heard; but *because* there are in fact no noises to be heard, it cannot be said that I actually *do* hear noises. If I knew about the irritated condition of my ears, I might certainly say 'I keep hearing noises in my head'; but this way of putting it makes it quite clear that I am not claiming to hear actual noises. But in saying 'I hear what sounds to me like a purring noise', I *am* claiming to hear an actual noise, and am saying how it sounds to me; and accordingly this statement would have to be retracted, if further investigation convinced me that there was actually no noise to be heard.

In order to eliminate this last 'inference' (namely that there is in fact some noise to be heard), it will clearly be necessary to avoid the assumption that I am actually hearing something. Nor is it difficult to do this. I can say 'It seems to me as if I were hearing a sort of purring noise'. In saying this I do not commit myself to any view about what is making the noise; I do not assume that it actually *is* a purring noise; I do not even assume that there is a noise at all. And therefore inquiries into the source, or the nature, or even the occurrence, of a noise could not possibly controvert what I say. I am *only* saying what *seems* to me at the moment: I am making no assumptions whatever (except the trivial and irrelevant assumption that I am correctly using the words that I utter). And thus I am making, by Berkeley's standards, a statement of immediate perception; I am simply saying what 'idea of hearing' it is that I now have, I am describing 'my own idea'. And no one could have a better right than I have to say what it now seems to me as if I were hearing.

*

One or two comments will help to make this quite clear.

(1) I think it is important to use the expression 'It seems to me *as if I were hearing* ...', rather than 'It seems to me *that I hear* ...' These expressions carry rather different sug-

gestions. If I say, for instance, 'It seems to me that I can hear a car', the suggestion is that I am inclined to *believe* that there is a car to be heard. (To say 'It seemed to me that he was very ill' certainly implies an inclination to believe that he was in fact very ill.) But in statements of immediate perception we do not want this suggestion at all. In saying simply what 'idea of hearing' I have, it would be unnecessary, and even wrong, to indicate what I am inclined to believe; besides, I might sometimes have the 'idea of hearing' appropriate (say) to there being a tiger in my room, when I know very well that no tiger is actually there. Suppose, for example, that a friend of mine has made some recordings in the depths of the jungle, and plays them over to me on my gramophone. I might naturally say, in congratulating him on their fidelity and vividness, 'It seemed to me exactly as if I were hearing the tigers growl in this very room' – the *sound* seemed to me exactly right, though of course I knew that no tigers were actually there; it did not really seem to me *that there were* tigers behind the sofa. (Normally, no doubt, I should say in a case like this '*It was* exactly as if ...' rather than 'It seemed to me exactly as if ...' But to say 'It was as if ...' exposes me to the possible objection 'It wasn't really', and is thus not eligible as a statement of immediate perception.)

(2) The example I have just used will serve to raise some interesting points about the *description* of 'ideas'. Suppose I say, 'It seems to me as if I were hearing tigers growl.' One might be inclined to say that this cannot be a statement of immediate perception, since it mentions tigers, which are certainly not 'sensible things' and cannot be 'immediately perceived'. (I mean by this that a tiger is not *an* idea; I am not pre-judging the question whether or not it is a *collection* of ideas.) But this objection would be beside the point. For the expression 'tigers' is not here used in saying *what* I hear (as in 'I can hear tigers'), but only in *describing* my 'idea of hearing'. I am trying to indicate what sort of sound it seems to me as if I were hearing, by mentioning what it is that commonly makes that sort of sound. (To put it in Berkeley's way:

I am seeking to characterize my idea by saying in what *collections* of ideas an idea of this kind is typically a member.) This way of describing sounds is very common, and when available it is usually the best. We can of course describe sounds in other ways – as loud or soft, reedy, or penetrating, or harsh, high-pitched, whining, or booming, and so on. But one of the best and easiest ways is to mention what sort of thing makes that sort of sound, or in what conditions that sort of sound is heard – 'like the sea', 'like the wind in the trees', 'like a violin', 'like a cat' are descriptive phrases of this kind. For seeing, our vocabulary is rather more extensive. In describing my 'ideas of sight', I can make use of all the adjectives of shape and colour; and this vocabulary is much more varied and discriminating than that for the direct description of sounds. Even in this case, however, the other method is usually more compendious and convenient. Compare, for instance, the description of a picture. We could certainly, if we wished, describe the colours and shapes of every distinguishable area of paint; but our audience would usually get a much clearer impression if we said that the picture was of a fat red-faced man in a brown suit, seen in left profile and sitting on a garden seat under a cherry tree. (Abstract paintings would have to be described by the other method.) Similarly, it would often be simpler to characterize my 'visual impressions' by saying 'It seems as if I were seeing boats on a lake', than by attempting to say what shapes and colours seem to be in my visual field. (But if my 'impressions' are very unusual, I might have to describe them as I would an abstract painting – for, just as such a painting is not 'of' familiar objects, my visual impressions may sometimes not be of the sort that one has in seeing any familiar object.) In the description of smells and tastes we are nearly always constrained to mention the objects which ordinarily have those smells and those tastes; for the reason that we have hardly any vocabulary in which to describe them in any other way.

However, it does not matter for the logic of statements of immediate perception which method of description we choose to employ. For the logical character of such statements is determined by the phrase 'It seems to me as if I were . . .'; it is this that excludes assumptions, 'inferences', 'commitments', and shows that I am speaking only of 'my own ideas'; what comes afterwards serves only to characterize the idea, and it does not matter very much how this is done. It is true that we could only use the method of reference to familiar objects if we already knew how to recognize and to speak of familiar objects; but this does not matter to Berkeley's case. (He need not and, I think, does not maintain that we learn to characterize separately our own ideas, *before* we learn to speak about common objects.) It is also true that this method of description increases the risks of *mis*description – if, for example, I seek to characterize a sound by saying that it is the sort of sound that an oboe makes, it is possible that I may have forgotten or otherwise be mistaken about the characteristic sound of an oboe. (Perhaps the sound that it seems as if I were hearing is actually more like a clarinet or a flute.) The method of what I have called 'direct' description – that is, by such adjectives as 'oval', 'pink', 'loud', 'high-pitched', 'bitter', 'sweet', and so on – is comparatively simple and involves less risk of error; it is, on the other hand, usually less intelligible to others, and besides our language is by no means rich in adjectives of this kind. It would be extremely difficult and perhaps impossible to convey to someone the exact quality of the sound of an oboe, without calling it 'the sort of sound that an oboe makes'.

But in any case, the essential feature of a statement of immediate perception is that it *begins* 'It seems to me now as if I were . . .'; its conclusion is a matter of taste and convenience, and does not affect the logical character of the statement.

(3) It might be thought that our account of statements of immediate perception is a misrepresentation of Berkeley's view; and this feeling is, I think, sufficiently natural to deserve some special scrutiny. The objection would presumably run as follows: Berkeley says that ideas are *immediately perceived*. (In fact he usually says that they are perceived, but

his omission of the word 'immediately' is a slip that we must correct on his behalf.) But if so, it is surely clear that a statement of immediate perception ought to begin with the words 'I immediately perceive ...', not with a phrase so cumbrous, uncommon, and different as 'It seems to me now as if I were ...' It is clear that, when I am having an idea, Berkeley means that I am actually *having* what may be called a 'perceptual experience', not that it merely *seems* as if I were seeing, hearing (etc.), something. Does not the account we have offered somehow abolish the actual *having*, the immediate perception, of ideas, and replace it by a mere 'seeming as if' – an entirely different matter?

But this objection is misplaced. It is quite true that, if we took Berkeley at his word, it would be natural to phrase a statement of immediate perception in the form 'I immediately perceive ...' But of course if we do this we at once encounter the difficulty that the *meaning* of this expression is quite obscure. What exactly is the force of the adverb 'immediately'? What is the difference between 'immediate perception', and perception? In using the expression 'It seems to me now as if I were ...' we are not *altering* Berkeley's view, but trying to make it quite clear what his view is; we are trying to show how his own demand, that a statement of immediate perception should involve no 'inferences', can actually be satisfied. Certainly we may say that to have an idea, to 'perceive immediately a sensible thing', is to have a 'perceptual experience', but then our account has no tendency to deny this. To say 'It seems to me now as if I were seeing ...' is obviously to say (making no 'inferences', no assumptions) that I actually *am* having some 'idea of sight'. We do not in this way overlook or abolish the actual 'immediate perception' of ideas, and replace it by 'mere seeming'; for it is exactly *when* it seems to me as if I were seeing ... that I actually *am* immediately perceiving an idea of sight. Certainly we do eliminate the phrases 'I see ...', 'I hear ...', etc., in favour of 'It seems to me as if I were seeing ...' etc.; but then Berkeley's view quite clearly requires us to do this. For he makes it quite clear that from a statement of the form 'I immediately perceive ...' it does *not* follow that I actually *am* seeing, hearing, etc., anything at all – I may be dreaming, imagining, having a hallucination. I may, in fact, have ideas, or if we choose to say so 'perceptual experiences', even though there is actually nothing at all to be seen or heard, tasted or smelled. Ideas may, as he says, simply 'arise in my fancy'; and in such a case, though I 'immediately perceive' ideas and 'it seems to me as if' I were seeing something, it would be a complete mistake to speak as if there were something that I actually *do* see. I 'see in the mind's eye', perhaps; but this is only another way of saying that I do not really *see*. The fact is that, in saying what 'idea of sight' I have, I must not say what I am actually seeing – I must not say 'I see an aeroplane'; I must not even assume that I am really *seeing* anything whatever; I must say nothing at all which (apart from misdescription) could be falsified by further experiences of my own or of other people. And I do not know of any familiar (intelligible) form of words which exactly meets these requirements except our version 'It seems to me now as if I were seeing ...' This formula serves to make it clear that I *am* having some 'perceptual experience', while committing me to nothing that could be contradicted by further perceptual experiences; and this is exactly what Berkeley requires. Such expressions as 'I see something red and oval', or 'I see an oval, red patch of colour', do not in fact satisfy his demands (though he himself often speaks as if they do). For the observations of other people might establish that there is actually nothing to be seen; and then such statements would have to be retracted, and replaced by 'It *seems to me* as if I were seeing something'. *I* have these 'ideas', even if no one else has any similar ideas 'coherent' with these, and even if I am actually *seeing* nothing at all. Our formula, then, does actually satisfy Berkeley's own demands.

There are two points which are liable to cause confusion in this matter. Firstly, it is natural to say that even in dreaming or having hallucinations there do occur 'visual experiences'. (Seeming to *see* pink rats in *delirium tremens* could be called a 'visual experience', as distinct from seeming to *feel*, say, moths in one's hair.) Now it has often been assumed that to say 'I see . . .' is to 'describe my visual experiences'; and hence it appears to follow that, *whenever* I have a 'visual experience', I could properly say 'I see' something. But, as we have already pointed out, to say 'I see . . .' is *not* to describe any 'visual experiences'; it is to claim that something is actually there to be seen. And hence, if there are actually no pink rats, then, whatever 'visual experiences' I may be having, it is not true that I see pink rats; indeed, if I am having a hallucination (and not merely, for example, *mistaking* pink bedroom slippers for pink rats), it is not true that I see anything at all. And this leads to the second point. If we are speaking of someone who has, and is known to have, hallucinations, we often do not bother to go on emphasizing that he really saw nothing at all. We say of the drunkard that he 'saw pink rats', of Macbeth that he 'saw a dagger', and so on. This is the easiest way of saying what 'visual experiences' they had, and leads to no misunderstanding provided, of course, that everyone knows we are speaking of hallucinations. But from the fact that we sometimes say 'Macbeth saw a dagger', it does not follow that he really did see anything at all; indeed, if anyone drew this conclusion from our words, we should say 'You don't understand – he was having a hallucination. There was not really any dagger to be seen, it just *seemed to him* as if he were seeing a dagger.' People may, in short, have 'visual experiences' without *seeing* anything at all; and in fact in hallucinations and (possibly) dreaming, this is exactly what occurs.

Such, then, are statements of 'immediate perception', statements about the 'sensible things' that we 'immediately perceive', about the 'ideas of sense' that we actually have. 'It seems to me as if I were hearing the sound of an oboe.' I 'make no inferences' – perhaps there is no oboe, perhaps not even any sound at all. I am speaking only of 'my own' idea, of what is 'in my mind', in the sense that I say only what it *seems to me* as if I were hearing, and do not make any assumptions about the experiences of other people nor yet about any further experiences of my own. It is as if I were speaking about my own sensations; no one else's observations are at all relevant. Just as, in saying 'I have a pain in my ankle', I am saying how *I* feel, so in saying 'It seems to me as if I were hearing the sound of an oboe' I am saying how things seem to *me*. It is for this reason that Berkeley can excusably speak of 'ideas or sensations', and can say that 'ideas have not any subsistence without a mind'. Just as a sensation must be *somebody's* sensation, so an idea must be *somebody's* idea.

We are now in a position to reconsider the central puzzle of Berkeley's philosophy.

*

He argues, it will be remembered, in this way. Suppose that I say 'I see a table'. This is not, of course, a statement of immediate perception; it involves an inference. What I *immediately* perceive, on this as on all other occasions, is an idea. What inference is it, then, that I make in saying 'I see a table'? Clearly it cannot be the case, as Locke thought it was, that I infer the presence behind the idea that I have of a (necessarily) invisible, unobservable 'external object'; for such an inference could never conceivably be checked, it would be invalid and is indeed not intelligible at all. It *must* be then that I am inferring (taking for granted) that I could, and would if I took suitable steps, see and feel, perhaps hear and smell, other *ideas*: and also (since tables can be observed by other people) that others would in suitable circumstances be 'affected with' similar ideas. If in my account of what I see I try to mention something *other than* the ideas that I (and others) have (and could have), I should be attempting to mention something *other than* 'sensible things', the things that we can immediately perceive; and this would not only be obviously wrong in an account of something that I see – it would violate the conditions of meaningful speech. For our words can only be given sense by reference to things that human beings do and can experience; it is a delusion to suppose that we could speak intelligibly of 'objects', if these were something quite other than the ideas that we do actually have. So that, if we want a short phrase to sum up the matter, we can say that the table is a 'collection of ideas'. When I say that I see it I have a particular idea; and (if what I say is true) God has, and I and others could have, a great many more. There can be no reference in my words to anything other than this collection of ideas. But an idea, we have found, exists 'only in the mind'. The table then (and any other so-called 'material object', anything and everything that we say we perceive) is a collection of things which exist 'only in the mind'. But what is true of all the parts must be true of the whole; and hence the entire observable universe, 'the whole choir of heaven and furniture of the earth', can exist only in the mind. Its *esse* is *percipi*; 'it being perfectly unintelligible ... to attribute to any single part of [it] an existence independent of a spirit.'

To make clearer how it is that Berkeley diverges from Locke, we may consider the following question. Suppose that I say 'I see an orange on the sideboard'. Now Locke and Berkeley both admitted that I might have the 'idea of sight' that I now have, both when there really is and when there is not an orange on the sideboard. What then is the difference between the cases when there is, and when there is not, an orange?

Now Locke's answer to this looked very simple. If there really is an orange on the sideboard, then the idea that I now have is caused by, and is in some respects a copy of, an 'external' physical object of the kind called 'an orange': if there is not, I may have a similar or even indistinguishable idea, but it then is not caused by a physical orange but in some other way – for example by a piece of wax or coloured paper, or merely by some trick of the light.

This account, however, does not work. For suppose that I look at a Christmas stocking at the end of my bed. About halfway down there is an angular bulge; and I say 'It looks to me as if there were a model boat in that stocking'. Now of course, given a bulge of that particular shape, there might or might not be a model boat inside. What then is the difference between the cases where there is, and there is not? Here the answer is obvious enough. There really is inside the stocking what, on the basis of the bulge, it looks to me as if there were, if and only if that bulge in the stocking is in fact made by a model boat. Then how am I to tell whether there really is a model boat or not? Of course I can put my hand into the stocking, pull out whatever is inside, and see what it is.

But this shows where Locke's account breaks down. How am I to tell whether the idea that I have is or is not caused by an 'external' orange? By some process analogous with the actual extraction of the bulge-making object fom the stocking? No; for, according to Locke, no such process is possible. The 'external' orange is itself quite inaccessible to observation; all that I can do is to have some more ideas (as if I examined all the other bulges in the stocking). I cannot get at the *cause* of all these ideas; this is in principle inaccessible to me. It is as if to pull the model boat out of the stocking were a thing that in principle I cannot do; I can only observe the bulges and make a guess at what is behind them.

Berkeley saw very clearly that this is not a tenable view. Locke makes it seem quite impossible for us ever really to be sure that we see an orange; for when we say that we do, we are always, he tells us, guessing at inaccessible causes, and our guesses could not conceivably be checked. How absurd, too, to say that the 'real', physical object is something we never see or touch, taste or smell! Oranges are not tasteless, intangible, invisible; it is often perfectly certain that we see an orange; it cannot be that in saying 'I see an orange' I am making a mere untestable guess at the presence of something I do not see and never could see. Such an account is worse than false; it is simply nonsense.

And so Berkeley took what seemed to be the only alternative. It seems to me as if I were seeing an orange. Now if there really *is* an orange, then if I go closer and look again, feel and sniff, and call in my neighbours to look and feel and sniff too, to me and to all of us it will go on seeming as if we were seeing an orange. If it is only paper we shall soon find the difference; and if there is really nothing at all on my sideboard, then it will no longer seem to us, as we come closer, as if we were seeing something there. When I have my 'idea of sight' and say 'I see an orange on the sideboard', I am not guessing that behind my idea there lies an invisible, indetectible *cause*; I am taking for granted that I and others could, and would if we took suitable steps, have innumerable other *ideas* of a suitable kind. The orange just is the collection of all of these; and when we have actually had enough of them we can say with perfect certainty that there is, there really is, an orange on the sideboard.

Yes, one might say, this sounds more sensible than Locke. But what about the orange on the sideboard when no one is there? It may then be true, that *if* certain conditions were satisfied (observers were in position for observing and engaged in doing so), then it *would* seem to each of them as if he were seeing (etc.) an orange, and as if it seemed to the others as if that were so. But what is there *now*, when no observers are observing?

To this Berkeley has his answer ready. It would be absurd, he thinks, to suggest that the actual (unobserved) orange on the sideboard is a collection of merely *hypothetical* ideas; unless these ideas do actually exist in some mind, we cannot say that the orange itself exists. But all ideas exist in the mind of God. There is certainly an orange on the sideboard when no one is there; that whole collection of ideas is still in God's mind, though none of its items is now in the mind of any human being. The general case can be stated as follows: Every material thing is a 'collection of ideas'. Any statement about any material thing is really (can be analysed into) an indefinitely large set of statements about what it seems, or in suitable conditions would seem, as if the speaker and other people *and God* were hearing, seeing, feeling, tasting, smelling – that is, into an indefinitely large set of statements describing the ideas of which any material object is a collection. It is clear then that nothing is 'without the mind'; for any such statement about a material object is analysed into a set of statements, each of which mentions some 'spirit' (human or divine) *by whom* the ideas that constitute the object are actually had. This reference to a 'spirit' cannot be eliminated, for every idea must be *somebody's* idea. It must always seem *to someone* as if . . .

*

Now we can return to the old and obvious objection. If all that I immediately perceive is *my own ideas*, is it not as if I were always in a dream? Is there no such thing as the waking perception of real, physical objects? Surely it might *seem to me* as if I were seeing an orange, even in a dream or a vision – this might *seem* to be so, even if no orange at all were actually there. Is not Berkeley somehow obliterating the distinction between *appearance* and *reality*?

Of course Berkeley replies that he is doing no such thing. 'There is a *rerum natura*, and the distinction between realities and chimeras retains its full force' (P. 34). He is not obliterating the distinction between appearance and reality, but rather trying to make clear what this distinction is. For suppose that it seems to you as if you were seeing an orange. You say that there might be no orange really there, and of course this is perfectly true. But what exactly does it *mean*? Clearly it means this – that if you altered your position or felt with your hands, or called in your neighbours to look and feel too, it might *no longer* seem to you as if you were seeing and feeling an orange, nor as if it seemed to your neighbours as if that were so. Your first 'idea of sight' might turn out to be 'irregular', not 'coherent' with your own further experiences. But if, on the other hand, there *is* an orange there, then to you and to all your neighbours and to anyone else it will or would always seem as if you and they were seeing, touching, etc., an orange. This, then, *is* the difference between reality and appearance – reality is, one might say, *consistent seeming*; we speak of 'appearance', *mere* seeming, when how things seem at first is not consistent with how they seem at other times, to others, or in other conditions. What possible reason could you have for saying 'There is an orange on the sideboard', except that it consistently seems as if that were so? And when you say 'It *only* seemed as if that were so', what reason could you have for saying this except that it now *no longer* seems as if that were so? This is surely the only way in which the appearance-reality distinction can be made intelligible; it is Locke, not Berkeley, who would lead us to 'scepticism' in this matter.

But Berkeley's words leave, all the same, a lingering doubt; and, with care, we can show that this doubt is indeed well-founded.

Suppose I say 'I can see an orange on the sideboard, but really there is no orange there'. It is plain that I contradict myself; I am both claiming, and denying, that there is an orange on the sideboard. But suppose I say 'It seems to me as if I were seeing an orange on the sideboard, but really there is no orange there'. Here I do not contradict myself; for the whole force of saying, 'It seems as if ...' is to allow for '... but not so really'. But this is fatal to Berkeley's case; the force of 'It seems as if ...' cannot be conjured away. If the sentence 'It seems to me and to God, and it would seem to anyone else, as if there were an orange on the sideboard' *means the same as* 'There is an orange on the sideboard', then to assert the first of these and to deny the second would be *self-contradictory*. But in fact this is not the case. 'It seems to me and to God and to absolutely everyone as if there were an orange on the sideboard, but really there is no orange there' – there is no self-contradiction in this. If it seems to everyone as if they were seeing an orange on the sideboard, it might be *silly* to say 'But no orange is really there'; but there is no *contradiction* in saying so. Indeed, the whole point of the expression 'It seems as if ...' is to make this non-contradictory. However many people give 'their own impressions', it *makes sense* to say that they are all mistaken; and hence to say 'There is an orange on the sideboard' *cannot* mean the same as saying that everyone had or has, will have or would have, the impression that there is. And thus the common suspicion that Berkeley is some-

how neglecting the distinction between what *seems* and what
is turns out to be justified. Not in the crudest and most blatant
sense – he provides us with *a* version of this distinction, in the
form of a distinction between 'consistent seeming' and *mere,*
irregular, 'incoherent seeming'. But this distinction is *not
enough*. For even 'It consistently seems so' does not mean the
same as 'It is so really'; one could say 'It consistently seems so,
but it is not'. In the course of translation into Berkeley's
terms 'the distinction between realities and chimeras' has not
quite vanished, but it does *not* 'retain its full force'.

*

But this is not the end of the matter: we must somehow break
the deadlock between Locke and Berkeley. For it seemed to
Berkeley that one could not disagree with his views, without
thereby assenting to the far more obviously inadequate views
of Locke: just as, conversely, it seemed to him that one could
not reasonably disagree with Locke, without thereby accepting his own doctrines. And this view of the matter has enjoyed a very long life. Philosophers were found, well into the
present century, discussing perception as if the only possibilities were versions of Locke's position, or of Berkeley's.

Berkeley would argue as follows. Whenever we perceive anything at all, we have certain 'ideas of sense'; and if there are
things that we never do perceive, still they must be *perceivable*
things, and this is to say that we *could* have (and God does
have) 'ideas' in perceiving those perceivable things. Thus, if
one says that statements about material things *cannot* be
translated into equivalent sets of statements about ideas, one
can only be suggesting, as Locke suggested, that statements
about material things refer to something which is *not perceivable*. Since perceiving just is having (and expecting to
have) ideas, to deny that objects just are collections of ideas
must be to say that they, or some elements in or constituents
of them, are not and cannot be perceived. But this is to raise
the spectre of Locke's (and Malebranche's) unperceivable,
blank, stupid, inert, utterly redundant 'real external world';

surely we do not want any other world than the world that
we can and do perceive, nor does it make sense to believe in or
even to wish for some other world. But if this is admitted, it
must be admitted that the material world is a collection of
ideas; and this is to say that any statement about the world is
equivalent to a collection of statements about ideas, and hence
that '*esse* is *percipi*'.

But we must not be swept off our feet. For *all* that we have
said so far is that statements about material things, though
they *can* be translated into Berkeley's terms, do not mean the
same as the versions supplied by his translation. Our reason
for saying this certainly might be what Berkeley boldly
assumes that it must be; it might be that our ordinary
statements refer to something unperceivable, which Berkeley's versions cannot do. But this is not the only possible
reason.

The following example will help to clear the air. Suppose
that the question is put to a jury: is the accused guilty or not
guilty of the offence alleged in the indictment? Evidence has
been produced, and it is, let us assume, strongly in favour of
the supposition that he committed the offence. The jury retire,
and on returning are asked to give their verdict. Now suppose
that the foreman says 'We are sure that all the evidence produced in court, and also any other evidence that might be or
might have been produced, supports the view that the accused
committed the offence'. But this, it would be objected, is not
enough; the jury has not given a *verdict*. Their business is to
say 'Guilty' or 'Not guilty', not to review or restate or sum up
the *evidence*. But at this point Berkeley would intervene.
Surely, he would say, in saying what all the conceivable evidence tends to show the jury must be regarded as having
already given their verdict; what the foreman said must be
equivalent to the verdict 'Guilty'. For if to say 'Guilty' is to
say something *more than* this, it must be in part at least to
say something about the accused for which there is *no evidence*. But there are no extra, mysterious facts about the
accused, *other than* what the evidence has established; hence

to say 'Guilty' *must* be to say the same thing as what the fore-man has said already.

But in fact it is clear that this is not so. It is true, of course, that a foreman pronounces the verdict 'Guilty' *because*, and only because, he and his fellows are sure that all the evidence supports the view that the accused committed the offence; in so doing he is not saying something for which there is no evidence, but pronouncing a verdict precisely *on* the evidence. But to state the reason, the whole reason, for pronouncing this verdict is not the same as to pronounce the verdict itself. If the foreman says 'We are all quite sure that all the evidence supports the view that the accused committed the offence', then he has, simply in that he has not said 'Guilty', *not* pro-nounced a verdict. He has stated an excellent, indeed a com-plete, *reason* for pronouncing a verdict, but he has not yet pronounced it. In order to get this done he must be asked, not to make up his mind or collect new evidence or go beyond the evidence, but simply to *say* something different – to pronounce a verdict, by saying 'Guilty'.

Now the difference between saying 'There is an orange on the sideboard' and saying 'It seems to everyone as if there were an orange on the sideboard', is very similar to this. If we ask 'What is there on the sideboard?', and get the answer 'It seems to me and would seem to everyone else as if there were an orange', we could say that the answer does not tell us what there actually *is* on the sideboard, just as the foreman's first remarks did not actually constitute a verdict on the accused. It may be true, as Berkeley often insists, that one could have no better *reason* for saying 'There's an orange' than that it seems and would seem to everyone as if that were so; but still, to say only how it seems and would seem to everyone is to fall short of saying what actually *is* the case. And in saying this we do not imply that there are or could be additional reasons for saying 'There's an orange', but only that to give all the reasons why one might say this is not the same as actually saying it. Our example also brings out one further point. Just as Berkeley is (I think) properly accused of blurring the distinction between reality and appearance, so the foreman in our example could be accused of blurring the distinction between conviction and acquittal. For to say 'All the evidence supports the view that the accused committed the offence' does not logically exclude the statement '... but he is not actually guilty', just as to say 'It seems to everyone as if there were an orange' does not exclude the addition '... but actually there is not'. Berkeley does not of course maintain that there are no oranges, nor even that we often think there are when there are not; but still, his translation of the statement that there is an orange on the sideboard does not *contradict* the supposition that there is not. Similarly our foreman need not maintain that no crimes are committed, nor even that verdicts are often wrong; but still, his way of speaking does not enable him to express the jury's conclusion that the accused is guilty, in a way which contradicts the suggestion that he is not. There is an essential logical difference between discussing evidence and pronouncing verdicts – a difference which cannot be abolished by any amount, however vast, of piling up evidence, however conclusive. So long as we go on talking only about evidence, we shall never pronounce a verdict. Similarly, there is an essential logical difference between saying how things seem and how they are – a difference which cannot be removed by assembling more and more reports of how things seem. If we go on talking only of how things seem, we shall never arrive at a statement of how things are.

Berkeley's view is in fact exceedingly paradoxical. For, normally, the whole point of talking about 'my own impressions', or about anyone else's impressions, is precisely to leave room for the possibility that my and their impressions were mistaken or misleading. The essential function of the language of 'seeming' is that it is *non-committal* as to the actual facts. In saying then that objects are 'collections of ideas', Berkeley is seeking to abolish, not merely a difference, but an actual contrast. He is maintaining that statements of the form 'It seems as if ...', statements about 'our own ideas', really can amount to saying exactly what they are normally used to avoid saying – namely 'There is ...' It is, of course, this which justifies the very commonly held, but less often correctly expressed, opinion that he is conjuring away the difference between 'realities and chimeras'. The whole vocabulary which he recommends is that which we normally employ in order to *avoid* saying what is really the case.

*

A schematic version of these arguments may be helpful. Both Locke and Berkeley are occupied with this question – How is our knowledge of the material world derived from our immediate perception of our ideas? Or, to put it in another way, How could a statement about a material object be derived from statements about ideas?

Let $S_1, S_2 \ldots S_n$ be a set of statements about ideas, and M a statement about a material object. Locke represents the connexion between these as follows: we assert '$S_1, S_2, S_3 \ldots S_n$ – *therefore* (by a causal inference) M.' (Compare 'There's a bulge here, and another bulge there – *therefore* there's a model boat inside.') But this account seems to Berkeley all wrong; the causal inference would be invalid, and the statement M, supposed to be about an unperceivable 'external body', would be flatly unintelligible. And so he presents the argument differently, like this; 'S_1, S_2, S_3, etc. ... therefore M' – where 'M' is regarded simply as a *way of asserting* 'S_1 and S_2 and S_3 and S_4 and ... S_n'; the 'inference' being that, since S_1 and S_2 and S_3 are true, therefore the whole series up to S_n is true. M, the statement about the material object, just *is* the conjunction of S_1 and S_2 and ... S_n, the statements about ideas (the object *is* a 'collection of ideas'). The inference, then, is not from S_1, etc., to M, a statement of a quite different sort; but from S_1 and S_2 and $S_3 \ldots$ to ... S_n – from a certain number of statements about ideas to an indefinitely large number of statements *also* about ideas. To assert M is implicitly to assert an indefinitely large conjunction of statements about ideas. And in this case the inference is not in-

valid, as in Locke's account it was; for its validity can be
tested by further observations; and the statement M is certainly intelligible, since it is a conjunction of statements about
ideas which are all well understood.

Our objection to Berkeley can be put in a similar form.
We have argued that M *cannot* be merely a conjunction of
S_1 and S_2 and ... S_n, for the reason that it is not logically
impossible to hold that M is true, but S_1, etc., false, nor that
M is false but S_1, etc., true. 'It seemed to everyone as if there
were an orange, but there was not'; 'There was an orange, but
it did not seem to anyone as if there were.'

How can we say this without agreeing with Locke? The
answer, I think, is clear enough. Locke argues that we pass
from S_1, S_2, etc., to M by a causal inference. This is, as Berkeley well saw, an untenable view. But this is by no means the
only alternative view to Berkeley's own. For suppose that you
and I and many others, looking at my sideboard, each say
'It seems to me as if I were seeing an orange'. Now this way of
speaking is specifically designed to enable each speaker to
avoid assuming a consensus of opinion; in these words each
of us gives his own impressions, quite independently of any
supposed facts or anyone else's impressions or assertions. But
if, as in this case, we find that there is a consensus of opinion,
it is *reasonable to drop* this deliberately non-committal way
of speaking; it would indeed be unreasonable to persist with
it. Each of us can reasonably say 'I see an orange' – for there
is, in view of the plain consensus of opinion, no further point
in restricting ourselves to stating merely our own impressions.
And the case for dropping our non-committal idiom would
become stronger, if in due course it seemed to each of us as
if we were touching and smelling an orange; the consensus
would thereby be made more convincing still.

Now what exactly has happened in this case? We have not
inferred from S_1, etc., a conclusion about an unperceivable
'external body'; on the contrary, we all concluded that we
saw an orange. Nor have we inferred, from the fact that it
now seems to us as if we were seeing an orange, that it will

and would consistently seem so to us and to anyone else. No; we have simply *stopped using* the language of 'seeming', saying instead that we *see* an *orange*. This is (obviously) not to speak of an unperceivable thing; but it is also to speak in a quite *different way* from that in which we say how things seem. The two ways of speaking are not, of course, unconnected; what made it reasonable to say 'We see an orange' was precisely our consensus of opinion on how things seemed (just as what makes it reasonable to say 'Guilty' is that the evidence supports the view that the accused committed the offence). If S_1, S_2, S_3, etc., are true, it then becomes *reasonable* to say 'M'; but to say 'M' is by no means, as Berkeley supposed, simply a short way of saying 'S_1 and S_2 and S_3 and ... S_n'. What we do is to jump from one way of speaking to another – of course not arbitrarily. If there is reason to be non-committal, we say 'It seems as if ...'; but if then there is general agreement on how things seem, we no longer have reason for being non-committal; or, to put it the other way round, we have good reason for changing to the other way of speaking, in which we say how things *are* and not only how they seem.

Statements about material objects are no more *unconnected* with statements about 'ideas', than verdicts are unconnected with evidence; but statements about ideas are no more the *same* as statements about material objects, than statements of evidence are the same as verdicts. And to stop talking about ideas and to talk about material objects is not to refer to *unperceivable* things; for it is to talk about objects which (in that way of speaking) we can say that we see and touch, taste, hear, and smell.

*

How did Berkeley come to think that his own doctrine was obviously, even necessarily, true? I think that by far the most important reason was that, in spite of his brilliant criticism of Locke, he still took Locke too seriously. Having rejected certain parts of Locke's opinions, he was too easily satisfied with what was left. A second reason was, I believe, that he unwittingly exaggerated his own most able attack on 'abstract ideas'.

(1) Locke had maintained that there exist 'spirits' (he called these 'immaterial substances'); ideas; and 'external bodies', material substances, which *caused* ideas to arise in the minds of 'spirits'. Now Berkeley might have argued, and indeed he ought to have argued, that this entire scheme is confused and confusing; he should have scrapped it entirely and started all over again. But he did not do so; instead, by exceedingly able and effective arguments, he attacked it in detail, extruded from it certain indefensible elements, and built up much of his own theory out of the remainder. His critical arguments were thoroughly convincing. He exposed the absurdity of 'material substance'; he pointed out that of Locke's 'external bodies' we could not possibly know anything, not even that any such things existed; and he argued that a language intelligible to human beings must refer to what human beings can and do experience. But he did not conclude from this that Locke's whole theory is tangled and ought to be dropped. By saying 'There is no such thing as material substance' or 'There are no external bodies', he did not mean to reject the whole theory from which he was dissenting; on the contrary, he did accept almost the whole of it, *except* for the doctrine that there is material substance and there are external bodies. He simply deleted this item from Locke, and held that *there are* only 'spirits' and their 'ideas'.

And from this all the rest flows almost inevitably. If there are (besides spirits) only ideas, then material objects *can only* be collections of ideas; and if there are only ideas, all statements about the material world must ultimately be about ideas. To say that some statement is not about ideas *must*, apparently, be to say that it is about some unperceivable thing; for the only possible things other than ideas would be Locke's 'external bodies'. Thus, we must either say that *'esse* is *percipi'* (that *there are* only ideas), or that there exist unperceivable 'external bodies'. But Berkeley has certainly shown that this second alternative is quite unacceptable; it *must* be,

then, that '*esse* is *percipi*'; that only ideas exist, and all statements about the world are about ideas.

In this way, Berkeley's analysis of statements about material
things (which is in any case by no means unplausible) seems
also to have a quite conclusive 'ontological' backing. It is not
only *plausible* to say that statements about material objects
can be analysed into sets of statements about ideas; this *must*
be so, he thought, for there *are* only ideas. Locke's 'external
bodies' have definitely perished in ignominy, and only 'ideas'
are left in the field.

But all this is a philosophical illusion. Why should we suppose that, when Locke's 'external bodies' disappear, we really
are left only with 'ideas'? To say that 'there are only ideas'
can only be to do one of two things – it is either to assume
that, except for the needless excrescence of 'external bodies',
Locke's theory is entirely correct; or it is to assert, in a fatally
misleading way, that Berkeley's own analysis of statements
about material things is right. In neither case does Berkeley's
analysis receive any effective *support*. For the doctrine that
only ideas exist is either a bad way of stating that analysis
itself; or else it is to accept quite uncritically the fragments
of another demonstrably vulnerable theory. I am sure it would
not be correct to say that Berkeley arrived at his own view
solely through uncritical acceptance of Locke's surviving doctrines; for I think it will have become clear that he offers
arguments, by no means transparently fallacious, on his own
behalf. But I am no less sure that his surprising conviction
that his own theory was *obviously* right was due to his inadequate scrutiny of Locke. He was so sure, and indeed quite
rightly so sure, that he had killed off 'matter' and 'external
bodies', that it came to seem as if dissent from his own views,
refusal to admit that 'there are only ideas', must be a return
to the theory that he had annihilated.

Another matter of great importance is that, at one point
where Locke had gone definitely wrong, Berkeley goes right –
but not, as he perhaps naturally assumed, to the place at
which Locke was seeking to arrive. This is in the matter of

'deriving' statements about things from statements about ideas, of deriving M from S_1, S_2, S_3, etc. Now Locke held that the inference to M from S_1, etc., was causal; in this he was certainly mistaken, and any such inference would be invalid. Berkeley points out that, on the other hand, there is no objection to inferring ... S_{27}, S_{28} ... S_n from S_1, S_2, S_3 ... We cannot, from statements of how things seem to some people, infer a conclusion about an utterly unperceivable thing; but we can infer a conclusion about how things *would* seem to other people. And so we can; this is indeed an unexceptionable kind of inference. But to say that this is a valid kind of inference is not the same as to say that it is the way in which M can be derived from S_1, S_2, etc. Not at all; it is simply to say that from S_1, S_2, etc., we can reasonably infer S_{27}, S_{28} ... S_n. Whether or not this amounts to inferring that M, is an entirely different question, and a question to which the answer is No. If we must ask how M can be 'derived' from S_1, etc., I think the proper (though doubtless too brief) answer would be this – that if S_1, S_2, S_3, etc., are true, it is *reasonable to stop* talking in the 'S-language' and to assert M instead. If to fifteen people and after thirteen experiments it seems as if they were all seeing an orange, we might validly infer that to other people and after yet more experiments it would still seem to all of them as if that were so; but we could with equal reason decide to *stop* saying only how things seem, and instead to say 'There is an orange on the sideboard'. Berkeley rightly assists that the possible inference is valid; but he quite wrongly assumes that to make this inference is *the same* as to say 'There is an orange on the sideboard'. This is a very natural mistake, and one in which numerous philosophers have followed him; but it is for all that a mistake, and a serious one.

(2) The second reason for Berkeley's conviction that he was right is to be found in his discussion of 'abstract ideas'. He realized, and argued with force and originality, that it is a mistake to suppose that for every noun there is some *one thing* of which it is the name. The abstract noun 'motion', for ex-

ample, is not the *name* of an 'abstract idea' or an 'abstract entity', but a word that we use in speaking generally about moving things and how things move. Abstract nouns, in fact, are not names of unperceivable abstract things, but ways of speaking of *perceivable* things. But what then are perceivable things? To this of course Berkeley answers 'Ideas'. But he is then obliged to regard even common nouns like 'orange' and 'tree' as if they were *abstract* nouns. For certainly neither word refers to *an* idea. Hence it seems to follow that to use the words 'an orange' must either be a way of speaking of numerous *ideas*, or else it must be construed as referring to an unperceivable, as-if-abstract, entity. But the discussion of such words as 'motion' has established the absurdity of the latter view; and hence the first must be correct. To speak of an orange must be to speak compendiously of an indefinitely large collections of *ideas*.

Now it is clear enough that Berkeley is on the right lines in his discussion of 'motion'. If someone says 'The motion of the planets is orderly and predictable', it is indeed natural to say that he is talking about the planets – namely, telling us how they move. In order to check what he says we observe the planets. If we think of the matter otherwise, we may fall into the trap which Berkeley warns us against; we may come to think that observing the planets is somehow not enough; that we ought to be observing not them, but 'motion', and that in some way 'motion' always eludes us. There is thus good reason for saying that to speak of the motion of the planets is simply to speak of how the planets move, and not of some 'abstract' thing quite other than the planets. But suppose that someone says 'The orange on the sideboard is not quite ripe'. Here it is natural to say that he is referring to the orange, that we must look at the orange to see whether what he says is true. What reason is there to say that he is talking about numerous *ideas*, that the orange is not *an* object but a *collection* of ideas? It is clear that there is no reason, independently of Berkeley's doctrine that perceivable things are really ideas and that what we call objects are really collections of these. But, because he maintained this doctrine, it seemed to him as if denying that to speak of an orange was to speak of ideas was analogous with denying that to speak of motion was to speak of moving things. And since he was (rightly) convinced that the latter denial was misleading and dangerous, it seemed as if the former must be, for the same reasons, mistaken too. And hence his assertion that objects just *are* collections of ideas became identified in his mind with his effective and vigorous dismissal of abstract ideas. But this too was really an illusion. The attack on abstract ideas appears to support his account of material objects only if we assume in advance what it is supposed to establish; and thus we are arguing in a circle.

Berkeley had put himself into a kind of strait-jacket. By questioning only part of the theory of Locke he had made it appear that to say 'There are only ideas' was a necessary consequence of his rejection of 'matter' and 'external bodies'; and by saying this, and that only ideas are perceivable, he had also made it appear that to say 'Objects are collections of ideas' was a necessary consequence of his attack on 'abstract' ideas. In this way he came to identify his critical arguments with his own most curious and startling positive doctrines. He made it seem impossible to dissent from these doctrines without falling back into mistakes which he had indeed most effectively pilloried. His own doctrines, so he believed, followed necessarily from his critical findings; if there are no 'external bodies', there are only ideas – if there are no 'abstract' ideas, objects must be collections of particular ideas. In order to escape from this strait-jacket it is essential to recognize the possibility that Berkeley could be correct in what he denies, without necessarily being correct in what he asserts; if we overlook this possibility, we shall be forever impaled on the cleft stick of false alternatives.

It follows that we can now safely abandon the difficult view that all things must always be perceived by God. If we always said only how things seemed to observers, and also wished to make statements about objects perceived by no *human* observers, then it would obviously be necessary to suppose that some non-human observer was always to hand, *to whom* it seemed as if so-and-so ... But if, as it has turned out, it is not the case that our ordinary statements are really conjunctions of statements of how things seem to observers, we need make no such supposition. Nothing prevents us from saying that there are oranges on the sideboard, but no one at all perceives them. When we drop the language of 'seeming', we drop also the mention (essential in that idiom) of observers to *whom* it seems as if ... Hence, as a general doctrine '*esse* is *percipi*' is, by these arguments at least, not proved.

*

It is a curious but I think an evident fact that Berkeley's general case owes both its plausibility and its strangeness to the same cause – namely, to his failure ever to make clear to himself and his readers what he meant by 'ideas'. When he calls these 'sensible things' and 'the things that we perceive', it seems most plausible to say that statements about the material world refer to these things and to them only; but then it seems most paradoxical to say that they exist 'only in the mind', that they are 'sensations', and that each of us perceives only 'his own ideas'. On the other hand, when we come to see that a statement of 'immediate perception' is a statement of how things *seem* to the speaker, it then looks natural enough to say that ideas are 'sensations', and 'only in the mind'; but then it at once seems wholly wrong to regard our ordinary statements as conjunctions of statements of 'immediate perception', as being only 'about ideas'. Berkeley's own statement of his case has a false simplicity, a false plausibility, and also a very startling effect, almost wholly because of these unrecognized ambiguities and complexities in his use of the word 'idea'; he chooses, no doubt unconsciously, that sense of the term which best suits the argument at any particular stage, and so constructs a case which has seemed to many people at once irrefutable and fantastic. But it is actually neither of these things; nor, when the mists are cleared away, does it even appear so.

10

THE IDEA OF EXISTENCE

I MENTIONED in the last chapter that the doctrine that *'esse* is *percipi'* depends partly, but not *entirely*, on the view that only ideas are perceivable, that material things are collections of ideas. This is certainly the most apparent, and perhaps also the most interesting, ground on which Berkeley puts forward his surprising thesis. But he has an additional and quite separate reason, which never emerges very explicitly, and which seems to have been very commonly overlooked. That there must have been some such additional reason is, however, quite clear on a little reflection.

For it is not only on the existence of material things that Berkeley holds strange views. He holds also that the 'esse' of persons, of 'mind, soul, or spirit', is 'percipere' (P.C. 429, etc.); and in the *Principles* he affirms it as a 'plain consequence that the soul always thinks', for its existence cannot possibly be 'abstracted' from its cogitation. It is clear, in fact, that he did not take the existence of material things to be 'percipi' only because of his views on what material things were; he was quite generally perplexed by the notion of existence itself, in the case of 'spirits' no less than in the case of 'bodies'. To attribute the doctrine that *'esse* is *percipi'* solely to the view that material things are collections of ideas would be to leave quite unexplained the no less peculiar doctrine that the *esse* of 'spirits' is *percipere*.

Examination of this question will show, I think, that Berkeley had not wholly taken to heart the admirable arguments of his own *Introduction*; he offends against his own good advice.

The difficulty seems to arise in the following way. Men had come to think, according to Berkeley, that from the various things they perceived, and from the various 'operations' of their own minds, they could abstract a 'most general idea', to which they proceeded to assign such names as Being, Entity, or Existence. 'I own, indeed, that those who pretend to the faculty of framing abstract general ideas do talk as if they had such an idea, which is, say they, the most abstract and general notion of all; that is, to me, the most incomprehensible of all others' (P. 81). For suppose that, according to the recipe for abstracting, we ignore, or 'think away', every feature of any given objects except their existence – what is then left in our mind's eye, what have we 'framed'? Clearly enough, nothing whatever. If I eliminate every particular feature of each object I am left with nothing; I have eliminated the entire content of my ideas. There is thus no 'abstract general idea' of Existence. Then what *particular* ideas does this word refer to? And here we discover a disconcerting fact – that there are *no such ideas at all.* Is existence a colour, one of the ideas of sight? It is not. Is it then a sound or a smell, a taste or a feeling? Obviously it is none of these. But there are no other ideas apart from these; in the whole corpus of our ideas there is, then, nothing at all to be picked out as an idea of existence. Of this Berkeley had been fully assured ever since he was making his notes in 1707. 'This I am sure, I have no such idea of Existence or annext to the Word Existence' (P.C. 671). And he finds it significant that those who profess to have it are at a loss to point it out among their ideas; for if there were any such idea at all it should be the most common and familiar of all our ideas.

Suppose now that I sit at my desk and look at my pipe. What I see, there can be no question whatever, exists; equally it cannot be questioned that I exist. But what exactly is meant by saying this? I am not saying what colour my pipe is, nor how it smells and feels to the touch; I am not, in fact, describing any of the ideas that I now have. But what is there in the situation supposed, except these ideas, of none of which I speak when I say that my pipe exists? Clearly the only point we have not yet mentioned is that *I have* these ideas, I perceive my pipe. So that, if to say of my pipe that it exists is to say anything at all, it must be and can only be to say that it *is perceived*. If the existence of my pipe is not itself one of the ideas that I now perceive, there is only one thing left that it possibly could be – namely the perception of these ideas. And what about my own existence? All that is occurring, all that can be said about me, is that I now perceive these ideas. Hence to say that my pipe exists can *only* be to say that it is perceived; and to say that I exist is to say that I perceive it. What else could the word 'exist' possibly mean? Apart from describing the 'sensible qualities' of objects, what can be said about them except that they are perceived? And apart from saying what 'operations' a spirit performs, can anything be said about it at all? The 'esse' of spirits must be to perform these operations; and of objects it must be to be perceived. Furthermore, that this is so is quite independent of the view that objects are 'collections of ideas'.

Now undoubtedly the word 'exist' is a curious word; it needs to be handled warily. There is even a serious danger in asking what seems the quite natural question, what 'to exist' means. For phrased in this way the question can be very puzzling. If we ask what 'to exist' *means*, we may be led to ask what we are saying about an object, when we say that it exists; and the answer appears to be, nothing whatever. For to say something *about* an object, is, for instance, to say what its properties are – its colour, shape, size, and so on; or to say to whom it belongs, how old it is, or how expensive to buy. But to say that it exists is not to speak in any of these ways; it is rather to say simply that *there is* something–about which we could speak in these ways though we do not do so in saying that it exists. In talking *about* an object, its existence is implied, or assumed, or presupposed, but not stated. But if we are saying nothing about an object when we say that it exists, does the word 'exist' mean anything at all?

It is also not at all easy to clear one's head by thinking of common examples of the use of 'exist'; for in fact this word is not very commonly used. Certainly Berkeley goes far astray on this matter. 'The table I write on, I say, exists, that is, I see and feel it ...' (P. 3). But we may be quite certain that, in unphilosophical moments, Berkeley never did say such a thing as this. For consider how strange a remark it would be. 'The table I write on exists.' Could there be any point in saying this? For it has no intelligible contradictory. If he had said 'The table I write on is mahogany', this might have been untrue. Perhaps the table he wrote on was not mahogany, but walnut. But could one say 'The table you write on does *not exist*'? Obviously not. I could indeed say 'You are not writing on a table' – but on a desk, say, or a bureau; or 'You are not really writing on a table' – but only pretending, or having a hallucination. But I could not first admit that you are writing on a table, by referring to 'the table you write on', and then go on to deny that that table exists. For this would be self-defeating; it would be an attempt to deny, in the words 'does not exist', what is implied to be true in the words 'the table you write on'; the sentence is hopelessly at odds with itself. But 'The table I write on exists' is hardly less tangled; for here one appears to say of the table something already implied by one's reference to it. If no such table existed it would be nonsense to refer to 'the table I write on'; but if one does refer to it, it is utterly redundant to say that it exists. It follows from this that Berkeley is wrong to add '... *that is*, I see and feel it'. For though it makes no sense to say 'The table I write on does not exist', it makes quite good sense to say that I do not see or feel that table I write on – perhaps my eyes are shut, and my hand anaesthetized, or merely (a more likely case) not touching the table.

However, Berkeley is aware that there is some important difference between '... exists' and '... is mahogany'. For his point that there is no 'idea' of existence means, I think, that existence is not a 'quality' of anything. Our ideas, he often says, are of 'sensible qualities' – colour, taste, warmth, and so on; but when we say that something exists we are not ascribing a 'quality' to it. To have any qualities at all it must already exist; we imply that it does, in saying what its qualities are; but to say that it exists is not to mention any of its qualities.

He seems then to have argued in the following way. In any

significant utterance we *must* be speaking of one or other of two types of things – either of ideas, or of 'spirits' and their 'operations'. Now to speak of ideas is to speak of the 'qualities' of things that we perceive; but if to say that some object exists is not to ascribe to it any quality, it *can only* be to say that there is some spirit by whom that object is perceived. This is all that is left for the word 'exist' to do; if it is not used to ascribe a 'quality', it must be used to record the operation of some 'spirit' – namely, perception.

The question that seems to have defeated Berkeley is this: If I am not ascribing qualities to an object, nor speaking of the operations of a 'spirit', what could I possibly be doing in the words that I utter? Because, when I say that something exists, I am not doing the former, I *must* be doing the latter. For there seems to be nothing else that I could be doing.

An example may help to loosen this knot. Suppose that a librarian is at work in a library. His task is to compile a descriptive catalogue of the books; and for his own purposes he also keeps a diary in which he records his own experiences in doing so. He works in the following way. As he comes across each book he writes in his diary (say) '2.30 P.M. Inspecting *Treasure Island*'; he then writes the title, *Treasure Island*, on a card, and writes on the same card a brief description of the book. Suppose we now ask the question – 'When he is not describing the books, nor recording his own experiences, what can he possibly be doing? And here the answer is obvious – the other thing that he may be doing is recording the fact that a certain book is in the library, by writing its title on a card. He may be recording the *existence* of a certain book.

Here, then, we have three sorts of information. The librarian's diary tells us that he saw and inspected certain books. The descriptions on the cards record the 'qualities' of the books. And the fact that *there is* a certain book in the library is shown by the fact that its title is written on the card. The fact that there is no 'idea' of existence appears in this example as the fact that nothing *in* any of the books makes it correct to write their titles on a card; nor does the description of their contents include the *statement* that those books are in the library. And the conclusion that '*esse* is *percipi*' is analogous with the (here obviously mistaken) view that only the librarian's diary tells us what books are in the library.

Suppose now that I say that there are tigers at the zoo. If I am not describing the tigers, nor saying that the tigers are perceived, what can I be saying? I am, we might say, *listing* the contents of the Zoo. To say that there are tigers at the Zoo is comparable with writing the word 'Tigers' in cataloguing the Zoo's contents; and this is clearly different *both* from saying what the tigers are like *and* from saying that one sees or has seen or will see the tigers. In fact listing, and asserting existence, are curiously similar. The librarian would be making nonsense of his task if he listed a book on a card in his catalogue, and then wrote on the card 'This book is not in the library'. And similarly I would be breaking the rules of language if I said 'The tigers at the Zoo do not exist'. In each case we put, in the place where some description should be, a phrase that has no business to be there.

I think that Berkeley was misled in this connexion by the vagueness of his claim that 'language and knowledge are all about ideas, words stand for nothing else'. He had two excellent motives in saying this. First, he wished to establish the absurdity of Locke's notion that we could know of and speak of a completely unperceivable 'external world'; and also, he wished to insist that words like 'motion' and 'force' get their sense from the observable behaviour of moving things, and do not refer to elusive 'abstract' entities. But the claim that 'language is about ideas', taken together with the notion that our ideas are of 'sensible qualities', inevitably seemed to make a problem out of any sentences which are not used to ascribe qualities. Existential statements are the most conspicuous example; but statements of number and relation puzzle Berkeley no less. If I say 'There are 1,500 books in the library' I am not saying what sort of books are in the library, I am not saying what 'qualities' the books possess. (There is no 'idea' of number.) And so, just as a place for existence has to be found

in 'the operations of a spirit', number also is said to be a
'creature of the mind'. Again, if I say *Treasure Island* is next
to *Kidnapped*', I ascribe no qualities to either book. Hence, we
have no 'idea' of relation; and Berkeley observes, obscurely
enough, that all relations 'include an act of the mind'. In all
these cases he seems to be faced with the same problem. If all
language (except that in which we speak of 'spirits') is 'about
ideas', in the narrow sense of 'used to ascribe sensible qualities', it seems that all the array of statements which do not
ascribe qualities to things must be construed as recording the
operations of a spirit. Existential statements record the perception of ideas; statements of number record how ideas are
'arbitrarily put together by the mind'; statements of relation
record some (not further specified) 'act of the mind'; and so
on. Each of these doctrines leads to intolerable paradox and
oddity. But so long as Berkeley stuck to the strange notion
that to talk of 'ideas' can only be to ascribe sensible qualities,
he did not see how anything else could be said. The mind
seemed to offer the only home to statements not of the simplest
descriptive type.

It must, however, be remembered that Berkeley had come
very near to a more profitable view of these matters. He had
already seen that what makes a general term general is not
that it stands for a special kind of idea, but that it is *used* in a
particular way. He had seen also that we do not always use
words for conveying information about objects. But it seems
not to have occurred to him to ask quite generally of any
word 'How is it *used*?' Instead he asked 'To what *particular*
ideas do we use this word to refer?' And although this question served him well enough in his discussion of such words
as 'triangle' and 'motion', it led him seriously astray in discussing such expressions as 'exist', 'to the left of', and '1,500'.
For such words do not 'refer to particular ideas' at all, in the
narrow sense he gave to that phrase. And so he was obliged to
fall back on another use of words that he recognized – their
use in speaking of 'spirits' and their 'operations'.

*

Berkeley's observation about 'spirits' have received, perhaps, more attention than they deserve; for the fact is that he had formed hardly any views at all on problems about the mind and its doings.[10] It is clear enough that what first engaged his serious interest was 'our knowledge of the external world', problems about perception and the nature of physical objects on which he found himself in such sharp disagreement with Locke. It was with this group of problems in mind that he first laid down his principle that 'knowledge and language are all about ideas'. But could he have maintained this principle in discussing our knowledge and language about people and their minds?

At one time he certainly thought that this could be done. In P.C. 580–581 he wrote (anticipating Hume) that 'Mind is a congeries of Perceptions. . . . Say you the Mind is not the Perceptions but that thing which perceives. I answer you are abused by the words that and thing, these are vague empty words without a meaning.' But in the *Principles* he insists that the mind is something 'entirely distinct' from ideas, something which 'exercizes divers operations' about them. We have, he says, no 'idea' of 'spirit'. How then can he allow that we know what that word means? He replies that we have a 'notion' of spirit; but this is scarcely an answer to the question. For by saying that we have a notion of spirit he confessedly means to say no more than simply that 'we understand the meaning of the word'. This perfunctory introduction of the word 'notion' cannot fairly be taken, as it has sometimes been taken, as a retraction of his attack on 'matter' and 'abstract ideas', for he never suggests that we have 'notions' of anything *except* spirits and their operations; however, it must be admitted that he does not provide us with any clear account of such notions as these.

We need not pursue in very great detail problems on which Berkeley had so little to say. It must, however, be pointed out that, if he had seriously tried to say more, he would surely have encountered numerous difficulties. He appears in the end to have accepted Locke's opinion that a mind is an 'im-

material substance', but not to have taken serious account of
Locke's further contention that this idea is no less obscure
than that of 'matter' itself. His own words, indeed, suggest a
latent inconsistency. For he says that the *'esse'* of a spirit is
'percipere', sometimes *'velle'* or *'agere'*; and, as his perplexed
correspondent Johnson inquired, how can an action be the
'esse' of a substance? Surely to speak of something as a substance is to claim that *it* can somehow be distinguished from
what it *does*. And if Berkeley did not feel able to make this
claim, should he not have concluded that the mind is a 'collection of acts', just as an object is a 'collection of ideas'? But
here again he would have run into difficulties. For, as he
rightly points out in the *First Dialogue*, perception is not an
action at all. What account then would he be able to give of
his assumed distinction between an idea, and the mind in
which that idea is said to exist? Perhaps he would have had
to return to his early suggestion that 'Mind is a congeries of
Perceptions', and to maintain that an object is a different *kind*
of 'congeries' of the very same elements. If so, he would have
anticipated the views of Hume and of Lord Russell. Berkeley
would not, however, have wished to do this. For one thing, he
seems to have felt that such a view might possibly yield a
tenable analysis of perception, but not of 'volition'. But
chiefly, he would have been embarrassed by its implications
about the existence of God and of the soul – implications by
which neither Lord Russell nor Hume appear to have been
oppressed. It is perhaps permissible to guess that the long
delay in publication of his projected second volume, of which
so many years later he lost the unfinished manuscript, was
due in part to his inability to harmonize the outlook of his
early work with his theological and metaphysical beliefs. In
any event he did not do this, and indeed it seems likely that it
could not have been done.

11

SCIENCE AND MATHEMATICS

Iᴛ is natural that Berkeley should have thought it necessary
to say something about mathematics and about science, or
in the contemporary phrase, 'natural philosophy'. For he believed that in each of these inquiries much time and labour
was wasted to no effect, owing to the pernicious influence of
the doctrine of abstract ideas; and he also expected that ap-
peals would be made to them in supposed refutation of his
philosophical views. It seems that scientists are naturally inclined to agree with Locke; and certainly Berkeley's denial of
the existence of 'matter' must have seemed inconsistent with
the findings of contemporary physics, the so-called 'corpuscular philosophy'. Also, both scientists and mathematicians
appeared to assume the existence of unperceived, and indeed
unperceivable, entities; and how could this be, if 'esse is percipi'? There is some uncertainty in Berkeley's early treatment
of these topics, but in the end he arrived at views of remarkable originality, insight, and interest.

*

From the first Berkeley showed an admirable lack of patience
with attempts to bring science to the aid of philosophical
scepticism. Such attempts have long been, and still remain,
the stock-in-trade of those who seek to 'popularize' the sciences.
The usual suggestion is that plain men are constantly mistaken
in the simplest matters; 'We are miserably bantered, say they,
by our senses, and amused only with the outside and show of
things.' I think, for example, that my pen is a familiar object,
tangible, solid, and red; but 'science shows' that it is really
none of these things. In truth there are only certain 'particles',
spatially discrete, odourless, colourless, and agitated, which

(in some way that we can never fully comprehend) so operate upon my brain that I *seem* to see something solid and red. But here I am deceived by the 'show' of things. 'Their internal constitution, their true and real nature, you are utterly in the dark as to *that*.' It can however be said with certainty that 'they have none of them any thing in themselves, like those sensible qualities by us perceived'. Our benighted state may be good enough for most purposes. For 'ordinary practice does not require a nicety of speculative knowledge. Hence the vulgar retain their mistakes, and for all that, make a shift to bustle through the affairs of life. But philosophers know better things.' They know that the real physical world is in most respects, perhaps in all, utterly unlike what it seems to our senses to be; we are 'bantered' with grossly misleading perceptions. All this will be familiar enough to modern readers of popular expositions of science.

Berkeley's reply to this is that it rests on a radical misunderstanding both of ordinary language and of science. It is, he maintains, absurd to suggest that, when I claim to have a solid red pen in my hand, science could show that I am always mistaken. For the word 'pen', whatever a scientist might say, is ordinarily used to refer to just this sort of object; and the adjectives 'red' and 'solid' are used to characterize things of exactly this kind. It cannot be said that the 'real' pen is something quite unlike what I see and touch; for the word 'pen' is really, properly applicable to what I *do* see and touch, not to collocations of particles or atoms that I do not. No doubt what the scientist says of his particles is true; but then, in the proper use of the words 'pen', 'red', and 'solid', it is also true that I have in my hand a solid red pen. I should be 'bantered' by my senses if what I took to be red turned out to be really brown, or if there turned out to be no pen at all where I took this pen to be; but if the pen continues to serve all the purposes of a pen, always looks red in normal light, and is always there when I reach out my hand to pick it up, I am of course not 'bantered' in any way. I do not indeed see or feel the particles of which the scientist speaks; but then these are

not pens nor parts of pens; about them I say or believe nothing false, for I am not speaking or thinking of them at all. In
this conclusion, Berkeley suggests, even the professed scientific sceptic agrees. He may *say* that we are 'utterly in the dark'
– but 'suppose you are going to write, would you not call for
pen, ink, and paper, like another man; and do you not know
what it is you call for?' It is indeed a melancholy thing to be
'influenced by false principles to that degree as to mistrust our
senses, and think we know nothing of those things which we
perfectly comprehend'. Whatever may be meant by saying
that I am ignorant of the 'true and real nature' of things, I
certainly know a pen when I see one. (This topic is well discussed in the *Third Dialogue*.)

But if so, what are we to make of the 'corpuscular philosophy' itself? If the scientist is wrong in thinking himself
'ignorant of what everybody else knows perfectly well', what
has he discovered in his inquiries? Are his theories mere
nonsense? On this point Berkeley is at first undecided. He says
that 'to endeavour to explain the production of colour or
sounds by figure, motion, magnitude and the like must needs
be labour in vain. And accordingly we see the attempts of
that kind are not at all satisfactory' (p. 102). Again, in the
Second Dialogue, 'what connexion is there between a motion
in the nerves, and the sensations of sound or colour in the
mind? Or how is it possible these should be the effect of that?'
And Hylas is made to reply that he 'could never think it had
so little in it, as now it seems to have'. Berkeley observes, with
misplaced satisfaction, 'I need not say, how many hypotheses
and speculations are left out, and how much the study of
Nature is abridged by this doctrine'. Not merely abridged,
one might think, but eliminated; and how could this be
advantageous?

But this is not Berkeley's final view. His real contention is
not that the theories of scientists are useless or mistaken, but
rather that they are often misunderstood. They should not be
thought of as *contradicting* ordinary beliefs, but as *system-
atizing* them; and also, not as *explaining* events, but as 're-

ducing them to general rules'. Behind this last point, of
course, is his peculiar view on the 'real' nature of causation.
We may at our own risk 'speak with the vulgar' and say that
scientists discover the causes of events; but if we 'think with
the learned' we should admit that this is not strictly true. The
real 'efficient cause' of any event can be 'no other than the
will of a spirit', and with this the scientist has, professionally
at least, nothing to do. The true view, in Berkeley's opinion,
is that the scientist 'considers signs rather than causes'. By
experiment and hypothesis and further experiment, he discovers 'analogies, harmonies, and agreements' between events
– for example, between the falling of bodies to the ground, the
motion of the tides, and the orbits of the planets. These (at
first sight) quite disparate phenomena he finds can be 'reduced
to general rules', which 'extend our prospect beyond what is
present, and near to us, and enable us to make very probable
conjectures, touching things that may have happened at very
great distances of time and place, as well as to predict things
to come; which sort of endeavour towards omniscience is
much affected by the mind' (p. 105). Thus the scientist ob-
tains 'a greater largeness of comprehension' than other men.
He is able to see a particular phenomenon as 'a particular
example of a general rule or law of Nature', and thus he
thinks it 'justly accounted for'; but as for the real *explanation*
of things, this is 'not so much as aimed at'.

There seems to be no very good reason why Berkeley should
have insisted that reduction to 'general rules' is not explanation. He thinks that to call it so may induce us to overlook
the constantly exercised Power of God, and perhaps even to
think of physical things as exerting will-power or 'agency'
upon each other. But having warned us of these pitfalls, he
sometimes allows that the scientist does explain phenomena.
However, he also mentions, with some hesitation, the possibility of a different kind of explanation. If the true cause of
every event is the will of a 'wise and good agent', it should in
theory be possible to explain events by reference to this agent's
motives or intentions, thus really saying *why* events occur as

they do. Of this reintroduction of 'final causes' Berkeley is only prepared to say that 'I must confess, I see no reason why [this] should not be thought one good way of accounting' for events, and 'altogether worthy of a philosopher'. But the difficulty would be that we could hardly be sure that we had adequately judged the agent's motives; indeed, a claim to complete understanding might be thought to savour of impiety. But if no such attempt is ever to be made, Berkeley's 'real' explanations of the course of nature will remain somewhat vacuous. To say only that all is due to 'the will of a spirit' is to offer no explanation at all.

If, then, the scientist is concerned to discover 'general rules' in the workings of nature, enabling him to say what states of affairs are 'signs' of what others, it would seem that Berkeley is right in his claim that from his philosophy 'no reason can be drawn, why the history of Nature should not still be studied.' But what about 'esse is percipi'? The exponents of the 'corpuscular philosophy' appeared to speak of entities which they declared to be 'insensible'; and how could Berkeley accept such talk as this? Occasionally, both in the *Principles* and the *Dialogues*, as seems inclined to dismiss it as mere verbage, implying that the scientists' 'rules' can be adequately stated in terms only of ordinary objects – of falling stones, moving planets and rising tides, and so on. These he could accept as 'collections of ideas'. But later (for example in the *Theory of Vision Vindicated* of 1733) he recognized that the 'nature and motion of light' and the theory of Optics were commonly discussed in terms of the motion of 'insensible particles', and he recognized also the value of this proceeding. Now he could no doubt have maintained that these so-called 'insensible particles' were in fact perceived by God and thus no exception to his principles; but he was not satisfied with this rather arbitrary-looking solution. Instead, with the greatest insight and originality, he relied on a distinction between the *observed facts* of science, and the *theories* constructed to comprehend them. (He sets out this view in his short tract *De Motu*, published in 1721.)

His argument runs, briefly, as follows. What the scientist actually observes raises no difficulties; he observes the behaviour of ordinary objects. But he seeks also to formulate rules, or 'laws of nature', which will allow him to represent particular phenomena as cases of some general rule. Now the ideal is to formulate such rules with mathematical precision and the widest possible generality; and the attainment of this ideal is enormously assisted if we *suppose* light (for instance) to consist in the emission of 'insensible particles'. With the help of this supposition, a wide variety of observed phenomena can be subsumed under relatively simple rules, and both the formulation of and the inferences from these rules can be stated in mathematical terms. Thus are devised a number of special concepts – 'particle', 'atom' and the like – which are used, not in order to describe any observed *facts*, but in stating the general theory by which it is sought to account for those facts. 'They serve the purpose of mechanical science and reckoning; but to be of service to reckoning and mathematical demonstrations is one thing, to set forth the nature of things is another.' The scientist has not really discovered that *there are* 'insensible particles'; it is rather that it suits his purposes as a theorist to *say* so. We may indeed say of them whatever we please, so long as some theoretical purpose is served by what we say. If our theories can be most easily formulated by supposing all such particles to be spherical, let us by all means say they are spherical; but this is to simplify our theory, and not to 'set forth the nature of things'. It follows that there ought to be no conflict between the scientist and the plain man. The plain man says that grass is green; the scientist ascribes no colour to his 'particles'. But they do not contradict each other. For the plain man is speaking in ordinary language of what he *sees*, the scientist is using the language in which he *theorizes*. These two ways of speaking cannot conflict.[11]

This view would naturally lead us to expect that, in the course of scientific progress, the old concepts would be abandoned and theories stated in new terms. And this is actually the case. The 'particles' and 'corpuscles' of the early eighteenth century do not appear in the theories of the present day. Moreover, Berkeley's argument rightly implies that it would be misleading to say that we now know there are no such things; it is rather that, as theories and experimental findings develop, it is found convenient to state laws and 'rules' in different terms.

Berkeley saw what tangles the scientists produced by their lack of understanding of their own work; they were in his day terribly 'embrangled' in the web of their own vocabulary. Their theorizing had produced a mass of strange terms – 'conation', 'impetus', 'solicitation', 'primitive force', 'dead forces', 'virtues', and 'essences' – the *use* of which they seemed to have forgotten, asking instead impossible questions about their 'true meanings'. Berkeley diagnosed the fatal blunder as that of expecting always to find some *thing* as the 'true meaning' of every substantive. Of course this 'occasioned infinite mistakes'. 'Torricelli says that force and impetus are abstract and subtle things and quintessences which are included in corporeal substance as in the magic vase of Circe' – and naturally thought this very mysterious (*De Motu*, 8). Another much disputed question concerned so very familiar a phenomenon as motion. When one moving thing strikes another, is the resulting motion of the second *numerically identical* with the motion of the first? Does the *same* motion *pass* from one to the other, or is motion annihilated in one and a new motion instantaneously generated in the other? This is, Berkeley forcibly points out, a foolish dispute. We cannot sensibly argue about the 'identity' of a 'motion', as if it were a kind of object, like a baton, handed on from one thing to another. If we know how the objects themselves move, we already know all that is to be known. Force, motion, impetus, inertia, and the rest, if treated as 'subtle quintessences' concealed in and mysteriously conveyed from one object to another, are 'the mere shadows of scholastic things'. There may be no harm, or even great profit, in using such terms, provided we always remember what they are *used for*. The scientist in fact has two concerns – the actual observed behaviour of things, and the formulation of theories to 'account for' this, that is, to subsume it under the simplest and most general rules. Metaphorical terms like 'force' and 'attraction' should be used only in order to facilitate this work. Nothing but confusion can result from the idea that they name mysterious 'agents' or 'entities'. 'Just as by the application of geometrical theorems the sizes of particular bodies are measured, so also by the application of the universal theorems of mechanics, the movements of any part of the mundane system ... become known and determined. And that is the sole mark at which the physicist must aim' (*De Motu*, 38). The introduction of special scientific concepts is 'of the first utility for theories and formulations'; but if their purpose is forgotten, we may slide back into 'the obscure subtlety of the schoolmen', into a fog of insoluble perplexities and mystification. We may even, like Hylas, think ourselves 'ignorant of what everybody else knows perfectly well'.

*

Berkeley's treatment of mathematics shows marked similarities with his discussion of the sciences. Here too he was inclined to think, in his early days, that large parts of mathematics were simply mistaken and could on his principles be 'abridged', or even abandoned; but later he comes to concentrate rather on the proper *understanding* of mathematics.

In the *Principles* (119 and the following paragraphs) he is, as one would naturally expect, concerned to combat the idea that arithmetic treats of invisible, intangible, 'abstract' things called Numbers. He rightly points out that mathematicians (and others) are tempted to think of numerals as names of elusive, abstract things; and he regards this as needless and even pernicious nonsense. The danger is that some mathematicians, fired with the idea that they are probing the secrets of some high non-empirical realm, may 'dream of mighty mysteries' hidden in arithmetic, and may even 'attempt the explication of natural things' thereby. (There have been and are many curious examples of such infatuated numerology.)

Berkeley enjoins us to bear in mind the origins and the use of arithmetic; we shall then realize what is actually involved in computation. There are, in the first place, groups or collections of things, men or sheep or whatever they may be, that are to be 'numbered'; and there are counters, or strokes, or other signs, each 'made to signify ... some one thing of whatever kind they had occasion to reckon.' The system of strokes or signs then becomes elaborated into a conventional notation, and rules are formed for 'computing in signs'; and by a 'standing analogy' the signs can be interpreted as statements of number, enabling us 'rightly to sum up, divide, and proportion the things themselves that we intend to number.'

Furthermore, Berkeley was clearly aware of the difference between using arithmetic in 'reckoning', counting, and so on, and doing 'pure' mathematics. In the latter we 'regard not the *things* but the *signs*'. (He rightly does not say that numbers *are* signs.) We have the very clear and 'compendious' Arabic notation, and by following the rules for manipulation of these signs we can execute all kinds of calculations, 'deduce theorems from a great height of evidence', and indulge in countless 'high flights and abstraction'. But 'the reason why we can demonstrate so well about signs is that they are perfectly arbitrary and in our power, made at pleasure' (p.c. 732). And this activity, in Berkeley's opinion, becomes 'jejune and trifling' if we have in mind no practical problem. It should be always 'subordinate to practice'; for he thinks mathematics without application of no more importance than a jig-saw puzzle. This, he thinks, would be generally admitted (many mathematicians do admit it), if we understood what mathematicians are doing. They are not laying bare the secrets of the Realm of Numbers, but forming from one set of characters, by certain rules, another set, and so on – as if 'a man was all day making hard knots on purpose to unty them again', or devising difficult problems at chess so that he might have the satisfaction of solving them. Algebra he regarded as being, in itself, more 'trifling' still; for 'algebraic Species or letters are denominations of Denominations' (p.c. 758) – signs of signs, letters representing numerals, and hence doubly removed from the affairs of men. Skill in such calculation is not 'speculative knowledge'; ' 'tis what any one of common sense might attain to by repeated acts' (P.C. 368).

These vigorous protests against absorption in calculi for their own sake are understandable, and doubtless salutary up to a point. But it would be easy to cite instances of valuable mathematical work which was not known *in advance* to be of practical importance. If mathematicians never indulged in their 'high flights' except for some clearly envisaged practical purpose, applied mathematics would itself be the poorer. It might even be held that progress in mathematics is assisted by the quaint beliefs about numbers held by some mathematicians; the trouble these may cause arises outside mathematics itself. Some mathematicians might feel damped and depressed by the mere elaboration of sets of signs, and require the stimulus of some number-mythology. But at any rate Berkeley insists that this *is* mythology. 'Take away the signs from Arithmetic and Algebra, and pray what remains?' (P.C. 767.)

His early views on geometry were strikingly different, and have earned him a good deal of not wholly undeserved ridicule. He seems to have thought, naturally perhaps, that geometry was essentially *about the sensible world* and could not be assimilated to the pure calculi of arithmetic and algebra. He recognized, of course, that it was general; in proving theorems, for instance, about triangles, the geometer is not referring only to the particular figure he draws in his diagram, nor yet to any abstract 'triangle in general'; he is speaking generally about triangles, of any figure that fits the definition of 'triangle'. (The particular diagram is used as an *example* of the whole class of triangles.) But the proof still refers, in Berkeley's opinion, to particular figures and particular things – not indeed to this one or that in particular, but still to any actual triangular *thing*.

But it is clear that on this view we soon run into difficulties. Consider, for instance, the geometer's definitions. A point is said to have 'position but no magnitude', a line 'length but no breadth', and so on. Berkeley has to regard these definitions as simply mistaken. For suppose a line drawn on any surface, in any medium; however finely drawn it may be, it is simply not true to say that it has *no* breadth. And a point, however delicately made, must certainly have *some* magnitude. There are, in Berkeley's view, '*minima sensibilia*' – the very smallest things of which we can be sensibly aware; and it must, he thinks, be of these that the geometer intends to speak when he speaks of 'points'. But if so his definition is wrong. A *minimum sensibile* has indeed no parts, for it is itself a *minimum*; but anything which is a *sensibile* must be of *some* magnitude. It follows from this that we cannot say that a line is composed of an infinite number of points. This would be all very well if points had no magnitude; but since this is not so, any line must contain a finite and definite number of points. The only line that could be composed of infinitely many points, or that could be infinitely divisible, would be a line of infinite length; but this is a meaningless supposition. Nothing is actually infinitely divisible, and mathematicians are quite mistaken in speaking as if this could be so.

But there are consequences still more curious. If every line is composed of some definite number of points, and these points are *minima*, not further divisible, there will certainly be some lines which cannot be bisected. For if the number of points in the line is odd, it cannot be so divided that the two segments are equal; one segment must always contain at least one point more than the other. Again, Berkeley thinks it need not be the case that the diagonal of a square is incommensurable with the sides; for each contains some definite number of points, and the proportions between these numbers could be found. Furthermore, Leibnitz was certainly mistaken in maintaining (relying on 'infinite divisibility') that there is a one-to-one correspondence between the points in lines of different lengths; for the longer line *must* contain more points than the shorter. In one note Berkeley goes so far as to say that a geometrical proof that two lines are equal might be refuted by inspection of the lines with a microscope. On the whole, it cannot be said that Berkeley was right in thinking that his treatment of geometry would 'abridge the labour of study', or make that science more 'clear' and 'compendious'.

In the *Essay* Berkeley had held, consistently enough, that the subject-matter of geometry is 'tangible extension' only, not visible extension. Points are *minima tangibilia*, triangles and the rest are tangible shapes. In the *Principles* he no longer accords any special status to 'tangible objects'; geometry is said to treat of visible and tangible extension indifferently; and points are the *minima sensibilia* of either sight or touch. But in either case it is hard to make sense of this notion. What is the very smallest thing that can be seen or touched? It seems that there could only be *ad hoc* answers. For our powers of discrimination vary, in the case of seeing, with the degree of illumination, with the colour of the background, and with the general health and degree of fatigue of the observer. And the case of *tangibilia* is yet more complex; here it would be essential to ask, with what part of the body the supposed 'point' is to be touched. For not only are some parts much more sensitive than others; there are many points on the human skin which are not sensitive at all, so that a very small object might be felt at one attempt and completely missed at another. And is Berkeley consistent in all of this with his own principles? He says that there is in an idea nothing that is not actually discerned in it. But certainly a line drawn on paper is not *seen* as composed of a definite number of points; it looks continuous. It is not only that one has no idea how to make even a reasonable guess at the *number* of points in a line; it does not look as if it were made up of points at all. And should not Berkeley have concluded that it *is* not made up of points?

It seems clear that Berkeley is really committed to wreaking more havoc in geometry than he recognized. There may be points, but it will certainly be very hard to identify them. Lines are perhaps not composed of points at all; and also, is any line straight or of minimal breadth? Are there actually any geometrical circles? At best some parts of geometry could be regarded as *roughly* true; but much of it would have to be rejected as false, much as dubious, and much as nonsense.

It is perhaps not surprising that Berkeley should have adopted this disastrously empirical view of geometry. For the geometer does speak of points, lines, and angles; and these words really do have application in empirical contexts. We do use them to refer to things that we see and touch, and it is natural to assume that the geometer uses them in the same way. But it soon becomes clear that his definitions do not fit the points and lines and angles that we see; since, however, the deductive development of geometry depends in large measure on these definitions, we cannot say that they are wrong without playing havoc with the theorems deduced. A more reasonable alternative course would be to regard geometry itself as an abstract calculus, *applicable* (more or less roughly) to the physical world but not descriptive of its properties. To the deductive validity of geometry it does not matter in the least that the original definitions are said to be of 'points' and so on; this gives a clue to the field of application of the calculus, but also gives it a misleadingly empirical look.

And in fact Berkeley in later years did come to adopt this alternative view. In *De Motu* he observes that 'geometers for the sake of their art make use of many devices which they themselves cannot describe nor find in the nature of things'; and so far from denouncing this as a mistake, he says that it is 'of first utility'. The 'geometers' fictions made by mathematical abstraction' are of the greatest value, 'even if in the truth of things, and in bodies actually existing, they would be looked for in vain.' On one such point he explicitly contradicts his opinion of fourteen years before. In his notebook he had written, 'What do the Mathematicians mean by Considering Curves as Polygons? either they are Polygons or they are not. If they are why do they give them the Name of Curves? ... If they are not polygons I think it absurd to use polygons in their stead' (P.C. 527). But in *De Motu* (61) he takes a different view: 'A curve can be considered as consisting of an infinite number of straight lines. ... That hypothesis is useful in geometry.' Here even the use of the concept of infinity, formerly so much condemned, is taken to be legitimate.

In the *Analyst* also, published in 1734, we find a similar view. Here he is still the critic of mathematicians, but not for the old reasons. He is examining chiefly the notion of 'infinitesimals'; but he does not now simply affirm that there is in actual fact nothing that is infinitely small; he objects that in Newton's doctrine of 'fluxions' there are *logical* blunders and incoherencies. He makes here the important point that the notion of infinity raises no difficulties purely as a matter of notation; a series of integers may be increased, and a series of fractions diminished, without limit. But he rightly protested that contemporary expositors of mathematics made strange and logically incoherent assumptions. They would first introduce infinitesimals as if they were positive though exceedingly small quantities, and then cancel or 'reject' them on the ground that they were not positive quantities at all. It was as if they regarded an 'infinitesimal quantity' as lying somewhere between a positive quantity and zero, and in fact assumed it to be the one or the other according to convenience. Newton himself, as Berkeley might in fairness have remarked, suspected that there were logical tangles in his doctrine; but his zealous (and far less able) followers were enraged by Berkeley's intervention – there ensued a great outburst of mostly mediocre controversial writing. But Berkeley's logical scruples were not overcome; and he justified his criticism on the ground that a geometer's work must be assessed solely by the touchstone of logic. 'It must be remembered that I am not concerned about the truth of your theorems, but only about the way of coming at them; whether it be legitimate or illegitimate, clear or obscure, scientific or tentative. To prevent all possibility of your mistaking me, I beg leave to repeat and insist, that I consider the geometrical analyst as a logician, i.e., so far forth as he reasons and argues; and his mathematical conclusions, not in themselves, but in their premises; not as true or false, useful or significant, but as derived from such principles, and by such inferences' (*Analyst.* 20). The heat of the controversy was intensified by Berkeley's ostensible motive for launching it – a desire to show that mathematics itself contained 'mysteries' no less obscure than those of religion, and so that it could not support 'infidelity' by its pretensions to absolute clarity and evidence. But this is hardly a serious point; the interest of the discussion is that it shows how far Berkeley had moved from his curious early views on geometry, and that in the end he became in this field also a pioneer of 'Formalism'.

12

LATER YEARS

The Principles of Human Knowledge was published in Dublin in May 1710; and thus, by the time he was twenty-five years old, Berkeley had already completed his most important work. It soon became clear that few readers were disposed to take his views seriously. The difficulty is that, at first glance, he seems to be denying that anything is really real, solid, and substantial – 'matter does not exist'; a second glance to a great extent dispels this impression; but a third glance repeats in a modified form the verdict of the first. Most of his amused or irritated readers no doubt never went beyond the surface impression, that simple and familiar facts were enough to show that Berkeley was absurdly wrong – *of course* there are material things, *of course* we are not all dreaming. To Berkeley this seemed the crudest misrepresentation; 'whoever reads my book with due attention will plainly see that there is a direct opposition between the principles contained in it and those of the sceptics, and that I question not the existence of anything that we perceive by our senses.' In saying 'Matter does not exist' he means actually to *defend* our ordinary convictions against an insidious philosophical blunder. The question is not 'Do trees and chairs and houses really exist?'; for *of course* they do. Undoubtedly. The question is 'What does it *mean* to say that they exist?' No sane man would ask whether there *is* any distinction between appearance and reality, for of course there is. But Berkeley asks, What *is* the distinction? There is nothing 'sceptical' in either of these questions. His opponents, if anyone, are sceptics: for they answer these questions wrongly, and even make them appear unanswerable.

But then, if we take our third glance at the argument,

Berkeley's case looks less sturdy again and less true to 'common sense'. For he is certainly unorthodox in his view on the meaning of 'existence'; existence 'without a mind' is not, in spite of his confident assertions, a self-contradictory notion. And if we consider his language of 'ideas' really carefully (more carefully than he considered it himself), we shall find that he would make it impossible for us to *say* what is really the case; he allows us only to say how things seem. Certainly he is not refusing to recognize any distinction between appearance and reality; he does in fact analyse it as the distinction between consistent 'seeming as if', and purely temporary, accidental, or subjective 'seeming as if'. But this is *not enough*. A philosopher who allows us only to say how things seem, even how they consistently seem to everybody, is taking out of our hands the means of saying how things *are*, what *is* the case. A world inhabited only by speakers of Berkeley's language might look and feel and sound exactly the same as the world in which we now find ourselves; but life in such a world (as Berkeley really knew quite well) would somehow possess a very different atmosphere. There would have to be constant mention of 'spirits' (who have the 'ideas' that are spoken of); and not, as there now is, of a world that we think of as being quite independent of the presence in or absence from it of 'spirits'. Berkeley would have thought this a desirable change; but at least it must be allowed that it would be a *change*, and not, as he so often tries to persuade us, merely a more explicit version of our current practices. His critics were right in feeling uneasy, even if they did not see exactly why they were right.

*

Berkeley left Ireland early in 1713, in order to publish his *Three Dialogues* in London, and in general to see something of the world. Though his books had won few converts to his doctrine, he was accepted at once into distinguished literary circles. He was fortunate in being quite free from political prejudices; no party label could be fastened to him. In a pamphlet of this period, *Passive Obedience*, he manoeuvres with great dexterity. 'I shall endeavour to prove', he says, 'that there is an absolute unlimited non-resistance, or passive obedience, due to the supreme civil power' – a view most gratifying to Tories. But, he proceeds, we have also the right, indeed the duty, to inquire into the claim of a 'power' to be the *supreme* power; for 'tyranny' lacks God's sanction, and ought to be resisted. It is accordingly not surprising that he soon found friends in every party. He was the friend of Swift, of Addison and Steele and Pope, and took part in the affairs of the *Tatler*, the *Guardian*, and the *Spectator*. Swift speaks of Berkeley as ' a very ingenious man and a great philosopher'; Berkeley, perhaps more controversially, thought Swift, 'one of the best natured and agreeable men in the world'. Swift, then at the height of his influence, introduced Berkeley to the Court, and also to the Earl of Peterborough – an introduction which led to his visiting the continent later in the year. In the late autumn of 1713 he set out for Sicily as chaplain to the Earl. It is probable that, in Paris, he met and had some conversation with Malebranche; but the story that his dialectical skill and vigour brought on the almost instant death of that philosopher is, though striking, unfortunately an invention.

He returned to England in the summer of 1714, intending apparently to go back to Dublin when his leave of absence expired in the following year. (He was aware that some had been heard 'to murmur at my absence in the College'.) But in fact he did not go; it seems that he had now begun to take an interest in his own advancement in the Church. His first tentative steps, however, came to nothing, and in the autumn of 1716 he went abroad once more as tutor and travelling companion to the son of the Bishop of Clogher. For the next four years he remained abroad in this post, apparently wholly absorbed in the ordinary pursuits of the inquiring tourist and sightseer.

In 1721 he was at last back in Trinity College, having in his long absence become a Senior Fellow. But now he was seriously concerned with the question of preferment; and after some canvassing and manoeuvring (more by the College on his behalf than by himself – he was a bashful intriguer) he was appointed Dean of Derry in 1724. At about the same time he was, to his amazement, left £3,000 by Hester Van Homrigh (Swift's 'Vanessa'), 'a lady to whom I was a perfect stranger', who had apparently altered her will in his favour on the occasion of her violent quarrel with Swift. Although this surprising event did not impair his friendship with Swift, it involved him in several years of troublesome business and correspondence; and he might have regretted the whole affair, if he had not at this time begun to lay ambitious (and costly) plans for founding a college in Bermuda. This scheme came to take complete precedence in his thoughts over his responsibilities to his Deanery; and it was not until it had become hopelessly held up that he turned again to philosophical writing.

Berkeley himself was inspired with the highest dreams. Bermuda is equidistant from the points on the American mainland from which he proposed to draw his colonial and Indian students; it had, he was assured, the perfect climate; and it afforded no opportunities for his pupils, once arrived, to deviate into trade. The colonists and (it was hoped) the Indians were to take the degree of M.A., come to London if they wished and be there ordained, and would then return to their own people equipped as missionaries and apostles of culture.

However, one neglected fact would have been enough to dispel these visions. The island is 600 miles from the nearest point on the mainland, and it is certain that no college could have prospered, or even begun, if it had relied on its students to undertake that voyage in the conditions of the time. The docility of the Indians might well have been questioned; their aversion from long sea voyages was quite beyond question.

But for years Berkeley was a zealous and persuasive advocate of his plan. He described the island with every device of romantic advertisement; he drew out magnificent plans of 'The City of Bermuda Metropolis of the Summer Islands'; he wrote a poem, affirming prophetically that 'Westward the

Course of Empire takes its Way'. And when, at a dinner in London, he was mocked for his enthusiasm, he replied with such fervent eloquence and skill that all who were present stood up from the table crying 'Let us set out with him immediately!' In 1725 it seemed that this strange project might succeed, or at least be attempted. A charter was granted by the King for the erection of 'St Paul's College' in Bermuda; dukes, bishops, deans, and even bankers were set to raise subscriptions; and with a reservation stressing the need for proper financial backing, the plan was approved by the Attorney and Solicitor General. (Berkeley had paid 'expedition money to men in office'; but this was no exceptional move.) Subscriptions, however, were clearly not likely to be adequate, and in the end the whole scheme came to depend on a grant from public funds. But Berkeley made light of this obstacle. He discovered a suitable source for the money required, and George I was persuaded to instruct Sir Robert Walpole to arrange the affair. In fact, though Berkeley did not at first realize it, his chances of success were thereby sharply diminished.

He had by now secured such keen and influential supporters, and had based his appeal on such high and impressive grounds, that little open opposition was attempted. Many thought that trade should be promoted rather than religion, and others disapproved of educating dependent colonists. But in view of the tone which Berkeley had imparted to the question, they hardly dared to say so; and Parliament gave leave for his grant to be paid with only two dissentient votes. Walpole, however, to whom the plan seemed unpractical, was careful to accept no definite date for the actual transfer of the money; and in high political circles no haste was made. A year or two passed without any further progress.

This put Berkeley in a most difficult position. It seemed imprudent to leave England before his grant was actually secured; but it also seemed necessary to do something, for his subscribers were beginning to suggest that it was time for their money to be put to some use. Accordingly he decided to sail; in September 1728 he left Gravesend for Newport in Rhode

Island – not for Bermuda. It is possible that he had already begun to suspect that Bermuda was not quite suitable for his purpose; but in any case he felt that a place on the mainland would serve better as a centre for his remaining business. At Newport he bought a large plot of land, built a house, and waited for his projects in England to mature.

As might have been expected, nothing occurred. Walpole had never been convinced, and nothing was or could be done to convince him. In Berkeley's absence the critics, both those who thought the scheme impracticable and those who thought it dangerous and undesirable, ventured to express their hostility openly. The King's support, it appeared, was beginning to waver. And at last Sir Robert Walpole declared, tactfully enough, that all was over. 'If you put this question to me as a Minister,' he told the Bishop of London, 'I must and can assure you that the money shall most undoubtedly be paid as soon as suits with public convenience; but if you ask me as a friend whether Dean Berkeley should continue in America, expecting the payment of £20,000, I advise him by all means to return home to Europe.' In the late autumn of 1731 Berkeley was back in London.

He must have been consoled in some measure while in America by finding there one of the first serious students of his works. One Samuel Johnson, educated at Yale and afterwards first President of King's College, New York (now Columbia University), was at that time living at Stratford, Connecticut. He and Berkeley met several times and also corresponded, Johnson being evidently an impressed but still rather hesitant adherent of Berkeley's doctrines. He found them 'surprisingly ingenious', and confessed himself 'almost convinced'. (He also encouraged Berkeley with the remark that 'this way of thinking can't fail to prevail in the world, because it is likely to prevail very much among us in these parts'.) Berkeley welcomed the criticisms of a 'candid thinking man', but no detailed answers to Johnson's letters have survived.

*

Berkeley's own interests at this time had turned in a different direction. His long dialogue *Alciphron, or The Minute Philosopher*, was published in London early in 1732, and so must have been written almost wholly in America. At the time it attracted more notice than any of his other works. It was a contribution to the religious controversies of the first half of the eighteenth century, an attack on the Deists and 'free-thinkers' who, in varying degrees and with a varying mixture of argument and ridicule, diverged from orthodox Anglicanism. Berkeley devotes much space to an attack on Mandeville's not wholly serious *Fable of the Bees*, in which it was argued that most so-called vices were essential to the prosperity of society; and to the Earl of Shaftesbury's *Characteristics*, a somewhat stilted defence of 'natural' morality and of men as 'naturally' virtuous, with or without the sanctions of religious belief. No doubt he meant to be as fair as would be consistent with his controversial purpose; but his book has a disconcertingly polemical tone, and the proponents of the views he attacks are presented, for the most part, as caricatures. 'Lysicles' in particular, expressing the views of Mandeville, is made to speak in accents of foolish dogmatism; and 'Alciphron', though he preserves a certain gravity and decorum, is not accorded much talent for argument; the triumphs of the orthodox 'Crito' are easily won. It is on the whole not surprising that the fame of this elaborate work was short-lived. Butler's *Analogy of Religion*, published only four years after *Alciphron*, gives the impression of a much more serious concern with the problems and soon came to carry more weight with the public. In this case Berkeley was probably ill-advised in attempting the dialogue form. Though he manages it with remarkable skill, his assemblage of pseudo-classical figures is not well adapted to the discussion of serious views held by actual people. If, as in the case of the *Three Dialogues*, the speakers are wholly fictitious, the convention is not objectionable. But it must have irked Berkeley's opponents to see their own views poorly expressed by characters clearly foredoomed to dialectical defeat. No doubt *Alciphron* is an abler specimen of orthodox apologetics than most others of the period, nor is it less well argued than the tracts and treatises on the other side. But the disputes have by now lost most of their interest; scraps of philosophical argument are brought in from time to time, but the comparative tedium of the debate as a whole is not relieved by any new philosophical matter, nor even by the grace of Berkeley's style.

*

On his return from America he took a house in London. He was now in a rather difficult position. He was not personally blamed for the collapse of his Bermudan projects, but it was thought by some that he would have been better employed in converting the Papists of Derry than in laying large plans for the possible but remote conversion of American Indians. He himself thought, on the other hand, that if he now went to Derry at all he would be in danger of being permanently forgotten and passed over. Accordingly he remained in London; and in 1734 his prudence was rewarded. He was appointed Bishop of Cloyne, in the extreme south of Ireland, and in spring of that year he crossed to his diocese. Here, with his family (he had married in 1728), he settled down to the conscientious discharge of his duties and to increasingly anxious care of his own health. And it is to his amateur concern with medical matters that we owe at least the pretext for his last philosophical work – the extraordinary *Siris: a Chain of Philosophical Questions and Inquiries concerning the Virtues of Tar-Water, and divers other Subjects connected together and arising one from another.*

The first half of this very remarkable piece contains an account of the alleged medicinal properties of tar-water, with a recipe for making it, supported by a great deal of curious and speculative chemistry and physiology. Berkeley points out that tar preserves trees from the 'invenomed teeth' of goats, and claims that it will also cure a surprising variety of human ailments; he recommends his mixture particularly to 'sea-faring persons, ladies, and men of studious and sedentary lives.' It is possible that tar-water was, in fact, not entirely useless; and if Berkeley and large numbers of the public made for it highly exaggerated claims, in the then state of medical knowledge such excited zeal was at least excusable. Tar-water became for a short time immensely fashionable; and it retained until quite recent years a place on the shelves of the more traditional medical practitioners.

The transition to the philosophical argument is made by way of speculation on the true *cause* of physical phenomena in general. The claims of air, light, and fire to be the true 'vivifying principle' are debated, with quotations from Newton, Heraclitus, the Pythagoreans, the Stoics, Hippocrates, Vossius, and numerous other authorites of varying repute. But Berkeley is at pains to point out that most of these authorities either said, or darkly hinted, that Mind or Intellect must be enthroned as the true active principle in all phenomena. This leads him, by a quaint and tortuous path, to his familiar contention that 'corpuscularian philosophers', however successful in framing laws of nature, do not really explain any events; for in his view, to say *why* an event occurs requires something more than merely to demonstrate that it is a particular case of a general rule. He repeats that such a term as 'force' has a use only in framing 'mechanical hypotheses', and does not name an actual agent of physical motion or change. 'In all this we know or understand no more than that bodies are moved according to a certain order, and that they do not move themselves.' But this orderliness 'forms a sort of Rational Discourse, and is therefore the immediate effect of an intelligent cause. This is agreeable to the philosophy of Plato, and other ancients.' The type of true explanation, he suggests, would be the proof that an event of such and such a sort 'is so best' – that it tends to promote the Supreme Good aimed at by the one genuine Agent. (Many authorities, Egyptian, Greek, and Roman, are cited in support of this.) 'Real or true causes', he insists, are 'the object of theology, metaphysics, or the *philosophia prima*'.

All of this, though presented in a random, rambling

fashion, embedded in a tangle of imaginative scientific conjecture and weighed down with a mass of miscellaneous learning, is not seriously at variance with the views more temperately set forth in Berkeley's earliest works. More interesting are certain curious passages which, it has been claimed, show that in his later years he reverted to some belief in abstract ideas, or even to some sort of Platonic Theory of Forms. Plato is certainly often cited, and his works are said to be 'the touchstone of a hasty and shallow mind'. 'According to that philosopher, goodness, beauty, and virtue, and such like are not figments of the mind, nor mere mixed modes, nor yet abstract ideas in the modern sense, but the most real beings, intellectual and unchangeable; and therefore more real than the fleeting, transient objects of sense which, wanting stability, cannot be subjects of science, much less of intellectual knowledge.' And Berkeley himself speaks in a similar tone. 'The most refined human intellect, exerted to its utmost reach, can only seize some imperfect glimpses of the Divine Ideas, abstracted from all things corporeal, sensible, and imaginable. Therefore Pythagoras and Plato treated them in a mysterious manner, concealing rather than exposing them to vulgar eyes; so far were they from thinking that those abstract things, although the most real, were the fittest to influence common minds, or become principles of knowledge, not to say duty and virtue, to the generality of mankind. ... Nevertheless, as the mind gathers strength by repeated acts, we should not despond, but continue to exert the prime and flower of our faculties, still recovering, and reaching on, and struggling, into the upper region, whereby our natural weakness and blindness may be in some degree remedied, and a taste attained of truth and intellectual life' (s. 337, 341).

This strange language is indeed unlike the plain prose of his early books; but we cannot base upon these or other passages a secure claim that Berkeley had changed his mind. In so far as any intelligible views emerge at all from the serpentine paragraphs of *Siris*, they indicate not a change of mind, but a change of interest. His early insistence that 'mechanical' science provides no real explanation of anything is, though perfunctorily, repeated; and it seems that in his allusions to and echoes from Plato he is attempting, however dimly, to adumbrate the sort of thing that would give us genuine *understanding*. No doubt he had observed that one purpose which Plato proclaimed in his Theory of Forms was precisely that of providing a method of explaining, of rendering 'intelligible', the world. Plato's Forms were not, as he correctly points out, 'abstract ideas in the modern sense'; Plato was rather seeking, as Berkeley himself would have wished to do, to make good the supposed deficiencies of scientific explanation. The change that we certainly find in *Siris* is in attitude of mind, not in doctrine. In his early years Berkeley would never have indulged in such a disorderly display of quaint lore and learning; he would not have admired its air of profundity and mystery; and he would have attempted to present his 'chain of reflexions' as linked by arguments, not by haphazard suggestion and association. *Siris* is indeed a curiosity. So Gothic a piece would seem to have strayed from some later or much earlier period; it seems not to belong to the age of Locke, Berkeley, and Hume, to the middle of the eighteenth century. It was at one time much admired for this very reason; but those who prefer the daylight of Berkeley's other works will not regret that the vast controversial literature to which it gave rise was directed to the virtues of tar-water, passing over in silence the strange 'reflexions'.

*

Siris was Berkeley's last piece of writing of any length; he wrote no more philosophy. In the summer of 1752, when he was sixty-seven and already in bad health, he planned to make a visit of some length to Oxford, where his second son, George, had just been admitted to Christ Church. Presumably Oxford's prestige was still more alluring than that of his own college in Dublin; though Lord Shelburne, who entered Christ Church the following year, described the Dean as 'a gentleman though not a scholar', and the rest of the community as 'very low'. (At this same time Gibbon was passing in Magdalen what he regarded as the least profitable years of his life.) George Berkeley, who afterwards did well in the Church, was at first a young man of high and extravagant tastes; and though his father regarded his affairs with tolerance, he presumably wished to supervise at least the beginning of his son's education. He took a house in Holywell with his wife and daughter and lived there for several months, intending however to return to Cloyne in due course. But on Sunday evening of 14 January 1753, he suddenly died. A few days later he was buried in the cathedral at Christ Church. Curiously, the mural tablet erected by his wife to one *'inter primos omnium aetatum numerando'* gives the date of his birth, incorrectly, as 1679. He was in fact born in March 1685, and thus was nearly sixty-eight years old when he died.

13

POSTSCRIPT

Since the time of Locke and Berkeley philosophical discussion of perception, of 'our knowledge of the external world', has been unceasing. It has been prosecuted with enormous industry and ingenuity, but also with a certain lack of originality – a lack which is itself a striking tribute to the power of our seventeenth- and eighteenth-century predecessors. Their terminology has been abandoned – 'ideas' and 'impressions' have given way to '*sensa*', '*sensibilia*', '*sense-data*', and other such technical terms – but the questions they asked have continued to be asked and even their answers (with more or less modification) adopted.

The contemporary theory which is most closely related to Berkeley's is the elaborate and much-discussed Phenomenalism. This might be described, in the simplest terms, as 'Berkeley without God'. 'The table I write on, I say, exists, that is, I see and feel it; and if I were out of my study I should say it existed, meaning thereby that if I was in my study I might perceive it, or that some other spirit actually does perceive it' (P. 3). It has rightly seemed impossible to believe that, if I say 'There is a table in my study' (but no one perceives it), I *mean* that 'some other spirit', namely God, does in fact perceive it; it seemed impossible to maintain that God's perception (whatever that may be) enters into the *meaning* of such familiar remarks as 'There is a table in my study'. Hence the alternative view was preferred – 'if I were out of my study I should say it existed, meaning thereby that if I was in my study I might perceive it.'

The resulting theory took two forms. The simplest remained closely similar to Berkeley's own. Material things, which he called 'collections of ideas', were said to be 'families of sense-data' – with the difference that, whereas all ideas were supposed actually to exist 'in the mind of God', most of the sense-data in any 'family' would exist (occur, be sensed, etc.), *if* certain conditions (the presence of an observer) were fulfilled, In J. S. Mill's phrase, material things were said to be 'permanent possibilities of sensation'. A more sophisticated version avoids the misleadingly 'factual' look of such claims. It was rightly felt that to say 'Material things are families of sense-data' was to say something of a quite different sort from 'The O'Donnells are a family of Irishmen'; and the case was presented, certainly less confusingly, as a claim about language. Material things were said to be 'logical constructions' out of sense-data, and this was explained to be the claim that any sentence about a material thing could be translated (or analysed) into a set of sentences about sense-data.

Unfortunately even this modified case gave rise to a startling variety of difficult problems (most of them latent in, but passed over by, Berkeley). The term 'sense-datum' itself proved very puzzling, and numerous questions were raised about its use which have never, in fact, been properly answered. (Indeed, the word 'sense-datum', like the word 'idea' in Berkeley's time, has by now been so frequently *used* that many people seem merely to take for granted that its meaning is clear and well understood; though inquiry would show that this is very far from being the case.) There were also two more serious difficulties. First, it soon became apparent that the phenomenalist's translations, or 'analyses', could never in fact be carried out, since for no less than three reasons the number of sentences about sense-data required to complete any analysis would necessarily be indefinitely large. The sentence 'There is a table in my study' could be used to refer to *any* table, to an indefinitely large number of tables; any one of these could be observed in indefinitely many ways and from indefinitely many points of view; and the *conditions* in which any of the (indefinitely numerous) sense-data would actually be sensed would also require to be specified in indefinitely many sentences about other sense-data. Second, it was often felt to be impossible to hold that a *categorical* sentence ('There is a table in my study') could rightly be translated into a set of sentences about sense-data all of which (if the table is not perceived) would be merely *hypothetical*. Or, to put the same point in an older-fashioned way, it seemed inadequate to regard the actual table in my empty study as a *possibility* of sensation. For surely, when I say there is a table in my study, I am saying what actually *is* the case, not mentioning merely the *possibility* of anything.

Much time and talent has been devoted to attempts to meet these objections; the original theory of phenomenalism has been diluted and repaired until it has become somewhat difficult to discern, in the abundance of subtle detail, exactly what claim it is that is finally put forward. Moreover, one very important question seems almost to have been lost to view, or if raised is rather perfunctorily answered. This question is, what is the purpose of all this argument? If it turns out to be difficult to make phenomenalism really work, why should we *try* to make it work? What is the aim behind all the labour and ingenuity? This question is raised most insistently by the view that phenomenalism offers an 'alternative language' – that it shows us how to use 'sense-datum sentences' instead of our ordinary sentences about 'material things'. One naturally asks, why do we need an alternative language? Surely the language we already use serves our purposes entirely adequately. What is the point of devising 'theories' of perception, if all that these actually offer us is the possibility of speaking in ways in which, being already supplied with an adequate language, we really have no need to speak?

Three answers to these questions have been suggested, or (more commonly) assumed without any explicit statement.

(1) Some philosophers have not in fact admitted that our ordinary language is adequate. They have claimed to find in it confusions, and even contradictions, which though not seriously damaging for practical purposes are said to be theoretically most undesirable. Of this claim (which could be properly discussed only in very great detail) it can only be said here that most of the confusions said to be discovered by

philosophers in ordinary language seem to be of their own invention. This is understandable. Our ordinary use of words in speaking of the things we perceive is certainly very ordinary; we use this vocabulary in all our daily doings and become familiar with it in early childhood. But it is, however ordinary and familiar, exceedingly complex. It is accordingly very easy for a philosopher in a hurry, bent on other things or with other axes to grind, to misunderstand or at least to misrepresent our ordinary linguistic practices; and hence to build up apparent contradictions and confusions where in fact there are none. Berkeley's *First Dialogue* is full of very striking examples of this; he appears to score easy points against common language by putting into the mouth of his victim Hylas a variety of fantastic views which are supposed to be, but certainly are not, the views implied in the language of 'plain men'. And many other philosophers have enjoyed equally barren and Pyrrhic victories. It is of course always possible that any system of language may contain more or less latent contradictions and obscurities; but I think it could safely be said that a language in constant daily use is far less likely to be thus unsatisfactory than a technical vocabulary, devised rather *ad hoc*, which has never in fact been tested and shaped and modified by actual use.

(2) Berkeley, and many philosophers since, would argue that, although our ordinary language may serve well enough for practical purposes, it does not really *fit the facts*. But this view appears to rest on a confusion. To say that some statement does not fit the facts can only be to say that it is not *true*. If I say 'There is a table in my study', this does not fit the facts if, for instance, there is no table in my study but only a desk. On the other hand, if what I say is true, it fits the facts exactly. Indeed, what statement could possibly fit the fact that there is a table in my study more exactly than the statement 'There is a table in my study'? It is really tautologous to say that any true statement *exactly* fits the facts; it exactly fits those facts, or that fact, which it states.[12] There are of course, indefinitely many facts which are *not* stated in any statement; but it would

be most unreasonable to object to a statement because it fails to state facts which it does not state. For how could just that statement fit, or state, facts *other* than those which it states? It is, I think, often felt that such common remarks as 'I hear a car' do not fit the facts discovered by physiologists or physicists. But what can this mean? Obviously physicists and physiologists have not established that the statement 'I hear a car' is never *true*. What perhaps they have established is that in hearing a car there occur surprisingly complex physical events; they have discovered numerous facts about such an occurrence which earlier generations had never suspected. But then the statement 'I hear a car' neither states nor denies any of these facts; it merely states, with tautologous completeness, the fact that I hear a car. And this fact, the only fact that is at all relevant, is exactly 'fitted' by what I say.

The complaint that ordinary language does not 'fit the facts' is often confused with the quite correct observation that ordinary statements are often logically complex, and can be analysed into more verbose but logically simpler expressions. If I say of a marksman that he scored a bull, I say of him in very few words what could be said at greater length – for instance, that he aimed and fired a gun, the bullet from which passed through the central area of the target at which he was aiming. This lengthy statement does not *fit* the facts any better; but it states in plain terms what is stated in a more 'concentrated' form in the statement 'He scored a bull'. It is clear enough that Berkeley often felt inclined to object to the highly 'concentrated' character of ordinary language, but that he (and others who have shared his view) mis-stated the grounds of the objection. It is not that in using lengthier forms of words we are correcting the inaccuracy, or looseness, of ordinary language; we are not getting 'closer to the facts'. We are rather stating explicitly and in detail what is ordinarily stated in 'concentrated' form. But this again raises the question, why is this worth doing? And this leads on to my third point.

(3) What, after all, induces philosophers to interest them-

selves in perception? Partly, and in the present day very
largely, their interest is engaged by the extraordinary things
that other philosophers say on the subject; but beneath this
surface of merely civil war and parasitic activity, there are
certain problems which seem *naturally* to arise from reflection on the facts and the language of perception. In particular,
there seems to be a persistent tendency to fall into the problems seen so clearly in Locke. We begin by 'analysing' our
ordinary perception of material things into some more 'basic'
or more 'fundamental' awareness of more 'basic' and 'fundamental' things – ideas, impressions, sense-data, or whatever
it may be – and thereafter it is only too easy to construct an
account which makes it seem quite impossible that we should
ever know anything of the 'external world'. The ordinary
world, so to speak, seems to vanish irretrievably *behind* the
'ideas' or 'sense-data' that we have introduced.

There are two main routes, both of which we have already
noticed, by which we may arrive in this predicament. First,
reflection on such phenomena as hallucinations, in which
there occurs awareness of *something* though not of physical
objects, may lead us to say that that of which we are aware
in these cases is the only sort of thing of which we are ever
immediately aware; and thus that the existence and character of physical objects must be somehow inferred from
these 'data' of immediate awareness. It is then tempting to
draw Locke's conclusion that the real 'external world' is the
cause of that of which we are immediately aware, but that of
it we are never (strictly speaking) aware at all. Second, this
conclusion is apt to be reinforced by the fact that scientists
(who, we may think, really *know* the nature of the physical
world) seem to speak of the world as consisting of 'corpuscles',
or 'particles', or 'atoms', to which it makes no sense to ascribe
most of those properties that we wish to ascribe to the things
that we perceive. And thus we seem forced to recognize a
radical distinction between what we actually perceive, and
the physical world as it really is. Now some philosophers, and
many scientists, feel able to accept this position without dis-

comfort; but it certainly appears to be highly paradoxical. For if there were in fact such a radical distinction as this, the nature of what we actually perceive would appear to give us no clue to the nature of the physical world; and yet how, if not by the use of our senses, could we ever come to know anything about our environment?

There is no doubt that these are entirely serious problems, problems which arise very naturally from reflection on familiar facts and ways of speaking. And it is clear that one of Berkeley's main motives in devising his own way of speaking, his language of 'ideas', was precisely to free his own mind and the minds of others from any temptation to fall into the predicament we have outlined. He agrees with Locke that 'ideas' are the only things of which we are immediately aware; but there is, he would persuade us, no resultant problem about the inaccessibility of the physical world behind or beyond our ideas – for besides ideas there is nothing at all. To put the same point in another way: our ordinary language (and the language of scientists) neither makes, nor tries and fails to make, any reference to unobservable 'external' things; for everything that we say in those idioms could be said in the language of ideas, in terms which obviously do not have, nor conceivably could have, any such reference. There is nothing mysterious and hidden from us; for we could say and do all that we wish, with a language mentioning nothing at all but the undoubted, immediate 'data' of sense-perception. It is, I think, clear that this same motive underlies, whether avowedly or not, the labours of contemporary phenomenalists.

But this suggests an important question. Suppose that someone finds himself perplexed by the fact, as it appears to him from reflection on 'illusions' or the findings of scientists, that our ordinary language seems to imply some baffling reference to unobservable, mystifying 'external objects'. He is aware, he admits, of certain sense-data; but there seems to be an insoluble problem about the relation of these sense-data to the physical world. Now we may assure him, as Berkeley and the phenomenalist would do, that his perplexity can be resolved –

common language and the language of science is really in-
nocuous, for it can in fact be translated into the 'sense-datum
language' in which it is manifestly impossible even to *raise* the
questions by which he is baffled. But if we are to allay his discomfort, at least three conditions must be fulfilled – (1) our
'sense-datum language' must be intelligible to him; (2) we
must in fact be *able* to execute our offered translations; and
(3) our translations must be shown to be good and adequate
translations of ordinary language. If the first of these conditions is not satisfied, we shall merely inflict upon him additional problems; if the second is not satisfied, we fall under
some suspicion of bluffing; and if the third is not satisfied, our
efforts will be beside the point. But in fact none of these conditions ever has been satisfied. The so-called 'sense-datum
language' has generated a large variety of quite new difficulties; it is admitted that translations cannot actually be
done; and it is still widely and reasonably supposed that, if
they were done, they would not have the same meaning as the
sentences which they are alleged to translate.

The persistence, in the face of these difficulties, in attempts
to repair and improve upon phenomenalism is due, I believe,
to the influence of an unexamined assumption. It is assumed
that, unless we go on trying to devise some way in which
ordinary language can be translated into some less philosophically puzzling idiom, we shall be obliged merely to abandon the philosophical problems; if someone finds himself perplexed, we shall be able only to urge him not to worry, and
to point out that for practical purposes he gets on quite well.
But this is a very singular assumption. Why should it be
thought that the only way to resolve a problem raised in a
certain form of discourse is to *translate* that discourse into
something else? Even if such translation could be conveniently and satisfactorily done, this would still not be the *only*
thing to do. We might instead examine directly the use of
the puzzling locutions themselves; we might try to discover
why they seem puzzling, and to achieve proper understanding of them by finding out exactly how they and related ex-

pressions are actually used. This work would need to be done in any case before we could begin to translate our ordinary language into some other; for we must at least understand what we undertake to translate. But if we understood it really adequately, would not the need for translation disappear? Inspection of the terms and concepts of science might show us that the conclusions of scientists have in fact no tendency to *contradict* our ordinary judgements of perception; and inspection of ordinary speech might show that to say 'We are immediately aware only of sense-data' is not to deny that we often see tables and chairs. These points are of course precisely those which Berkeley and the phenomenalists seek to establish; but is there any good reason to suppose that the only method of establishing these points is to carry out a *translation* on the pattern proposed? I think there is not. Indeed, the acknowledged difficulty (or worse) of providing translations seems to show that this is *not* the right way to proceed. Certainly Berkeley and his successors are attempting to resolve perplexities which do indeed call for resolution; they are not amusing themselves with linguistic games; but it is very far from obvious that their attempts are on the right lines.

It could, I believe, be reasonably argued that Berkeley and his successors have been inclined to be over-ambitious. Berkeley, as we have seen, construed the statements that 'there are only ideas,' that knowledge and language are about nothing else, as true statements supporting (indeed entailing) his analysis of statements about material things; his analysis seemed to have 'ontological' backing. This belief was however illusory; the 'true statements' alleged to support his analysis were in fact disguised assertions of that analysis itself. But he was of course influenced also by respectable and even admirable motives. Finding that Locke had made it appear that the 'external world' was wholly inaccessible to observation, he sought to remove this baffling problem at a single blow. By adopting the language of ideas, in which we say only how things seem to observers, he hoped to eliminate even the possibility of supposing that there is something which forever eludes observation. Now this would indeed be excellent, if successful; but it is not successful. Berkeley's own way of speaking, and the languages of 'sense-data', etc., which followed, raised a variety of quite new problems, and in any case convinced few people that they were really equivalent ways of speaking.

Must we say, then, that statements about material things cannot be analysed at all? I do not think so. It has long been assumed that to offer an 'analysis' must be, and can only be, to offer some single-blow solution of the kind that Berkeley offered – some quite general recipe for translating the puzzling idiom into some other idiom supposed to be free from all problems. But this is prejudice. Why should not the analysis of a statement consist in a careful account of its actual use, directed to the understanding of the statement itself without proposing a dubious translation into some new and problematic terminology? Or if it be held that such descriptions could not be properly called 'analyses', we might suggest that in that case it is not analyses that we require. To assume that it is, and that analyses must be translations into other terms, is merely to make the covert assumption that philosophical problems can be resolved only in some such way as Berkeley supposed.

*

Philosophy has a strange power of spontaneous growth. If someone encounters a problem and offers a solution, his solution is apt to generate new problems, which become in turn the progenitors of further theories and yet more perplexities. There is thus a constant danger that the original problems may be simply forgotten – as, in the course of a long vendetta, no one may remember how it all began. It is always difficult, but sometimes essential, to shake off the accumulated superstructure of theory and go back to the beginning. The study of Berkeley, who was not too heavily burdened with accretions of detail, may help us to do this. It is in his case not too difficult to see what problems they were with which he was engaged – and hence not to overlook the possibility of attacking these problems by methods quite different from his. His example, and the subsequent history of philosophy, suggest that perhaps it is now time for philosophers to desist from the repair and renovation of such general theories as his, labours which in time yield sharply diminishing returns. Perhaps it is time to consider the possibility that nothing more can be achieved by his methods, and to undertake instead the proper investigation of the immensely complex vocabulary of perception in ordinary language. At the very least we shall thus be able to ensure that no time is wasted on problems due *merely* to imperfect understanding of language; and this would be, if not the end of the whole matter, at least a by no means inconsiderable gain – 'especially since there may be some grounds to suspect that those lets and difficulties, which stay and embarrass the mind in its search after truth, do not spring from any darkness or intricacy in the objects, or natural defect in the understanding, so much as from false principles which have been insisted on, and might have been avoided'. Berkeley would not, we may be sure, have wished to prohibit the application of this wise remark to his own philosophy.

BIBLIOGRAPHY

1. The earliest collected edition of Berkeley's writings was published in London and Dublin in 1784, probably edited by Joseph Stock. Another edition, by G. N. Wright, was published in London in 1843.

A. C. Fraser's edition of 1871 (Clarendon Press, Oxford: re-issued, with revisions, in 1901) was reasonably complete. But what must now be regarded as the definitive edition is *The Works of George Berkeley*, edited in nine volumes by A. A. Luce and T. E. Jessop (Nelson, 1948–57).

Many texts of the *Essay, Principles*, and *Dialogues* are readily available, for example in an Everyman's Library volume with an introduction by A. D. Lindsay (1910: re-issued 1957). The *Principles* and *Dialogues* have appeared in the Fontana Library (1962), with an introduction by the present writer.

2. The following works on Berkeley should be mentioned:

A. A. Luce, *The Life of George Berkeley*, Edinburgh, 1949.

D. M. Armstrong, *Berkeley's Theory of Vision*, Melbourne, 1960.

G. Dawes Hicks, *Berkeley*, London, 1932.

A. A. Luce, *Berkeley and Malebranche*, Oxford, 1934. *Berkeley's Immaterialism*, Edinburgh, 1945. *The Dialectic of Immaterialism*, London, 1963.

W. E. Steinkraus (ed.), *New Studies in Berkeley's Philosophy*, New York, 1966.

J. F. Thomson, 'Berkeley', in *A Critical History of Western Philosophy*, ed. O'Connor, New York, 1964.

NOTES

1. Professor Luce, in *The Dialectic of Immaterialism* (1963), makes admirably clear how these note-books should be read, and how Berkeley's apparatus of marginal signs should be interpreted. It is particularly important to appreciate that many *dicta* entered in the note-books were subsequently rejected by Berkeley himself.

2. This is a rather careless historical observation. The influence of Locke is indeed manifest in all Berkeley's major writings; but there is, by contrast, not much reason to think that he was himself taken seriously either by Hume or Kant. There is a respectful reference to him in Hume's *Treatise* (Book I, Section VII), but only one; and Kant's few mentions of Berkeley are distinctly patronizing. It is remarkable also that, while Hume's *Treatise* was published fourteen years before Berkeley's death, Berkeley's correspondence and later writings give no indication that he had ever heard of Hume.

3. My interpretation of Berkeley in the pages that follow has been questioned by D. M. Armstrong, *Berkeley's Theory of Vision* (1960), pp. 35–6.

4. I evidently overlook here that we may be said to touch things *with*, for example, barge-poles, when our physical contact with the things touched is 'indirect'.

5. It is probably wrong to imply, as I do, that 'General terms are names' *must* be a disastrous proposition; 'red', after all, *is* the name of a colour. It depends what calling a word a 'name' is taken to imply. I am afraid the line I take in the text on this point is very much of an over-simplification.

6. The paragraphs that follow should be read, as I suggest in the Preface, as reporting how Locke was interpreted by Berkeley; it has been argued that he attributed to Locke opinions which Locke did not really propound.

7. This is partly wrong. The crucial feature of the physical theory which Locke accepted – mostly from Gassendi and, of course, Newton – is really that it was a *mechanistic* theory;

Locke's primary qualities are those necessary to a 'body' as an element in a mechanical system. Solidity was not, as I say, 'thrown in'; it was of the essence of the case. The fact that the same qualities are, as Locke also suggests, essential to our everyday concept of a 'material thing' perhaps implies that that concept also is fundamentally mechanical. Cp. Fröhlich, 'Primary Qualities in Physical Explanation', *Mind*, 1959.

8. Mr Richard Robinson, of Oriel, in a private letter, has deplored my wording here, on the ground, which I accept, that 'there is no guilt in being confused'.

9. Notwithstanding the rather euphoric tone of my text here, it is this chapter which was particularly severely handled by J. L. Austin, *Sense and Sensibilia*, pp. 132–42, and also, as mentioned in the Preface, by Jonathan Bennett, W. F. R. Hardie, and J. W. Yolton.

10. Mr I. C. Tipton, making skilful use of Berkeley's *Commentaries*, has shown reason for regarding my statement here as considerably too sweeping. See his article 'Berkeley's View of Spirit', in *New Studies in Berkeley's Philosophy*, ed. Steinkraus (1966), pp. 59–71.

11. For critical discussion of Berkeley's position here, see Sir Karl Popper's 'Three Views concerning Human Knowledge', in *Contemporary British Philosophy*, Third Series, ed. Lewis (1956), pp. 375–88.

12. This unfortunate sentence is called by Austin a 'perverted little rigmarole', in his 'Unfair to Facts', in *Philosophical Papers* (1961), p. 110. His point, surely a correct one, is that 'fits the facts' is not, as I imply, a mere synonym for 'is true'.

INDEX